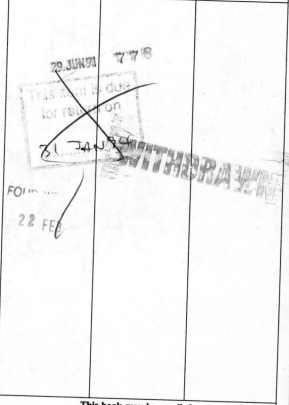

# Mr. Hawthorne Goes to England

*The Adventures of a Reluctant Consul*

**NATHANIEL HAWTHORNE AT THE TIME HE WAS NAMED CONSUL**
Early in 1853, the year he went to Liverpool as United States Consul, Hawthorne sat for this portrait by the well known artist, George P. A. Healy.

# Mr. Hawthorne Goes to England

*The Adventures of a Reluctant Consul*

JAMES O'DONALD MAYS

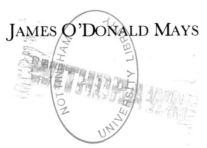

*...always they give a salute of two guns; but ... yesterday so many were thundered off because Mr. Hawthorne, the distinguished United States Consul and author, was leaving the shore, and honoring Her Majesty's steamship with his presence.*

– Sophia Hawthorne, as quoted in
*Memories of Hawthorne.*

## NEW FOREST LEAVES

*Burley, Ringwood, Hampshire*

**British Library Cataloguing in Publication Data:**

Mays, James O'Donald
  Mr Hawthorne goes to England: The adventures of a reluctant consul.
  1. Hawthorne, Nathaniel – Biography
  2. Novelists, American – 19th Century – Biography
  I. Title
  813'.3     PS1881.
  ISBN 0-907956-01-7

All quotations from the *The American Notebooks* and *The French and Italian Notebooks* of Nathaniel Hawthorne are from the editions by, respectively, Claude M. Simpson and Thomas Woodson, published as Volumes VIII and XIV of the Centenary Edition of the Works of Nathaniel Hawthorne, edited by William Charvat (1905–1966), Roy Harvey Pearce, Claude M. Simpson (1910–1976), and Thomas Woodson. Copyright © 1973 and 1980 by the Ohio State University Press. All rights reserved.

Set in 10/11 Baskerville by Pintail Studios Limited,
and printed in Great Britain by Pardy & Son (Printers) Limited,
both of Ringwood, Hampshire,
for New Forest Leaves, Burley, Ringwood, Hampshire.

For
STUART

# Contents

# Acknowledgements

The endpapers depict the Liverpool waterfront as it appeared during Hawthorne's consulship. The view is from a chromo lithograph by Joseph Shepherd and is reproduced with kind permission of the Liverpool City Libraries. (The ferry boats in the foreground very likely include some on which Hawthorne commuted daily between his Rock Ferry residence and Liverpool.)

The author also wishes to thank the following for permission to use illustrations on the pages indicated: New Hampshire Historical Society, frontispiece portrait of Hawthorne by G. P. A. Healy, 202; State Street Bank and Trust Company, Boston, 12; Bowdoin College Library, 13, 16, 18, 31, 195; Methuen London, Ltd., 31; United States Customs Service, 23, 30; Essex Institute, retouched version of etching by Schoff, 28; C. E. Frazer Clark, Jr., for items from his collection, 37, 75, 79, 123, 177, 180; Library of Congress, 38, 41, 49, 76, 115, 119, 153, 182, 201; U.S. State Department, Historical Office, 46, 110, 124, 168; Library of the Boston Athenaeum, 47; Stuart Beck, Royal Society of Marine Artists, 53; Liverpool City Libraries, 57, 61, 62, 63, 65, 66, 70, 71, 83, 85, 90, 92, 93, 98, 99, 121, 148, 154, 171, 173; Adelphi Hotel, Liverpool, 62; Tennessee State Library and Archives, 73; Church of the Latter Day Saints, 76; The Mitchell Library, Glasgow, 94; University of Bristol Theatre Collection, 95; The John Rylands University Library of Manchester (Gaskell Collection), 103; The Atkinson Library, Southport, 104; The American Numismatic Society, 108; National Portrait Gallery, 113, 176; Leamington Spa Library, 128; British Tourist Authority, 130, 131, 133, 134, 135, 142, 143, 145; Southampton Art Gallery, 136; Bodleian Library, 141; Biblioteca Nacional (Portugal) de Lisboa, 150; National Archives and Record Service, 153; Lt.-Col. Howard N. Cole, O.B.E., 161; Guildhall Library, City of London, 163, 165; Walker Art Gallery, 175, 178; Redcar (Cleveland) District Library, 188; Avon County Libraries, 190; Trinity College Library, Cambridge University, 191; Concord Free Public Library, 192; Houghton Mifflin Co., 201.

For documentation of Hawthorne's official duties the author is indebted to the Diplomatic Branch of the National Archives and Record Service, and to Dr. Mark F. Sweeney and Bowling Green University. Assistance in documenting Hawthorne's consular career also was provided by the Navy and Old Army Branch of the National Archives and Record Service; the U.S. Customs Service and the U.S. Maritime Administration.

The U.S. State Department's Historical Office and the former State Department Librarian, Lewis M. Bright, provided background on American consular regulations in Hawthorne's period. Much valuable reference material also was supplied by the Library of Congress and the U.S. Naval War College.

Mrs. Cleone Odell Stewart and the Modern Languages Association have generously given permission to quote from *The English Notebooks of Nathaniel Hawthorne* by the late Randall Stewart (copyright 1941 by the M.L.A. and 1969 by Mrs. Stewart). Likewise the publishers John Murray have permitted quotations from Julian Hawthorne's *Shapes That Pass* (1928). Use of Hawthorne's and his family's correspondence has been granted by Manning Hawthorne and the Essex Institute, and by the New York Public Library (Henry W. and Albert A. Berg Collection, the Astor, Lenox and Tilden Foundations). For most of the references to Hawthorne–Bridge correspondence, appreciation is due to the Bowdoin College Library. Passages from *The American Notebooks* and *The French and Italian Notebooks* of Nathaniel Hawthorne (Centenary Edition) are quoted, as indicated on the title page, by courtesy of Ohio State University Press.

Other sources granting permission to quote include the University of Iowa Libraries, Trustees of the Boston Public Library, Maine Historical Society (the John S. H. Fogg Autograph Collection), Houghton Mifflin Company, the Nathaniel Hawthorne Collection of the Clifton Waller Barrett Library, University of Virginia Library, *The New England Quarterly*, Yale University Library, The Houghton Library, Harvard University, and the New Hampshire Historical Society. For other assistance the author is grateful to Dr. Homer T. Rosenberg, Waynesboro, Pennsylvania; Mystic Seaport, Inc., Mystic, Connecticut; The Steamship Historical Society of America, Inc., New York,

N.Y.; the Concord (Massachusetts) Free Public Library; Dr. Lola Szladits and Ann Meronet of the Berg Collection, New York Public Library; Arthur Moncke and Mary H. Hughes, Bowdoin College Library; and Rita Gollin, State University of New York.

Assistance from British sources has been equally generous. Foremost among these have been the Liverpool City Libraries, in particular the Liverpool Record Office, to which the author made repeated visits over a period of nine years. Here is a real treasure house of materials contemporary with Hawthorne's consular period. For access to these items appreciation is due the City Librarian, Ralph Malbon, and Janet Smith and Naomi Evetts. Other useful background was provided by Miss J. Tarbuck of the Atkinson Library, Southport; the staff of Birkenhead Central Library; Mitchell Library, Glasgow; T. M. Dinan, Librarian of Lloyd's of London; M. K. Stammers and Dr. A. J. Scarth, Merseyside County Museums; Basil Greenhill, National Maritime Museum; John E. Vaughan, Tutor Librarian, University of Liverpool; Professor H. A. Jones, University of Leicester; Mrs. Norman Jones; R. D'O. Butler, Historical Advisor, Foreign and Commonwealth Office; A. P. M. Nixson, Oxford City Secretary and Solicitor, and J. P. Wells, Oxfordshire County Library; and J. W. V. Cumming, Archivist, Gibraltar Secretariat.

An enormous debt is owed the late Norman Holmes Pearson, Professor of English and American Studies of Yale University, for his suggestions and encouragement during the early stages of the author's research. For reading part or all of the manuscript, appreciation is due the late Professor Arlin Turner, Duke University; Professor Raymona Hull, Indiana University of Pennsylvania; Arnold Goldman, Professor of American Studies, University of Keele; Lewis C. Mattison, retired U.S. foreign service officer; S. R. Denny; and C. E. Frazer Clark, Jr., Hawthorne scholar and editor of the *Nathaniel Hawthorne Journal*.

I also want to thank Anton Cox and Terry Hood-Cree of Pardy and Son, Printers, and Eddie Hams of Pintail Studios Ltd., for their sensitive guidance and advice in the production of this work.

Finally, appreciation is due members of my family who, by their assistance and constant encouragement, enabled me to bring the book to fruition. Angela, Stuart and Melinda interrupted their studies to track down numerous references, while Mary was always present to render a judgment or help me over some critical point in the research, writing and production stages. Without their support, this work could not have appeared in its present form.

# Preface

When Nathaniel Hawthorne, the new United States consul to Liverpool, settled down to his duties in August of 1853, he had every reason for being pleased with the previous four years in America. After a difficult early life when supporting his family was a constant problem, he found the years 1850 to 1853 relatively happy ones with less concern about income. Indeed, this four-year period had been packed with literary success: three novels – *The Scarlet Letter*, *The House of the Seven Gables*, and *The Blithedale Romance* – as well as *The Snow Image*, *A Wonder Book*, and *Tanglewood Tales*.

Now removed to Liverpool, he could look forward to an equally exciting four years as United States Consul – in effect, a second career. Beyond the consular work and the security it afforded, England obviously held other attractions for Hawthorne. For one thing, it was his ancestral home – "Our Old Home," as he came to call it. England was also the nation whose literary figures he most admired. And no doubt he thought he would come away with ideas and plots for future works of his own.

Scholars will never agree whether Hawthorne's decision to become consul robbed American literature of untold great works just as the author seemed at the peak of his creative powers, or, as has been suggested, he may have already written himself out. This book does not join the argument, but seeks rather to document Hawthorne's four consular years. Insofar as possible, the actual words written or spoken by Hawthorne, his family, and his contemporaries have been retained.

Because Hawthorne's consular appointment grew directly out of the author's friendship with President Franklin Pierce, the book opens when "Hath" and "Frank" met as students at Bowdoin College. Here they formed the ties that were to bind them together to the end of their days. The account then proceeds chronologically until the family arrives in Liverpool. From the time Hawthorne became consul the book views the various aspects of his experience separately – the demands of his office, his family and social life, his relations with his superiors – especially Minister Buchanan, his travels, the causes he espoused, his ability as a writer of dispatches, his conception of Britain and her people, and his unending struggle to live as frugally as possible.

The volume ends with a glance at Hawthorne's last years and a brief assessment of his consular performance.

# The Chief People of the Book

**The Family Circle:**

NATHANIEL HAWTHORNE, sometime author, and United States Consul to the port of Liverpool, 1853–1857.
SOPHIA (PEABODY) HAWTHORNE, his wife.
Their children: UNA, born 1844; JULIAN, born 1846; and ROSE, born 1851.
FANNY WRIGLEY, the faithful English nurse-maid.

**Bowdoin College Classmates of Hawthorne:**

HORATIO BRIDGE, later Paymaster-General of the U.S. Navy.
FRANKLIN PIERCE, later President of the United States.

**Close Relatives:**

LOUISA, Hawthorne's younger sister and his favourite; ELIZABETH, his elder sister.
DR. NATHANIEL PEABODY, Sophia's father, and ELIZABETH PEABODY, her sister.

**Liverpool Consulate Staff Members:**

SAMUEL PEARCE, senior clerk, and HENRY WILDING, junior clerk.

**Close Friends of Hawthorne During the Consulate Years:**

In the United States: WILLIAM D. TICKNOR and JAMES T. FIELDS, his co-publishers.
In Britain: FRANCIS BENNOCH of London and HENRY A. BRIGHT of Liverpool.
MRS. MARY BLODGET, a renowned Liverpool boarding house proprietress.

**Some Liverpool Acquaintances:**

WILLIAM RATHBONE, Sr., and WILLIAM RATHBONE, Jr., merchants and philanthropists.
WILLIAM BARBER, merchant and one-time President of the American Chamber of Commerce.
WILLIAM BROWN, merchant, banker, Member of Parliament and benefactor.
HENRY YOUNG, bookseller and publisher.

**State Department Personages:**

The United States Ministers in London: JAMES BUCHANAN (later U.S. President) and GEORGE M. DALLAS (previously U.S. Vice-President), who succeeded BUCHANAN.
The U.S. Secretaries of State: WILLIAM L. MARCY and LEWIS CASS, who succeeded him.
JOHN L. O'SULLIVAN, an old friend of Hawthorne who became U.S. Minister to Portugal.

# I
# The Future Consul at Bowdoin College

Nathaniel Hawthorne was one of several passengers in the stagecoach that bumped and rattled along the road to Brunswick, Maine. Most were young men of his own age obviously bound for a common destination – Bowdoin College – for no other explanation could account for a lively band travelling through the sparsely populated countryside of America's newest state in the beginning of October.[1]

The year was 1821 and Bowdoin was about to open its doors for only the twentieth time since its founding. But if any of the young men in the coach had doubts over the academic health of the fledgling college, they did not show it. Certainly Nathaniel Hawthorne had no qualms and, indeed, considered himself lucky to be a prospective student. True, there may have been a time when his family had thought of sending Nathaniel to Harvard, but the prestigious Massachusetts college would have been rejected for at least two reasons. First, the required $600 in annual fees were more than Mrs. Hawthorne and her brothers could manage. As an impoverished widow of a New England sea captain, she found it difficult enough to provide life's necessities for Nathaniel and his two sisters, Elizabeth and Louisa. But the second reason for selecting Bowdoin over Harvard was more compelling: the family's intense pride in the new state of Maine.

Until 1820 Maine had been a mere province of the state of Massachusetts, but now it was a state on its own. One of Mrs. Hawthorne's brothers, Robert Manning, lived in Raymond, Maine, on Lake Sebago. Nathaniel had welcomed the departure from his native Salem, Massachusetts, to Raymond, where his mother lived off and on from 1816 to 1822, for he loved the Maine countryside. The Mannings had followed the progress of Bowdoin College with understandable pride and, when young Nathaniel early displayed literary tendencies, they were convinced he should study there. By 1821 Bowdoin had established for itself a solid reputation in New England academic circles, and several of its faculty members commanded national respect. The fact that Bowdoin's fees were a mere fraction of those at Harvard left no doubt in the Mannings' minds that Nathaniel should attend the Maine college.

Although he was a tall, well-developed lad of seventeen, Nathaniel was being shepherded to Bowdoin by his Uncle Robert. He may well have resented his uncle's presence in the company of fellow stagecoach passengers, but he had no choice. For all he knew, he might be returning home with Uncle Robert two days hence, should he fail to gain admission to Bowdoin. And even if he were accepted, it would be Uncle Robert to whom he would look for the greater part of his fees. Robert Manning may have harboured secret doubts about finding the money to meet his nephew's educational costs over the next four years, but he had none as to Nathaniel's fitness for Bowdoin and did his best so to impress the boy. An entirely different question may well have been foremost in Robert Manning's mind – his nephew's ability to adjust to Bowdoin's all-male environment after growing up in a family composed only of females. The boy's father, Nathaniel Hathorne (young Nathaniel decided to add the "w" while at Bowdoin), had contracted yellow fever and died in Surinam in 1808 when the future author was only four.

At eleven o'clock on the morning of October 2 the Brunswick-bound stagecoach was nearing its destination. Robert Manning need not have worried about his nephew's ability

## A STAGECOACH FRIENDSHIP

While en route to Maine's Bowdoin College by stagecoach, Nathaniel Hawthorne met Franklin Pierce. The two became lifelong friends, and Hawthorne's campaign biography helped Pierce to the American presidency.

to get along with young men his age. Indeed, he must have been agreeably surprised by the speed with which Nathaniel developed friendships on that eventful journey. One aspiring student was Alfred Mason, who explained that his father was a United States Senator for New Hampshire. Another was Jonathan Cilley, destined to represent the state of Maine in the American Congress. But it was Franklin Pierce – who had attended Bowdoin the previous year – whose life was to become inextricably linked with Hawthorne's.

Enrolling in an institution of higher education in the United States was gloriously uncomplicated in the early 1800s. After removing his belongings from the stagecoach, Nathaniel went to the president's office where he was told he would be examined for admission at two o'clock that same afternoon. He was anxious lest he be rejected, but Robert Manning made light of his nephew's concern and offered what encouragement he could. The young man's fears were unjustified, as Manning's letter home revealed: "At 2 o'clock he attended and in one hour returned, having been examined, passed, and a Chum appointed him."[2] The "chum" was Alfred Mason, one of his fellow stagecoach passengers.

Being a resident at an American college in the first quarter of the nineteenth century demanded considerable resourcefulness from students. Robert Manning wisely absented himself while Nathaniel and Mason made the arrangements and purchases essential to their stay. Two days later Manning returned and found the freshmen settled in their academic surroundings. Nathaniel conceded he "had traded more than he ever did before," and told his uncle the only unresolved problem was bedding. For his part, Manning was pleased the fees were no more than expected. He was nonetheless appalled that so much had been spent on furniture and books, and regretted leaving Nathaniel "so small a sum as after buying wood and candles [there hardly] will be sufficient to procure him those small articles which are absolutely necessary."[3]

Families eagerly await the first letter from a young person away at college and there is little doubt that William Manning, another uncle, was agreeably surprised to receive Nathaniel's initial impression:

BRUNSWICK, OCTR. 9TH, 1821

DEAR UNCLE,

   I suppose you have heard that I have entered college. I passed through my examinations as well as most of the candidates. I am very well contented with my situation, and do not wish to come back to Salem this some time. My chum is the Son of the Hon. Mr. Mason of Portsmouth. He has money enough, which is perhaps unfortunate for me, as it is absolutely necessary that I should make as good an appearance as he does. The Students supply their own Furniture for their own Rooms, buy their own wood, and pay 2 dollars a term for washing, 1 dollar for sweeping and bed-making besides various other expences.

**AN EARLY VIEW OF BOWDOIN COLLEGE**
This engraving dates from 1821, the year Hawthorne entered the college. Hawthorne's grades placed him in the middle third of his class, but homesickness and poverty made his undergraduate days detestable.

I board at Professor Newman's with three other Students. The Laws of the College are not at all too strict, and I do not have to study near so hard as I did in Salem. The 5 dollars you gave me has been of great use to me. I did not tell Uncle Robert that I had it, so that I was richer when he left me than he supposed. I hope I shall have no occasion to call upon you for any more this term. If I should be in want of any, I shall confidently apply to you. . . .

I remain
Your affectionate nephew

NATHANIEL HATHORNE.[4]

Hawthorne appears to have adjusted quickly to collegiate life. Having grown up in Salem and passed many pleasant days in Raymond, he would not have been too shocked at Bowdoin's austere setting. The campus embraced about thirty acres, much of it pine forest. The college's four modest buildings were grouped in quadrangular fashion; among them Maine Hall was to be his dormitory. On warm days the students were happy enough to abandon their sultry buildings for the welcome cool of the shady pines. Wild life, while not spectacular, was sufficient to interest the bored student. Pigeons and squirrels thrived in abundance and there were delectable salmon for the angler.

Bowdoin's curriculum was ideally suited to Nathaniel's literary bent. It was heavily weighted with the Greek and Roman classics, and considerable emphasis was placed on English compositions. Science and mathematics, although not favourites of Hawthorne, posed no great problem. But another feature, declamations, was abhorrent to him. During his first year they were given privately, but for the remaining period they had to be in public as well as private. His dislike of declaiming probably dated from an unhappy public speaking experience as a young boy in Salem. Although Hawthorne knew that to declaim successfully would enhance his scholastic standing at Bowdoin, he resisted. "Fines and admonitions were alike powerless," his classmate, Horatio Bridge, said. "He would not declaim."[5]

Nonetheless, Hawthorne could hardly survive the four years of Bowdoin's academic regime without making some appearance in public. When he did so, he seems to have performed very well. There were at least two occasions when he delivered orations that were well received by his fellow students and the Bowdoin faculty. One of these, "*De patribus conscriptis Romanorum,*" still survives in the college archives.[6] Hawthorne's rare public performances, however much dreaded, were to stand him in good stead later on when, as American Consul in Liverpool, he was expected to speak frequently at civic functions. The college's classics-oriented curriculum also provided other useful attributes to diplomacy with its emphasis on logic and objectivity in thinking, and its stress on clarity and accuracy in writing.

Writing was Hawthorne's forte. Even before enrolling at Bowdoin his literary bent was clearly established. As a teen-age boy he had tried his hand both at poetry and prose and while these efforts were juvenile, they nonetheless were unmistakable signposts of his future career. In college he most enjoyed writing English essays and translating Latin. His language professor later recalled that when the shy student presented himself at the mentor's private study, he submitted a composition which no other undergraduate could equal. His friend, Horatio Bridge, added that Hawthorne excelled in Latin, being blessed with the ability to write the language "with great ease and purity."[7]

But young Nathaniel, bookish though he may have been, was not a good student overall. By his own admission he was idle much of the time. He seems to have put little effort into those subjects which did not interest him. This lack of interest in some fields, and his unwillingness to declaim regularly, combined to deprive him of a role in Bowdoin's commencement programme. Yet, this mediocrity in the classroom appears not to have been a concern of Hawthorne; more pressing were his problems of deportment and making ends meet. Money matters, indeed, were to plague him to the end of his days and it was at college that he first learned the humiliation of begging. Although he had confidently written his Uncle William that he hoped to get through the first term without asking anyone for additional funds, he was mistaken in his optimism. By the end of the first month he was obliged to write his mother saying he would "make no objection to some money as I have had to buy Webster's Mathematics which cost $3.00 and am now almost out of cash."[8] Then another financial blow fell from a totally unexpected quarter – illness. He contracted measles and afterwards came the inevitable doctor's bill. Too embarrassed to apply to one of his uncles this time, he again appealed to his mother. This time she had nothing to send and, in the end, the uncles were obliged to come to his aid with a combined grant of $15. When his unhappy first term ended, the chagrined student wrote plaintively to one of his uncles. "I hope," he said, "you will call for me, for I long to get home."[9]

Hawthorne's bout of measles, his homesickness and his permanent state of poverty were hardly conducive to the start of a happy collegiate life. These drawbacks, however, were insignificant compared with the next drama at Bowdoin. In the middle of the second term a fire ravaged Maine Hall where Nathaniel now lived. Students counted themselves lucky to escape without injury, but some lost all their possessions. Nathaniel and his roommate, Alfred Mason, were luckier than most. Their room was on the ground floor and they managed to save everything. The little town of Brunswick was hard-pressed to find accommodation for the displaced students; Hawthorne and Mason appealed to Mrs. Adams, the lady who provided their meals, and she kindly took them in. Eventually the necessary repairs were made and the students returned to their old quarters.

The tedium of classwork was relieved as Hawthorne developed friendships and began to sample Bowdoin's official, and un-official, extra-curricular life. He was especially attracted to the activities of the Athenaeum, one of Bowdoin's two literary societies. The secret of these societies' popularity at Bowdoin, as at other American institutions, lay in their rivalry. Two societies on a campus meant that they could become collegiate counterparts of the two national political parties. Moreover, two societies guaranteed "pro" and "con" sides on any issue facing the nation. Thus, election year or not, the societies could be counted on for lively debate, fierce loyalties, and the making of lasting friendships. At Bowdoin the societies early acquired radical and conservative colourations. Nathaniel chose the Athenaeum, the radical stronghold, while conservative students joined the Peucinian. Three other passengers who had arrived by stagecoach with Hawthorne also belonged to The Athenaeum – his roommate, Mason, and Cilley and Pierce.

It was Franklin Pierce, of New Hampshire, who was to make the biggest impact on the Athenaeum. Quick to discern that the real power in the society resided in the chairmanship of the standing committee, he promptly got himself elected to this position. His deputy, however, was to be appointed and, perhaps to the surprise of many, he chose Hawthorne. As Pierce's right-hand man, Hawthorne was concerned with the entire range of the Athenaeum's programme – its declamations, debates, library, and social activities. Not unexpectedly, the periodic debates between the Athenaeum and the Peucinian attracted the interest of the entire Bowdoin student body and at times feelings ran high. On the social side, each attempted to outshine the other when the time came for their annual banquets – easily the highlight of the year. The societies were proud of their respective libraries, for books had not yet been cheaply produced. So great was the pressure brought to bear on members to donate volumes to the libraries that few could escape without contributing – however difficult their personal circumstances. Given the low state of the Hawthorne family finances and his prominence in the society as Pierce's deputy, young Nathaniel must have been distressed by his dilemma. Nonetheless, he dutifully joined with one or two friends and together they presented over twenty volumes for the shelves of the Athenaeum.

Another enthusiastic member of the Athenaeum was Hawthorne's friend, Horatio Bridge. He later recalled how the 1824 presidential election caused great interest at Bowdoin where each literary society identified itself with one of the major parties. The Athenaeum sided with the Democrats, the Peucinian with the Whigs. "The students," said Bridge, "showed their individual preferences as strongly as . . . the average voter at the polls."[10] Bridge added that he, Pierce, Cilley and Hawthorne were enthusiastic supporters of the Democratic candidate, General Andrew Jackson.

But the Athenaeum was not the only activity which brought together Hawthorne and Pierce. Bowdoin College at that time boasted a crude military training program, the forerunner of the Reserve Officer Training Corps which has produced so much American military leadership in times of crisis. Hawthorne humourously described his feeble efforts in the Bowdoin training program as "the only military service of my life." While quick to

**MAINE HALL, WHERE HAWTHORNE ROOMED**
It was here, during his second year at Bowdoin, that a fire broke out and damaged
the hall of residence so extensively that students had to move out.

admit his own shortcomings on the parade ground, he added that Pierce – a company
officer – "entered into this pastime with an earnestness with which I could not pretend to
compete."[11] Hawthorne was not the only one to recognize Pierce's qualities of leadership.
Bridge described him as an extrovert, immensely popular with his fellow students, and as
being "impulsive, not rash, generous, not lavish."[23] In a strange way the opposite natures
of Hawthorne and Pierce, the one shy and the other outgoing, seemed complementary, for
the two became close friends.

Wherever students live and work together they form unofficial clubs or groups which
sometimes provide opportunities for conviviality not possible in formal organizations.
Hawthorne, Mason, Cilley and a few others formed one such club whose major purpose
was to diversify the traditionally dull diet of the college boarding houses. Their "Pot-8-0
Club" met weekly to allow its members to feast upon roasted potatoes flavoured with butter
and salt, and washed down with "cider or some other mild drink."[13] The club's constitution provided that *"ardent spirits shall never be introduced."*[14] Because this passage was
underlined, it seems probable that beverages more potent than cider occasionally graced
the table. The preamble to the club's constitution stated the group's motive in simple
terms:

> We the undersigned subscribers being convinced that it is beneficial both to the
> health and understanding of man to use vegetable diet, and considering that the
> Potato is nutritious, easy of digestion, and procured with less difficulty and
> expense than most other vegetables, do hereby agree to form ourselves into an
> association under the name of the Pot-8-0 Club.[15]

If the convivial gatherings of club members escaped notice of Bowdoin's vigilant professors, the card-playing indulged in by Hawthorne and several of his friends did not. Towards the end of Hawthorne's last term of his freshman year Bowdoin's president, William Allen, was obliged to write Elizabeth Hathorne that her son had been guilty of playing cards at different times, and was being fined. The following day Nathaniel wrote his mother:

                                                                    BRUNSWICK, MAY 30TH, 1822
MY DEAR MOTHER,

    I hope you have arrived safely in Salem. I have nothing particular to inform you of, except that all the Card Players in College have been found out, and my unfortunate self among the number. One has been dismissed from College, two suspended, and the rest, with myself, have been fined 50 cts. each. I believe the President intends to write to the friends of all the delinquents. Should that be the case you must show the letter to nobody. If I am again detected, I shall have the honour of being suspended. When the President asked what we played for, I thought it proper to inform him it was 50 cts. although it happened to be a quart of wine, but if I had told him of that he would probably have fined me for having a blow. There was no untruth in the case, as the wine cost 50 cts. I have not played at all this term. I have not drunk any kind of spirit or wine this term, and shall not till the last week.

        I remain
                N.H.

I must have some money, for I have none left except about 75 cts. Do not show this.[16]


Nathaniel was not caught again at cards, but his name appears continuously in the college record of fines for the next three years. In fairness to him, it should be noted that some offences were merely violations of Bowdoin's puritanical code of regulations. For example, an entry dated May 17, 1824 reads: "*Bridge, Greenleaft, Hathorne,* and *Hale 2* [there were two Hales enrolled at the time] 25 cents each for walking unnecessarily on the Sabbath."[17] Hawthorne's other fines were for neglect of declamations, recitations, prayers, night worship, themes and forensics – in fact, his name appears under every category of fines with as many as three offences being listed in each of several headings.

Hawthorne did not enter into the religious life of Bowdoin College, although the opportunity was there. "A missionary society has lately been formed in college . . .," he wrote one of his aunts, "but it does not meet with much encouragement; only twenty-two of the students have joined it. . . . I suppose you would be glad to hear that I am a member, but my regard to truth compels me to confess that I am not."[18]

Despite his rebellion against college regulations and his mediocre record in the classroom, Hawthorne was not the totally miserable student he imagined himself to be. He clearly enjoyed his participation in The Athenaeum and the Pot-8-0 Club, and he made friends with two students who were to be loyal until the end of his days – Horatio Bridge and Franklin Pierce.

In his leisure moments, Hawthorne much preferred the company of Bridge. Three decades after leaving the lovely campus he recalled his many pleasant strolls with Bridge in

## THE MYSTERY OF A NAME

On Hawthorne's battered copy of Bowdoin College rules, his name is spelled variously as "Hathorne" and "Hawthorne." Just when, and why, he adopted Hawthorne has never been satisfactorily explained.

his dedication to him of *The Snow Image* ". . . we were lads together," he said, "at a country college, gathering blueberries in study hours under those tall, academic pines, or watching the great logs as they tumbled along the current of the Androscoggin, or shooting pigeons or grey squirrels in the woods, or bat fowling in the summer twilight, or snatching trout in that shadowy little stream which, I suppose, is still wandering riverward through the forest, though you and I will never cast a line in it again; two idle lads, in short (as we need not fear to acknowledge now) doing a hundred things that the faculty never heard of, or else it would have been the worse for us . . . ."[19]

Bridge, for his part, remembered the stealthy visits he and Hawthorne made to an old fortune-teller whose lively predictions must have amused and cheered the hearts of her youthful listeners. "After tea," he recalled, "Hawthorne and I often walked, silent or conversing according to the humor of the hour. These rambles sometimes ended at the unpainted cottage of an old fortune-teller who, from the tea-leaves in a cracked cup or from a soiled pack of cards, evoked our respective destinies. She always gave us brilliant futures, in which the most attractive of the promised gifts were abundance of gold and great wealth of wives. Lovely beings these wives of destiny were sure to be, some of whom she prophesized would be 'dark-complected' and others 'light-complected,' but all surpassingly beautiful. . . . To the discredit of the prophetess it must be said that the gold never came to us, but to each a very happy marriage without the dangerous procession of blondes and brunettes."[20]

During their walks at Bowdoin the two young men sometimes discussed their futures. Bridge was convinced that literary success would one day come to his friend, although Hawthorne never once voiced such a hope. "He listened without assenting," Bridge recalled, "but, as he told me long afterwards, he was cheered and strengthened in his subsequent career by my enthusiastic faith in his literary powers."[21] In dedicating *The Snow Image* to Bridge, Hawthorne freely acknowledged his collegiate friend's encouragement. "If anybody," he said, "is responsible at this day for my being an author, it is yourself."[22] Although Bridge's cheerfulness was an undoubted tonic to his friend's downcast nature, it was not enough to change his overall attitude to college. He remained impatient to leave and never ceased to be haunted by the spectre of expulsion for unpaid bills. Shortly after beginning his final year he poured out his feelings in a letter to his sister Elizabeth:

BRUNSWICK, OCTOBER 1st, 1824

MY DEAR SISTER,

Since my arrival I have put on my gold watch-chain and purchased a cane; so that, with the aid of my new white gloves, I flatter myself that I make a most splendid appearance in the eyes of the pestilent little freshmen. . . . I am very low-spirited and I verily believe that all the blue devils in Hell, or wherever else they reside, have been let loose upon me. I am tired of college, and all its amusements and occupations. I am tired of my friends and occupations, and finally, I am heartily tired of myself. I would not live over my college life again, "though 'twere to buy a world of happy days."

I must now come to the serious part of my letter, and truly I do it with a sad heart. There has been a new code of laws promulgated since the last term, from which I extract the following section, for the edification of all concerned, "If any bill is not paid within one month after the commencement of the next term, interest will be charged; and if not paid within *six months* from the date of the bill, there shall be an assessment of twenty cents for *every days neglect*, and the student, against whom the bill is made, *may be dismissed from college.*" My term bills remain unpaid for more than a year past. I do not ask for money, but thought it best that you should know how delightful are my prospects.

I can write nothing else that will be interesting to you. I hope that I shall hear from you soon, and do not let your letters be long. Notwithstanding I was so weary of home, I shall rejoice when I return to it, whether by dismission or any other cause. I am your affectionate brother, N.H. . . .[23]

Before leaving Bowdoin Hawthorne had one superb opportunity to display his rebellious spirit. College yearbooks or annuals, now an American fixture, were unknown as such at Bowdoin. There was, however, an agreeable substitute in the form of an assembled set of student profiles which provided a composite representation of the graduating class. The concept of the project was ideal so long as all students were willing to have their vignettes made. However, Hawthorne stubbornly refused and so did the faithful Bridge. The group did include a profile of Bowdoin's other literary giant-to-be Henry Wadsworth Longfellow. Partly because Longfellow entered college at a different time and partly because he belonged to the rival and conservative Peucinian literary society, Hawthorne did not know his fellow student well. In later life, when each was making his way in the literary world, their friendship flourished.

Although he had flouted many of Bowdoin's regulations, Hawthorne eventually was certified for graduation in the Class of 1825. The Board of Overseers did not at first approve of granting Bridge a Bachelor of Arts degree, but eventually relented. The highest ranking students were given speaking roles on the commencement programme, Longfellow electing to talk about "Our Native Writers". Hawthorne ranked only eighteenth in the class of thirty-eight seniors, but this position nonetheless would have entitled him to a role on graduation day except for one overriding problem. In a letter to his sister Elizabeth he explained what had happened, and why he was displeased with his Uncle John Dike's glowing report of his Bowdoin experience:

MY DEAR SISTER,

. . .. I am not very well pleased with Mr. Dike's report of me. The family had before conceived much too high an opinion of my talents, and probably formed expectations which I shall never realize. I have thought much upon the subject and have finally come to the conclusion that I shall never make a distinguished figure in the world, and all I hope or wish is to plod along with the multitude. I do not say this for the purpose of drawing any flattery from you but merely to set mother and the rest of you right, upon a point where your partiality has led you astray. I did hope that Uncle Robert's opinion of me was nearer the truth, as his deportment toward me never expressed a very high estimation of my abilities. . . .

Did the President write to you about my part? He called me to his Study and informed me that though my rank in the class entitled me to a part, yet it was contrary to the laws to give me one, on account of my neglect of Declamation. As he enquired Mother's name and residence, I supposed that he intended to write her upon the subject. If so, you will send me a copy of the letter. I am perfectly satisfied with this arrangement, as it is a sufficient testimonial of my scholarship, while it saves me the mortification of making my appearance in public at commencement . . . .

I shall return three weeks from next Wednesday, if I should not write, I wish to have 15 dollars sent me about a week before that time. You must answer this letter immediately, as I feel very anxious to hear from you all.

I am &
NATHANIEL HATHORNE[24]

There was an amusing sequel to President Allen's decision not to give Hawthorne a place on the graduation program. Thirteen other students, by virtue of their low class ranking, were also excluded. Undaunted by not making the elite upper bracket, these students and Hawthorne formed a group of their own who, for reasons unknown, called themselves "The Navy Club". In later life the Navy Club members did very well: one became a Doctor of Divinity, another a Congressman, one the Paymaster-General of the United States Navy, and another (Hawthorne) an eminent author. "Of the officers elected," said Bridge, "the D.D. was made Commodore, Hawthorne was Commander, myself Boatswain, and the most fun-loving of the party designated Chaplain. Every one had a title, from Commodore to Cook. The weekly suppers at Miss Ward's were very jolly; and some of the class, who, by reason of superior standing as scholars, were not entitled to membership, would fain have joined in the merry sessions of the club, but they were not admitted."[25]

Eventually graduation day arrived and the students duly received their diplomas. Then they scattered to make their way in the world, some – including Hawthorne – not bothering to return to the campus until many years later. Hawthorne's time at Bowdoin may have been a period of restlessness and unhappiness, arising mainly from his constant lack of funds, but he did form at least two staunch friendships. Horatio Bridge was to be a key figure in inspiring and launching his literary career, while Franklin Pierce would become the sponsor of his consular years.

# II
# Of Love and the Custom House

For many years after their graduation from Bowdoin College, Hawthorne and Pierce saw little of each other. Hawthorne wrote ceaselessly, but failed either to gain national recognition or to earn a decent livelihood by his pen. Pierce, on the other hand, found the path to political fame incredibly easy. Hawthorne, perhaps embarrassed by his lack of achievement, did not bother to seek out his old friend, but Pierce – at least on one occasion – dropped in on Hawthorne and the two cronies had a pleasant reunion.

In 1832 Pierce was elected Speaker of the New Hampshire legislature. Hawthorne was pleased, but not surprised. "I suppose," he wrote Pierce, "there is hardly a limit to your expectations at this moment, and I really cannot see why there should be any." He went on to predict, among these unlimited possibilities, that Pierce would become United States Senator, reach a high position in the War Department, and then go on to even greater honours. Amazingly, each of these predictions proved correct, but it was another sentence in Hawthorne's congratulatory letter that would return to haunt him in twenty years. "It is a pity," he said, "that I am not in a situation to use my pen in your behalf, though you seem not to need the assistance of newspaper scribblers."[1]

Pierce had married Jane Appleton, daughter of Bowdoin's president. Although each partner was devoted to the other, the union was not a happy one. Jane was shy and detested the public limelight. As Franklin advanced from one honour to the next, she found the ordeal increasingly difficult to bear. Despite his wife's uneasiness, Pierce's aspirations for the highest offices in the land were undiminished.

Meanwhile, Hawthorne's first novel, *Fanshawe: A Tale*, appeared and was loosely based on Bowdoin College. It was not a success and cost the author $100. Bitterly disappointed, he repudiated the work and vowed that it would never be reprinted. In the years that followed he produced many short stories and sketches, most appearing anonymously as was the prevailing custom. Bridge, ever the frank advisor, despaired at Hawthorne's insistence on anonymity and urged him to let his name be known. No doubt he was pleased, therefore, when in 1836 Hawthorne agreed to become editor of the *American Magazine of Useful and Entertaining Knowledge*. So, too, was Franklin Pierce who immediately asked him to "enter my name as subscriber to the magazine." Then, in a friendly rebuke, he added: "If you do not write to me soon, Hath, I will never write a puff of the 'American Magazine,' or say a clever thing about its editor."[2] But Hawthorne's bid for prominence was short-lived; the journal failed and he once more was left without regular income. He continued to write short stories and managed to survive only through the sheer volume of his output.

As a college student, Hawthorne could not picture the day when he might become a married man. So confident was he of bachelorhood that he readily entered into a wager with his friend, Jonathan Cilley, on November 14, 1824, that he would not be married twelve years later.[3] The wager was a barrel of the finest Madeira wine. Their mutual friend, Horatio Bridge, was entrusted with the wager document. Bridge, like Cilley, must have considered Hawthorne a candidate for early marriage, for Nathaniel was extremely handsome with "dark, brilliant, and most expressive eyebrows, and a profusion of dark hair," To Bridge he seemed to have ideal qualities; he was "manly, cool, self-poised, and brave."[4]

Yet Bridge was obliged to notify Cilley on November 14, 1836, that Hawthorne was still unmarried, and thus had won the Madeira wager. Cilley was surprisingly reluctant to keep his word. Bridge told Hawthorne he might never receive the wine. "Cilley," he said, "has written me in a manner inconsistent with an intention of paying promptly, and if a bet grows old it grows cold."[5] Cilley, the politician, had the nerve to propose that the barrel of wine be delivered at the next Bowdoin College commencement service at which "as many of our classmates as could be mustered" would share the prize.[6] Bridge did not hesitate to give his own view that "A bet of a barrel can only be intended for the individual's use who wins."[7]

During the difficult years when Hawthorne was establishing his reputation, it was Bridge who most encouraged and supported the author. He would not be shaken from the belief that his old Bowdoin classmate was destined for literary greatness, but he had difficulty in convincing Hawthorne of his true ability. In 1836, impatient over Nathaniel's lack of confidence, he went to the publisher, Samuel Goodrich, and made a bold proposal. Would Goodrich, he asked, tell Hawthorne to put together a book of tales from those had appeared in periodicals, and submit them for publication in a book? Goodrich doubted the volume would sell, but when Bridge offered to guarantee costs, he agreed. Not even the publisher's subsequent overture convinced Hawthorne the book would succeed. On Christmas Day, 1836, Bridge was obliged to chide the author for his continued lack of confidence. "Whether your book will sell extensively may be doubtful," he explained, "but that is of small importance in the first book you publish. At all events, keep up your spirits till the result is ascertained. . . . The bane of your life has been self-distrust. This has kept you back for many years . . . ."[8] The book appeared in March, 1837 and sold fairly well, but the publishing house itself soon fell upon bad times and failed. Hawthorne was left without remuneration, but his *Twice-Told Tales* had the result for which Bridge had hoped. Thanks in part to a favourable review in the *North American Review* by Longfellow, America woke up to the fact that it had a brilliant new writer.

The year 1837 also saw Franklin Pierce win a remarkable victory at the poll. He became the youngest member of the United States Senate at the age of thirty-three. Citizens of New Hampshire no doubt were overjoyed at this latest triumph of their brilliant young politician, but the victory came as no shock to Bridge. "And so Franklin Pierce is elected Senator," he wrote Hawthorne. "There is an instance of what a man can do for himself by trying. . . . He is a good fellow and I rejoice at his success." Then, with Nathaniel's welfare in mind, he added: "He can do something for you perhaps. The inclination he certainly has. Have you heard from him lately?"[9] Despite Bridge's expectation, Pierce was not yet in a position to act on behalf of his friend.

Hawthorne gladly would have married had he felt the income from his pen to be enough to support a family. But he knew only too well it was not, and asked Cilley, now Congressman for Maine, to use his influence in obtaining for him the Salem postmastership. Cilley readily agreed, and began the task of wooing the appropriate politicians. He had hardly taken up Hawthorne's cause when he became involved in a duel with a Kentucky Congressman, and was killed. The loss of an old friend and, with him, the chance of finding immediate employment, was shattering.

He was rescued from his miserable plight late in 1838 when friends approached the future historian, George Bancroft, who headed the Boston Custom House. Bancroft agreed to appoint Hawthorne weigher and gauger, a position that paid him $1500 annually. Hawthorne was grateful even for this small income which he could not then hope to match from writing. In a letter to Longfellow, he admitted to an additional advantage. "I have no

**"MINE IS A HEALTHY WEARINESS"**
Here at the Boston Custom House
Hawthorne became intimately acquainted
with the ways of seafarers. He found the work
tiring, but the experience was to prove useful
when he became a consul years later.

reason," he said, "to doubt my capacity to fulfil the duties, for I don't know what they are. They tell me that a considerable portion of my time will be unoccupied, the which I mean to employ in sketches of my new experience, under such titles as . . . 'Scenes in Dock,' 'Voyages at Anchor,' 'Nibblings of a Wharf Rat,' 'Romance of the Revenue Service.'"[10] George Hillard, a Boston attorney, invited Hawthorne to lodge at his home while employed at the Custom House. Hawthorne accepted; this was but the first of several acts of kindness extended by Hillard to the struggling author.

Hawthorne arrived early at the wharf each morning, for the dock labourers drew wages based on the number of hours worked, and it was his duty to see that they worked well. The long hours were tiring, but he did not care. "Mine," he said, "is a healthy weariness, such as needs only a night's sleep to remove it. But from henceforth forever, I shall be entitled to call the sons of toil my brethren. Years hence, perhaps, the experience that my heart is acquiring now will flow out in truth and wisdom."[11] This last prophecy was indeed fulfilled fifteen years later when, as consul in Liverpool, he championed the cause of America's wretched seamen.

Hawthorne remained at the Boston Custom House only two years, but when he left he was richer, both materially and spiritually. Of the $3,000 he had earned he managed to save nearly half. Of far greater value was the knowledge he had gained of the maritime world. His experience taught him the importance of listening with equal attention to captain and crew, a precaution that was to help him gain an insight into conditions aboard American vessels when he became consul.

During his employment in the Boston Custom House, Hawthorne kept a diary. Excerpts from it portray the drama which attended the arrival and departure of vessels, and the delightful rogues whose lives were centred in the Boston docklands. One entry details his impression of a dismal little British schooner in mid-winter, "Most of the time," he said, "I paced the deck to keep myself warm . . . . Sometimes I descended into the dirty little cabin . . . and warmed myself by a red hot stove, among biscuit barrels, pots and kettles, sea chests, and innumerable lumber of all sorts – my olfactories, meanwhile, being greatly refreshed by the odor of a pipe, which the captain or some of his crew was smoking. But at last came the sunset, with delicate clouds, and a purple light upon the islands, and I blessed it, because it was the signal for my release."[12]

Hawthorne's magnificent powers of description, destined to reach fruition in the four years immediately preceding his consular assignment, received great stimulus during the lonely years between college and marriage. Although his Custom House work left much to be desired in income and dignity, it led directly to his great period of writing.

A typical diary passage, in which Hawthorne instantly transports the reader into the Boston waterfront scene, describes the antics of a boy from Malaga – perhaps only ten or eleven years old – who came to the port aboard an American coal ship. "It is really touching," he wrote, "to see how free and happy he is – how the little fellow takes the whole wide world for his home, and all mankind for his family. . . . He is a Catholic, and yesterday being Friday he caught some fish and fried them for his dinner in sweet oil, and really they looked so delicate that I almost wished he would invite me to partake. Every once in a while he undresses himself and leaps overboard, plunging down beneath the waves as if the sea were as native to him as the earth. Then he runs up the rigging of the vessel as if he meant to fly through the air.[13]

Liverpool was the principal port of embarkation for millions of immigrants who came to the United States in the nineteenth century. Boston was the landing point for those who had staked their futures in New England, and many went straight from the docks to the region's thriving factories. Hawthorne was a witness to this human drama and his diary records the arrival of an immigrant ship. The English brig *Tiberius* landed some seventy girls who were earmarked for factory jobs. "Some," noted Hawthorne, "[are] pale and delicate-looking, others rugged and coarse. The scene of landing them in boats at the wharf stairs, to the considerable display of their legs – when they are carried off to the Worcester railroad in hacks and omnibuses. Their farewells to the men – Good-bye, John, etc., – with wavings of handkerchiefs as long as they were in sight."[14]

Boston's Long Wharf may have been an uninspiring sight to some, but to Hawthorne it was a mirror of the worldly needs of man. His diary describes a huge pile of cotton bales, unloaded from a New Orleans ship, "twenty or thirty feet high, as high as a house." There were also barrels of molasses, casks of linseed oil, and iron bars being landed from another vessel with the dockside scales waiting to receive them. "To stand on the elevated deck or rail of a ship, and look up the wharf, you see the whole space of it thronged with trucks and carts removing the cargoes of vessels, or taking commodities to and from stores. Long Wharf is devoted to the ponderous, evil-smelling, inelegant necessaries of life . . . ."[15]

Despite the guaranteed income and other advantages gained from his days on the Boston waterfront, Hawthorne was far from happy with the Custom House job. Because he had obtained his position through political patronage, he came to resent the work and looked upon his fellow government employees as dull, spineless men. He vowed he would never again have anything to do with politicians. But, faced with a continuous precarious existence – could he be sure he would not be tempted by some future handout from the hand of Uncle

Sam? To the nagging problems of his financial future and his annoyance with some Custom House workers, Hawthorne now added another dilemma which had something of bitter and sweet. He was becoming increasingly fond of Sophia Peabody, the comely daughter of a Salem dentist. Their love letters began in earnest in 1839 and Hawthorne was not long in realizing that Sophia had to be the only girl in his future. What was maddening was the realization that his Custom House position was tied to political favour, and that he could lose it as quickly as he had come by it.

Some scholars regard Hawthorne's letters to Sophia as among the most beautiful in the realm of courtship. Julian Hawthorne, commenting on them long after his father's death, said they express "a single hearted love and reverence."[16]

Sophia had never enjoyed robust health and she was honest enough to emphasize this deficiency as one reason why Hawthorne might find her unacceptable. But he would not hear of it. "If my little Sophie – mine own Dove – cannot grow plump and rosy and tough and vigorous without being changed into another nature," he wrote in April, 1839, "then I do think that for this short life she had better remain just what she is."[17] Hawthorne's earliest love letters begin with "My Dearest" and end "Your own friend," but quickly progress into the language of true love. Sophia is not long in becoming "Dearest," "Best Beloved," and even "Dearissima," and his endings – "Your Own" and "Thinest" – reveal his deep feelings.

Although the contents of love letters seldom convey their original passion when made public in later years, Hawthorne's letters to Sophia constitute an exception. One letter, for example, took as its theme Sophia's name, and before he has ended his playful study of it, he cleverly managed to combine it with his own. For most of the courtship period he unabashedly called his true love "Sophia Hawthorne" and referred to himself as "husband." Sophia, for her part, very early in the romance, reciprocated by calling herself his wife. When, in August, 1839, Hawthorne received Sophia's first letter in which she subscribed herself as his wife, he was ecstatic with joy. "I kiss that word when I meet it in your letters," he wrote, "and I repeat over and over to myself, 'she is my wife – I am her husband.' Dearest, I could almost think that the institution of marriage was ordained, first of all, for you and me, and for you and me alone; it seems so fresh and new . . . ."[18]

Hawthorne then went on to picture, sometimes in great detail, his future with Sophia at its centre. In one letter he proposed the precise manner in which the family library would be developed. "Very dearest," he said, "I wish you would make out a list of books that you would like to be in our library, for I intend, whenever the cash and the opportunity occur together, to buy enough to fill up our new book-case, and I want to feel that I am buying them for both of us. . . . We shall prize every volume, and receive a separate pleasure from the acquisition of it."[19]

In June, 1840, after receiving a letter from Sophia extolling the beauty of Concord, he vented his despair and loneliness. "Would that we could build our cottage this very now," he said, "this very summer, amid the scenes which thou describest [in Concord]. My heart thirsts and languishes to be there, away from the hot sun and the coal-dust and the steaming docks, and the thick-pated, stubborn, contentious men with whom I brawl from morning till night . . . ."[20]

Hawthorne's unhappy days in the Boston Custom House came to an abrupt end with the inauguration of William Henry Harrison as President in March, 1841. Thousands of supporters of outgoing President Martin van Buren were dismissed. Hawthorne submitted his resignation and left in January of the new year. Comforting though it had been to look forward to regular pay, he had been far from content as a mere weigher of cargo. He was impatient to get on with his writing, especially since that exciting creature – Sophia Peabody – had entered his life. He wanted desperately to marry, for he was now thirty-six and was convinced that Sophia was meant for him. But how was he to support her? Torn between his love and the need to earn a living, he turned to Brook Farm – the nineteenth century American farm commune – as a possible solution. He reasoned that if he liked life there, Sophia could join him later. In April, 1841, he made up his mind and joined the community, contributing a large portion of his meagre savings accumulated from his years in the Custom House. He arrived in the middle of a raging snowstorm, an event which he lost no time in describing to Sophia. His first letter from Brook Farm, and others which immediately followed, reveal Hawthorne's rare gift of combining romance with a tinge of humour:

Oak Hill, April 13th, 1841

Ownest love,

Here is thy poor husband in a polar Paradise! I know not how to interpret this aspect of nature – whether it be of a good or evil omen to our enterprise . . . I laud my stars, however, that thou wilt not have thy first impressions of our future home from such a day as this. Thou wouldst shiver all thy life afterwards, and never realize that there could be bright skies, and green hills and meadows, and trees heavy with foliage, when now the whole scene is a great snowbank, and the sky full of snow likewise. . . . Dearest, provide thyself with a good stock of furs; and if thou canst obtain the skin of a polar bear, thou wilt find it a very suitable summer dress for this region. Thou must not hope to walk abroad, except upon snow-shoes, nor to find any warmth, save in thy husband's heart.

Ownest wife, I like my brethren in affliction very well; and couldst thou see us sitting round our table, at meal-times, before the great kitchen fire, thou wouldst call it a cheerful sight. . . . Wert thou here, I should ask for nothing more – not even for sunshine and summer weather; for thou wouldst be both, to thy husband.

Now farewell, for the present, most beloved. I have been writing this in my chamber; but the fire is getting low, and the house is old and cold; so that the warmth of my whole person has retreated to my heart, which burns with love for thee.[21]

When Hawthorne came to write *The Blithedale Romance* twenty years later, he freely admitted in the preface that he had drawn from "actual reminiscences" at Brook Farm. Indeed, his arrival at the Blithedale commune was under almost identical circumstances as those described in his first letter from Brook Farm to Sophia – during a fierce snow-storm in the month of April. For a time he considered building a house on the farm so that Sophia could join him, but eventually came to realize that he – like many another at Brook Farm – had not found the proper niche in life. So, in October of 1841, he said good-bye to his friends and left. He had no regrets, not even for his investment which he doubted would ever be returned.

Hawthorne now turned his whole attention to the perplexing problem of marriage. He was learning to live with the uncertain financial situation which had plagued him since he first took up his pen. And there was no question but that Sophia was to be his bride. But when? An old obstacle to their union arose again – the reluctance of Hawthorne's sisters and, at times, his mother, to accept Sophia into the family. Sophia could not understand this and asked time and again to talk with Hawthorne's sisters, but they steadfastly refused to see her.

"Belovedest," wrote Hawthorne in a desperate attempt to explain, "I know not what counsel to give thee about calling on my sisters, and therefore must leave the matter to thine own exquisite sense of what is right and delicate. . . . I think I can partly understand why they appear cool towards thee, but it is for nothing in thyself personally, nor for any unkindness towards my Dove, whom everybody must feel to be the loveablest being in the world.[22]

As late as May of 1842, when the marriage was imminent, the rift had not been healed. It was not for lack of trying on Sophia's part. In this month she had written a touching letter to Elizabeth and Louisa, seeking their approval. Hawthorne hastened to give Sophia a report of how it had been received. "Thy letter to my sisters was most beautiful," he said, "– sweet, gentle, and magnanimous, such as no angel save my Dove could have written. If they do not love thee, it will be because they have no hearts to love with."[23] A month before the wedding date Mrs. Hawthorne capitulated. "It seems," wrote Hawthorne to Sophia, "that our mother had seen how things were a long time ago. At first, her heart was troubled . . . but, gradually and quietly, God has taught her that all is good, and so, dearest wife, we shall have her fullest blessing and concurrence. My sisters, too, begin to sympathise as they ought, and all is well. God be praised!"[24] The wedding took place on July 9, 1842, in the home of Dr. and Mrs. Peabody in Boston, with the Rev. James F. Clarke officiating. The minister was never again to see Hawthorne in real life, but would outlive him and return to preach at his funeral twenty-two years later.

The couple settled at The Old Manse in Concord, and Sophia quickly adapted to her new role as dutiful wife of a writer. In a letter to a friend she explained that "my dear lord began to write in earnest, and then commenced my leisure, because, till we meet at dinner, I do not see him." She usually referred to Nathaniel as "Mr. Hawthorne" or "my lord" but rarely by his first name. In the same letter she said nature had come off second best in the competition to win their hearts. "The treetops waved a majestic welcome, and rustled their thousand leaves like brooks over our heads. But the bloom and fragrance of nature had become secondary to us, though we were lovers of it. In my husband's face and eyes I saw a fairer world, of which the other was a faint copy."[25] Two weeks later Sophia was just as ecstatic in describing to Mary Foote the happy routine of the home. "In the afternoon and evening I sit in the Study with him," she said, "It is the pleasantest niche in our temple. We watch the sun together, descending in purple and gold, in every variety of magnificence, over the river." She went on to depict their evenings: ". . . we are gathered together beneath our luminous star in the Study, for we have a large hanging astral lamp, which beautifully illumines the room with its walls of pale yellow paper. . . . Except once Mr. Emerson, no one hunts us out in the evening. Then Mr. Hawthorne reads to me. . . . Such a voice, too – such sweet thunder!"[26]

Sophia's bliss continued to ride the crest of the wave. In another letter to her friend Mary Foote she related how, during the confining months of winter, they had decided to study German together. "I knew a little," she said, "just enough to empower me to hold the rod, and be somewhat impertinent, and I have entire pre-eminence in the way of pronunciation. But ever and anon I am made quite humble by being helped out of thick forests by my knight, instead of my guiding him. So we teach each other in the most charming manner . . . ."[27]

In the autumn of 1843 Sophia wrote Mary that Nathaniel had succeeded at an entirely

**SOPHIA HAWTHORNE**
The Hawthornes were living at The Old
Manse in Concord in 1844 when their first
child was born. Sophia was 36 at the time.

new venture – gardening. "Mr. Hawthorne," she said, ". . . has cultivated his garden a
great deal, and as you may suppose, such vegetables never before were tasted. When
Apollos tend herds and till the earth, it is but reasonable to expect unusual effects."[28] On
Christmas Day Sophia found time to sing her husband's praises in a letter to her mother.
"Apollo boiled some potatoes for breakfast," she said. "Imagine him with that magnificent
head bent over a cooking stove, and those star-eyes watching the pot boil! In consequence,
there never were such good potatoes before." Dutiful wife that she was, Sophia had looked
forward to preparing a special dish for her husband's Christmas feast, but her plans went
astray. "I intended," she said, "to make a fine bowl of chocolate for my husband's dinner,
but he proposed to celebrate Christmas by having no cooking at all. At one o'clock we went
together to the village, my husband going to the Athenaeum, and I to Mrs. Emerson's,
where Mr. Thoreau was dining. On my way home I saw in the distance the form of forms
approaching. We dined on preserved fruits and bread and milk – quite elegant and very
nice. What a miracle my husband is!"[29]

Their first child, a girl, was born on March 3, 1844, and was christened Una after
Spenser's heroine. Hawthorne explained to his friend, George Hillard, why the name was
chosen.

> I thank you for your kind and warm congratulations on the advent of our little
> Una – a name which I wish you were entirely pleased with, as I think you will be
> by and by. Perhaps the first impression may not be altogether agreeable, for the
> name has never before been warmed with human life, and therefore may not
> seem appropriate to real flesh and blood. But for us, our child has already given
> it a natural warmth, and when she has worn it through her lifetime, and
> perhaps transmitted it to descendants of her own, the beautiful name will have
> become naturalized on earth . . .

Hawthorne cherished Hillard's friendship and went on to confide some of his innermost thoughts. "I find it a very sober and serious kind of business that springs from the birth of a child," he said. "It ought not to come too early in a man's life – not till he has fully enjoyed his youth – for methinks the spirit can never be thoroughly gay and careless again, after this great event." Then his thoughts turned to his struggles to make ends meet – now accentuated by the arrival of the first child. "God keep me from ever being really a writer for bread!" he said. "If I alone was concerned I had rather starve, but in that case poor little Una would have to take refuge in the alms-house – which here in Concord is a most gloomy old mansion."

Hawthorne then shared with Hillard his and Sophia's delight over Una's first smile. "She has already smiled once . . .," he said. "I was inclined to attribute it to the wind, which sometimes produces a sardonic grin, but her mother, who was the sole witness of the phenomenon, persists that it was a veritable smile out of the child's mouth and eyes."[30]

When Una was only thirteen days old, Sophia arranged for her to be taken to Hawthorne's study. "Great was his surprise," she said, "to see his little daughter coming to him!"[31] Through letters to her family and friends, Una's progress to that blissful time which every family awaits – sleeping through the night – was finally achieved. By August Sophia was able to report that Una "woke a little after four this morning, and when I first opened my eyes upon her, her feet were 'in the sky'."[32]

But the old bugbear of financial insecurity again darkened the Hawthorne threshold. Una's arrival, blessed event that it was, meant additional expense. "The only way we can make money now," Sophia told her mother, "seems to be to save it . . . you know we cannot live cheaper anywhere or anyhow than thus."[33] To her friend Mary Foote she dropped a hint of concern. "I do not know," she said, "what is in store for me, but I know well that God is in the future, and I do not fear, or lose the precious present by anticipating possible evil."[34] However impoverished the Hawthornes were, they detested charity. Sophia was acutely embarrassed when a Concord friend, Mrs. George Prescott, wished to give a helping hand. In a letter to her mother Sophia explained that Mrs. Prescott "is perpetually doing for me what she will not allow me to pay for, and often what I cannot pay for. . . . She papered my kitchen with her own hands, and would not let me even pay for the paper."[35]

Despite Hawthorne's vow that he would never have anything more to do with politicians, he confided to a friend in 1844 that he might consider another government job – if he could get it. "If we have a Democratic administration next year," he said, "I shall again favor Uncle Sam with my services, though I hope in some less disagreeable shape than formerly."[36] When the Democratic party's choice, James K. Polk, emerged victor, Hawthorne's friends promised to start fathoming the pork barrel of patronage to see if some morsel could be found for the author.

Happily, there was Baby Una to distract the couple from their money woes. Hawthorne continued to sing the child's praises to those he met and wrote. He offered Bridge a double recipe for happiness: marriage and parenthood. "If you want a new feeling in life," he said, "get married." As to Una's pulchritude, one fact was obvious. ". . . she," he vowed, "will be the prettiest young lady in the world."[37]

These forlorn days were further brightened when Bridge and Franklin Pierce once turned up without notice. "Mr. Hawthorne was in the shed, hewing wood," Sophia said, "[when] Mr. Bridge caught a glimpse of him and began a sort of a waltz towards him. Mr. Pierce followed, and when they reappeared, Mr. Pierce's arm was encircling my husband's blue frock. How his friends do love him!"[38]

At the time of his visit with the Hawthornes, Pierce was District Attorney for New

## "I AM TURNED OUT OF OFFICE!"
The Salem Custom House offered Hawthorne employment for three years, but his unwillingness to become a tool of local politicians led to abrupt dismissal. He pleaded for work of any kind, saying he would not "stand upon my dignity."

Hampshire, having resigned his seat in the United States Senate three years before. During his service in Congress he consistently chose to remain aloof from the emotive issues of the times. But these frailties were unrecognizable to Hawthorne, for his eyes could see only the genial Frank Pierce of college days. Neither did Sophia, then or thereafter, have occasion to doubt Pierce's sincerity and loyalty.

This was the first occasion when Sophia met Pierce. "My impression," she said afterwards, "is very strong of Mr. Pierce's loveliness and truth of character .... My husband says Mr. Pierce's affection for and reliance upon him are perhaps greater than any other person's. He called him 'Nathaniel,' and spoke to him and looked at him with peculiar tenderness."[39]

In vain did Pierce, Bridge and others seek a suitable government position for Hawthorne. Several offers were put to him, but most involved moving away from home, and this Hawthorne firmly resisted. Suddenly the crisis became acute; Sophia was again with child. Hawthorne feverishly attempted to collect old debts and to borrow small sums. None of these measures helped substantially. Then, when the owner of The Old Manse wanted to

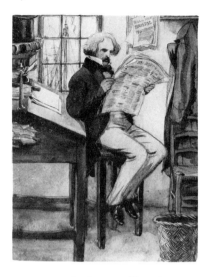

## CUSTOM HOUSE EMPLOYEE

Some of the most scathing descriptions of civil servants are found in Hawthorne's introduction to *The Scarlet Letter*. Yet he was obliged to accept employment in two custom houses when his pen failed to provide adequate means for living.

repossess the house, Hawthorne was obliged to leave Concord and go to Salem where he moved in his family with his mother.

Almost beside himself with worry, he appealed to his friend Horatio Bridge. Suppose, he said, the child (Sophia's next, due in June) should come before a job was found – what then? Bridge could only respond with renewed appeals to the Democratic Party bureaucracy. In an attempt to be helpful, Ralph Waldo Emerson, philosophically pointed out that many other people were in debt – some of whom were far worse off than Hawthorne. He suggested the impecunious author should try whistling away his cares. Sophia was not amused. "It is wholly new for him to be in debt," she wrote her mother, "and he [Nathaniel] cannot 'whistle' for it'."[40] Hawthorne's long wait ended in April, 1846, when President Polk approved his appointment as Surveyor for the port of Salem. The President had defeated the stork in a close race, for the Hawthornes' only son, Julian, was born a mere two months later.

The salary for the Salem post was only $1,200 a year, but it provided a welcome and reliable $100 every thirty days and, for the time being, the old anxiety about where the next mouthful of food was coming from could be put aside.

As surveyor Hawthorne was in charge of several junior employees – men who knew nothing of his literary endeavours. To his great delight, they accepted him as one of themselves. Although Salem had been a busy port in New England's early history, it was now in decline and there was some pressure to reduce the staff of the Custom House. The time came when Hawthorne was ordered to dismiss two temporary inspectors. He recalled all too vividly his own recent financial difficulties, and was determined not to dismiss the pair unless absolutely obliged to. He thus incurred the wrath of the Salem Democrats when he attempted merely to suspend the two men. The unpleasant incident was but an omen of worse things to come; happily, he was unaware of his growing unpopularity with Salem's Democratic Party chieftains.

Two of Hawthorne's Custom House associates, Zachariah Burchmore and William Pike, were special favourites. Burchmore was as fine a clerk as the job called for, Hawthorne said, and besides, possessed a rare sense of humour. A sample of Burchmore's wit emerged in a pithy promissory note made out to Hawthorne:

SALEM, Jan. 27, 1848, – For value received I promise to pay Nathaniel Hawthorne four pence in sixty years. – Z. BURCHMORE.[41]

Pike, on the other hand, was a philosopher of sorts. Hawthorne thought highly of him and once wrote Franklin Pierce: ". . . there is an old fellow at Salem who has more brains than either of us."[42]

Hawthorne's task in the Custom House required him to certify official records, collect duty, and stamp goods with a stencil bearing his name once the required fees had been paid. In his spare time he turned over in his mind various plots which he hoped to turn into fiction when time permitted. It was while performing the Custom House chores that he developed the theme for his masterpiece, *The Scarlet Letter*. Although his duties were uninspiring, Hawthorne applied himself assiduously and could, when occasion demanded, become as tempestuous a customs official as ever boarded a ship. An old friend, referring to Hawthorne's days in the port of Salem, recalled an attempt by a rough, overbearing captain to throttle the customs inspector. The amazed master, said the friend, "was met with such a terrific uprising of spiritual and physical wrath that the man fled up the wharf and took refuge in the Office, inquiring, 'What in God's name have you sent on board my ship as an inspector?!'"[43]

But mischief was still afoot in Salem politics, and Hawthorne was its target. His dislike of politicians, especially the Salem party bosses who felt he owed obeisance to them, was bound to cause ruffles. He had been happy enough to avow party allegiance in a nominal way, but no more. This seeming indifference on the part of someone who owed his position to party patronage was intolerable to Salem Democrats, and they vowed to get rid of Hawthorne. They therefore joined in a smear campaign with the opposition Whigs, who now took up the initiative, and there was little Hawthorne could do to check it. In March of 1849 he wrote his friend George Hillard about this organized effort to oust him. "I don't think this ought to be done," he said, "for I was not appointed to office as a reward for political services, nor have I acted as a politician since."[44]

Three months later he startled Hillard with the latest development. "I am turned out of office!" he exclaimed. He went on to plead for Hillard's help in finding "anything . . . in the way of . . . literary employment, in connection with a newspaper, or [even] as corrector of the press to some printing establishment, etc." His pathetic appeal continued: "I shall not stand upon my dignity; that must take care of itself . . . . Do not think anything too humble to be mentioned to me."[45]

# III
# A Pen Helps a Friend

"My dear father," wrote Sophia when the news of her husband's dismissal broke, "Mr. Hawthorne received news by telegraph today [June 8, 1849] that he is turned out of office headlong. I have written to mother, and told her, fearing she would hear of it accidentally. We are not cast down at all, and do not be anxious for us. You will see by my letter to mother how we are hopeful and cheerful about it, and expect better things . . . ."[1] In the letter to her mother she repeated the same thought, but went on to say that he had never liked the job in any case, and was now "rather relieved . . . that it is taken out of his hands, and has an inward confidence that something much better and more suitable for him will turn up."[2]

Sophia's next letters to her parents were bitter against the Democrats and the injustice done to her husband. She related the galling charge which had been levelled against Hawthorne – that he "had been in the habit of writing political articles in magazines and newspapers!"[3] The accusation, she explained, had been made by a prominent Salem citizen who had been backed up by the signatures of thirty other men. "Can you believe it?" she implored, "Not one of these gentlemen knew this to be true, because it is *not* true; and yet, for party ends, they have all perjured themselves to get away his office, and make the President believe there were plausible pretexts."[4]

Hawthorne's initial reaction was to fight the system which had left him so embittered. But the confrontation with politicians, now fully in the public eye, was both distasteful and painful, and he determined to put the episode behind him. He had earlier considered moving to Lenox and the recent unpleasant events persuaded him to accelerate his plans. Meanwhile, his financial plight did not escape the notice of his faithful band of friends. George Hillard devised a plan whereby he, and others, could assist their old friend without afflicting humiliation. His letter to Hawthorne read:

> It occurred to me and some other of your friends that, in consideration of the events of the last year, you might at this time be in need of a little pecuniary aid. I have therefore collected, from some of those who admire your genius and respect your character, the enclosed sum of money, which I send you with my warmest wishes for your health and happiness. I know the sensitive edge of your temperament, but do not speak or think of obligation . . . . Could you know the readiness with which everyone to whom I applied contributed to this little offering, and could you have heard the warm expressions with which some accompanied their gift, you would have felt that the bread you had cast on the waters had indeed come back to you. Let no shadow of despondency, my dear friend, steal over you. Your friends do not and will not forget you.[5]

Hawthorne read Hillard's touching letter in the vestibule of the Salem post office, and it drew tears to his eyes. In his reply to Hillard, he said: "it is sweet to be remembered by one's friends . . . and bitter, nevertheless, to need their support."[6] In the final paragraph of his reply he explained that the money would ease his life for quite a while, but added if he were to keep his self-respect, he must vow never again to need such help. Moreover, he resolved to repay the money as soon as he was able.

Hillard was not the only person who came to Hawthorne's rescue. John O'Sullivan, who had edited the now defunct *Democratic Review* for which Hawthorne had contributed many stories, now mysteriously resurrected $100 from the publication's assets. And his surprise must have been very great indeed when his dear Sophia presented him with $150 which she had carefully put aside during his years as Surveyor of the Custom House. But all these bonanzas, welcome as they were, would not tide over the growing family for long, and Hawthorne knew that he must now look to his pen.

Once the aftermath of the Salem Custom House affair subsided, he applied himself vigorously to *The Scarlet Letter*. James T. Fields, whose firm was to publish most of his output, read a portion of the book in draft, and was so enthusiastic that he urged Hawthorne to rush its completion. Fields' encouragement was a great tonic, for Hawthorne had despaired halfway through the novel when his mother had died. Now spurred on, he finished the story in February of 1850. Fields had said he would print 2,000 copies of anything Hawthorne wrote, but *The Scarlet Letter* should merit a print order of 5,000. Hawthorne was fearful that Fields' faith in the work was misplaced, and decided to read out the conclusion to Sophia. "It broke her heart," he said later, "and sent her to bed with a grievous headache,"[7] True to Fields' prediction, the book did well, selling out at once and going into a second printing. An ungrateful Salem now realized it had a literary giant in its midst, but it was too late. In the summer of 1850 Hawthorne moved to Lenox as planned, and the very first income from *The Scarlet Letter* was used to provide decorations for the home. Although the book sold well, not everyone was pleased with it. One church publication complained that a "French influence" had crept into American literature and even his old friend, George Hillard, could not resist taking a dig at the book's sombre tone. "For my own taste," he said, "I could wish that you would dwell more in the sun. . . . . "[8]

While living in Lenox Hawthorne came to know Herman Melville who had settled at nearby Pittsfield after his most recent trip to England and Europe. Although the future consul was fifteen years Melville's senior, the two writers instantly became good friends. Melville had just published his *Redburn* and its vivid account of Liverpool and its beggars was bound to have become fixed in Hawthorne's mind.

The years 1850–1853 saw Hawthorne reach the peak of his literary career. Capitalizing on the success of *The Scarlet Letter*, Fields brought out a new edition of *Twice-Told Tales*, as well as *The House of the Seven Gables*, *The Snow-Image*, *A Wonder Book*, *The Blithedale Romance*, and *Tanglewood Tales*. Hawthorne was being talked about by every literate American, and his works were also selling well in Britain. But royalties were small and even a highly successful author had difficulty in making ends meet. There was, however, one glorious advantage: for the first time since his marriage to Sophia, he was totally self-sufficient through his writing.

Now no longer obliged to rely on Uncle Sam's benevolence, he could afford to look back upon his Custom House experience with philosophical amusement. In his introduction to *The Scarlet Letter*, he said a visitor to the Custom House might find a row of old figures reclining in old-fashioned chairs tipped on their hind legs against the wall. "Often," he said, "they were asleep, but occasionally might be heard talking together, in voices between speech and a snore, and with that lack of energy that distinguishes the occupants of alms-houses, and all other human beings who depend for subsistence on charity, on monopolized labour, or anything else but their own independent exertions."[9] These men, he added, made much fuss about little matters, but thanks to their obtuseness, managed to let greater ones slip between their fingers. In the literature of many lands there are pungent references to slow-moving civil servants and *fonctionnaires*, but Hawthorne's description of his Custom House colleagues must surely rank among the most biting in print. Not unexpectedly, some of his former colleagues – as well as Salem citizens in general – were displeased at the jibes. Fortunately he did not have to endure their abuse in person, for Lenox was far enough away to allow him to escape any intended vindictiveness.

Having been so outspoken about Uncle Sam's minions, Hawthorne hoped the income from his pen would forever prevent his being included among their number. Though his present circumstances were much improved and his future outlook rosy, his hope of being utterly independent of government patronage was to be short lived. Yet Hawthorne could not have wished for better publishers than James T. Fields and William D. Ticknor. Fields was regarded as the foremost promoter in the publishing business at the time and possessed an uncanny instinct for choosing just the right moment to bring out his clients' works. He pressed Hawthorne for more and more, and it was largely to Fields' constant prodding that so many titles appeared during Hawthorne's "golden years" (1850–1853). Ticknor, by contrast, was quieter; he and Hawthorne established a rapport which is rarely achieved between publisher and author. The two became intimate friends and remained so until the end of their days. "Tick," as has been often pointed out, was not merely Hawthorne's co-publisher. He was also his financial counsellor, banker, business adviser, travelling secretary, provisioner, broker and confidant.[10]

Hawthorne's brief period of financial independence was also made happy by the arrival of his and Sophia's third and last child. A month before the birth in 1851, Sophia seems to have anticipated correctly the child's sex and name. Writing to her mother of the forthcoming event, she said, "I am so happy you feel serenely about my little 'flower' . . . . After such a winter and spring as I have passed, of tranquil and complete joy, with mountain air and outlines to live upon, I do not see how this new Hawthorne-bud can be otherwise than a lovely and glad existence."[11] The child, a girl, was promptly named Rose – which Hawthorne affectionately altered to Rosebud. He hastened to write his sister Louisa that she had another niece. Now he would have three "playmates," for he liked nothing better than romping with the children. But Rosebud, Hawthorne thought, was somehow different. He attempted to explain why to his sister-in-law, Elizabeth. "It does seem to me," he said, "that I feel a more decided drawing of the heart towards this baby than either of the other two, at their first appearance. This is my last and my latest, my autumnal flower, and will be still in her gayest bloom when I shall be decidedly an old man . . . ."[12]

In the same letter he lamented that he had been, and still was, too poor to afford life insurance, which he readily admitted was a good thing for those lucky enough to have regular incomes. "But I have never seen the year since I was married," he told Elizabeth, "when I could have spared even a hundred dollars from the necessary expense of living."[13] Such an admission, coming at the peak of Hawthorne's literary popularity, speaks volumes about the plight of writers in the middle of the nineteenth century. Their works could go into numerous editions and their names could be the talk of a nation's literary circle, but all too often there was little reward for the author.

In November of 1851 the Hawthornes moved to West Newton in the outskirts of Boston, not far from the experimental commune, Brook Farm. Here the family lived until the following summer, but it was long enough to allow him to ponder on his Brook Farm experience and develop it into his novel, *The Blithedale Romance*. Up to now Hawthorne had lived from hand to mouth, in houses either rented or belonging to relatives. The time had come, he reasoned, when he owed it both to himself, and his wife and children, to accomplish the dream of every free man – home ownership. But could he afford it? Where should this home be and, even if he found it, would the family be happy there?

In the early part of 1852 Hawthorne learned that the house belonging to Bronson Alcott, the philosopher and educator (and father of Louisa May Alcott) was for sale. He viewed it in a snowstorm and, although the conditions were hardly the best for gaining a fair impression, decided to take it, In the first week of June, Sophia, Una and Rose arrived in Concord in advance of Hawthorne and Julian. Sophia, in a letter to her mother, relates the drama of moving into her very first home. "... at four o'clock the hackman drove me to 'The Wayside.' The cartman," she said, "had tumbled all the wet mattresses in a farthest corner of the barn and I had them all pulled out to dry. . . . A good deal was accomplished in three hours, when they went home to supper, leaving me and Una in quiet possession of our home."[14] Sophia marvelled at how the old house was magically transformed through the combined efforts of the painters, paperers, and carpenters. She and Una worked hard to make the place look habitable by the time Hawthorne arrived with Julian.

Sophia need not have worried, for her husband instantly fell in love with the house and grounds. He told a friend that The Wayside was surrounded by more of a thicket than a forest, but nonetheless provided excellent shade against the summer sun. "I spend many delectable hours there in the hottest part of the day," he added, "stretched out at my lazy length with a book in my hand, or some unwritten book in my thoughts."[15]

Home ownership, Hawthorne discovered, had its problems as well as its pleasures. Only two days after moving into the house, he found himself hard-pressed to pay the workmen. He hurriedly wrote Ticknor that he had promised the men $100 at once, and the rest later – but he hadn't even the $100. Would Ticknor, he asked, rush him a draft for this amount?[16] His financial worries eased momentarily when a note arrived from Fields in England, saying he had succeeded in obtaining £200 for *The Blithedale Romance*. But the respite was short-lived. By mid-July he was obliged to appeal to Ticknor again. "I am reduced to a penniless condition," he said, "and Mrs. Hawthorne has thirteen cents in ready money. Please to send a small supply – say twenty-five dollars – as speedily as possible."[17]

Improving The Wayside and making ends meet were not the only distractions for the Hawthornes after their move to Concord. The summer of 1852 was memorable for an entirely different reason – one that was to have far-reaching effects on the author's life. This was presidential election year and if the Democrats had any chance of winning, they would have to come up with a candidate acceptable both to the North and the South. That seemed highly improbable, given the red-hot issue of slavery which already had divided both the country and the party. Lewis Cass and James Buchanan ran neck and neck through 48 ballots of the Democratic national convention, and the contest for the party nominee was still deadlocked. When neither candidate was willing to give way, delegates turned to the only compromise figure who seemed capable of drawing votes from all parts of the nation – Franklin Pierce. But was this little known man from New Hampshire really presidential calibre? After his sensational start in the state legislature, he had gone to Washington, first as Representative (1833) and later (1837) as Senator. He quit as Senator in 1842 to become District Attorney for New Hampshire. His future as a national figure appeared more promising when war erupted with Mexico and President James K. Polk made him a general. The war lasted just long enough for Pierce to share the victor's laurels. With the 1852 convention hopelessly deadlocked, the Mexican War general seemed as good a bet as any for the Democrats. On June 5, on the 49th ballot, Pierce was nominated. The Democrats at last had a candidate, but would he be a winner? An old farmer from Pierce's own state of New Hampshire had his doubts. "Frank does well enough for Concord," he said, "but he'll be monstrous thin, spread out over the United States."[18]

**TICKET TO THE WHITE HOUSE**
Without Hawthorne's biography it is doubtful that Franklin Pierce could have been elected American president in 1852. Written under pressure and interrupted by news of the tragic death of his sister Louisa, the book was regarded by Hawthorne as not being of a high literary standard.

LIFE

OF

FRANKLIN PIERCE.

BY

NATHANIEL HAWTHORNE.

BOSTON:
TICKNOR, REED, AND FIELDS.
M DCCC LII.

A popular biography was the only sure method of publicizing a political candidate and Hawthorne sensed that the time might not be far away when he could be asked to do one for his old Bowdoin College friend. Anticipating Pierce, he dashed off a letter immediately after the Democratic convention. He hoped by doing so to dodge the assignment and give Pierce time to find someone else. "It has occurred to me," he said, "that you might have some thoughts of getting me to write the necessary biography. Whatever service I can do you, I need not say, would be at your command, but I do not believe that I should succeed in this matter so well as many other men. It needs long thought with me in order to produce anything good."[19] This sounded quite final, but could Hawthorne – if actually approached by Pierce – refuse his old friend? Meanwhile, Horatio Bridge and Hawthorne pondered over Pierce's chances of winning the presidency. "[He] is playing a terrible game and for a tremendous stake," Hawthorne wrote. "On one side power, the broadest popularity, and a place in history; on the other . . . oblivion, or death and a forgotten grave."[20]

Even if Hawthorne wanted to avoid writing his friend's campaign biography, he greatly valued loyalty, and the more he looked at Pierce's chances of gaining the presidency, the more he realized his old college mate needed all the help he could get. In a nutshell, the question was, could Pierce beat the Whig candidate – the popular Winfield Scott? A Virginian, he was deeply respected, and had been a professional Army man with a commendable record dating back to the War of 1812. Moreover, he was a cultured and intelligent officer whose rigorous Army training programme had gained him the title of "Old Fuss and Feathers." Thus the American electorate in 1852 was faced with the unusual dilemma of choosing between two generals who had been comrades-in-arms in the Mexican War. The dilemma was compounded by the issue of slavery and anyone who hoped to win was bound to take a soft stand on this question, for the vote of the South was necessary to victory. But how, Pierce asked himself, could he – a relatively unknown

**FRANKLIN PIERCE**
Although Pierce was an ineffective and unpopular president, Hawthorne's loyalty to him never wavered.

Northerner – make his views known to the public, easily and quickly? A truly national press did not exist, and there was no other medium save the printed page. Common sense left Pierce, ever the practical politician, no other choice. He urgently needed a flattering campaign biography and Hawthorne was the man to write it. Their friendship would guarantee favourable treatment, and Hawthorne's reputation as the nation's foremost author insured wide readership. When these hard facts were put to Hawthorne, he knew he had no choice.

"Mr. Hawthorne did not feel as if he could refuse a boon to an old friend," Sophia wrote her mother. "He knew that it would subject him to abuse, and that the lowest motives would be ascribed to him, but . . . he never cares a *sou* what people say."[21] In agreeing to write the biography Hawthorne not only clinched the presidency for his old Bowdoin friend, but also put a seal upon his own future. With the exception of *The Marble Faun* (1860), he was finished as a novelist. His "great period" had been the immediate four years past, when virtually all of his best work was published. His consulship over the next four years resulted directly from his decision to write Pierce's campaign biography. Now he was to be catapulted into an entirely new, second career, from which would spring one of the most entertaining accounts of a consular experience ever recorded.

Hawthorne felt obliged to explain to his publisher, James T. Fields, why he had agreed to write the biography. "I have consented," he said, "somewhat reluctantly . . . for Pierce has now reached that altitude where a man careful of his personal dignity will begin to think of cutting his acquaintances. But I seek nothing from him, and therefore need not be ashamed to tell the truth of an old friend."[22] To Bridge, he explained that after a friendship of thirty years, it was impossible to refuse Pierce "at the great pinch in his life."[23] Having agreed to do the biography, Hawthorne set to work with great zeal, for the book had to be completed and circulated to the voting public with all possible haste. The imposed speed went against Hawthorne's pattern of work, but he had no choice. On July 13 he told Ticknor he had made no progress because of "the sluggishness of the people who ought to furnish the materials."[24] Eleven days later, with the long-awaited information in hand, he was able to give Ticknor a slightly better report. "I shall set to work tomorrow," he said, "and shall not show my face till it is finished."[25] But he was unaware of a staggering blow which would befall him within the next forty-eight hours. His sister Louisa, to whom he had been closely attached since childhood, drowned after leaping from the burning steamer *Henry Clay* in the Hudson River. The loss of Louisa stunned him, but the urgency of the biography enabled him to put aside the shock of her death until quieter times. He worked frantically and by July 27 told Pierce, "I am taking your life as fast as I can – murdering and mangling you. God forgive me, as I hope you will."[26] By the end of August he had completed the work, now entitled *Life of Franklin Pierce*, and his old friend was thereby nudged one step nearer the White House.

The ordeal of turning out the biography, coupled with the shock of Louisa's sudden death, left Hawthorne a drained man. Sophia was worried, but at length was able to write her mother that "Mr. Hawthorne feels better now, and looks natural, with living color." Then, in a reference to his sister, of whom she was very fond, Sophia poured out her heart: "Poor, dear Louisa! It is harder and harder for me to realize that I shall never see her again. And she had such a genuine joy in the children." During those hectic weeks when the biography was in the making, Sophia was obliged to assume full responsibility for the children. The Wayside, with its little hill, was ideally suited to separation of father from family. "I thank heaven that we possess a *hilltop*," she confided to her mother. "No amount of plains could compete with the value of this."[27]

Sophia's world may have been idyllic, but Hawthorne's was not. Many who remembered his friendship with Pierce and hoped for plums of patronage, now sought him out. Some indeed were old acquaintances; others were simply office-seekers. He listened patiently to their flattery, and agreed to do what he could if Pierce was elected. But he had no more heart for politicians now than when he was turned out of the Salem Custom House. Although Pierce was now a serious contender for president, Hawthorne continued to view him as an old Bowdoin friend – now grown up. In the preface to his *Life of Franklin Pierce* he explained his position: "The author of this memoir – being so little of a politician that he scarcely feels entitled to call himself a member of any party – would not voluntarily have undertaken the work here offered to the public."[28]

Hawthorne subscribed to travel as the best therapy for the overworked and ailing, and arranged to shake off the torpor into which he had worked himself by taking a three-week vacation. Most of it would be spent on the Isles of Shoals, off Portsmouth, New Hampshire, by himself, but first he planned to attend the fiftieth anniversary celebration of his old college, Bowdoin, in Brunswick, Maine. The occasion was the first time he had seen many of his old friends since graduation nearly a generation before, and his impression was not unlike that of most former students belatedly attending their first class reunion. His former classmates seemed to Hawthorne a miserable bunch of decrepit old men whose heads looked as if they had just emerged from a snow shower. He considered this transformation truly remarkable, especially since he himself felt as young as the day he had left Bowdoin. On pondering this phenomenon, he realized that each aging face he encountered was but a mirror in which he beheld his own reflection.[29]

On the Isles of Shoals, Hawthorne was able to relax for the first time since beginning the Pierce biography. He enjoyed the company of the other visitors, joining in evening sing-songs, and seeing the various points of interest on the island. Pierce took time out from his busy campaigning to visit him briefly, but this was the only occasion during the vacation when he was jolted back into the real world. He could not bear to be away from Sophia, even for a short period. He felt compelled to write, always employing his quaint, affectionate style. In a letter sent from Portsmouth he begged Sophia first to kiss the children, and then "Kiss thyself, if thou canst – and I wish thou couldst kiss me."[30]

The children greatly missed their father, but for Sophia the parting was even more painful. "I could not eat sitting opposite his empty chair," she confided to her mother, "and I lost several pounds of flesh." Little Rose mourned for her father and chatted away about him, all the while staring at his portrait. But the separation did not last long, for in mid-September Hawthorne returned. Sophia related how the remarkably sensitive Una – on the day of her father's arrival – missed riding home from the station with him. She had been dispatched to the village with the family mailbag sometime before Hawthorne's train was due. Sophia explained that Una might well spot her father, and in that case she would have the thrill of driving home with him. Sure enough, she saw Hawthorne as he arrived, but he was gone in a flash (apparently not seeing her), and Una continued with her postal chore. Sophia asked, on her return, why she hadn't left the letters – which were not that important – and immediately joined her father. "Oh," replied Una, "I did not know but it would be wrong to go back *only because I wanted to.*" For the next two hours she sat with the family in the study, listening to her father's adventures, and saying very little. When she went to bed, she touchingly told her mother that her head "has tingled so, ever since I saw papa, that I can hardly bear the pain! Do not tell him, for it might trouble him."[31]

While Hawthorne was on the Isles of Shoals his *Life of Franklin Pierce* appeared. The opposition Whigs were furious because so respected an author as Hawthorne had given the nation such an impressive picture of Pierce. They raged, and called the biography Hawthorne's latest "romance."[32] But the Democrats were delighted. In New York City they asked for, and received permission to print 5,000 copies in a cheap edition for gratuitous distribution. Southerners, who may have had doubts earlier about Pierce's stand on slavery, had no qualms now. In a key passage setting forth the Democratic candidate's views, Hawthorne affirmed: "Pierce fully recognized, by his votes and by his voice, the rights pledged to the South by the Constitution." Just in case anyone missed the point, Hawthorne went on to explain Pierce's stand on freeing slaves. ". . . the evil of abolition would be certain, while this good [freedom] was, at best, a contingency," he wrote.[33] The South was pleased for Hawthorne's Pierce seemed squarely on its side. Moreover, Pierce's words appealed to those in the North who believed in the South's position on states' rights. But what of those in the North who considered slavery the *only* issue?

Abolitionists were incensed with Pierce's views on slavery and especially by Hawthorne's seeming justification of them. Reaction was swift. Hawthorne told Horatio Bridge "the biography had cost me hundreds of friends here in the North, who had a purer regard for me than Frank Pierce . . . and who drop off from me like autumn leaves, in consequence of what I say on the slavery question. But," he vowed, "they were my real sentiments and I do not now regret that they are on record."[34]

Reaction of the leading journals of the day was mixed. Predictably, the *Democratic Review* was sympathetic towards the life of Pierce. "It omens well for Frank Pierce's administration," it said, "[in] that his biography, modest, unassuming as it is, deficient as it is in everything which could attract to lucubrations of the high-falutin' order of literary genii, is the first which has attracted the attention of a proved and elegant writer . . . who . . . is respected abroad and beloved at home."[35] E. A. Duyckinck, writing in the *Literary World*, was kinder still. He called the work "honorable and desirable and, as for the charge that Hawthorne had written the biography to gain public office, declared if this were indeed so "we should like to see it happen oftener . . . ." Neither did he agree with those who thought it inappropriate for writers to hold office. "Literary men," he said, "may and ought to take an active part in the affairs of the world, and there is no province where they are more wanted than the political."[36] Britain's *Westminster Review*, on the other hand, thought the work very

**PRESIDENT PIERCE LEAVING WILLARD'S HOTEL**
Inauguration day, March 4, 1853, was one of mixed feelings for Pierce. While grateful to receive the highest honour his country could bestow upon him, he and Mrs. Pierce had lost their only surviving son, Benjamin, in a railway accident only weeks before. Mrs. Pierce was not up to the usual inauguration day festivities and the traditional ball was cancelled out of respect to her.

poor. "It does the author no credit," it said in an unsigned essay. Then it went on to criticize the quality of Hawthorne's prose: "The writer is clearly out of his element; his genius forsakes him; and his usual thoughtfulness is replaced by declamatory panegyric."[37]

Hawthorne sensed the Pierce biography was not up to his usual standard, for he was reluctant to talk or write about it to his friends. He did not even bother to send a copy to Bridge, excusing himself because it was not "fairly one of my literary productions."[38] Indeed it mattered not that the book was mediocre; what counted was that it was written by a leading author who portrayed Franklin Pierce as the man of the hour. As one writer concluded, when Hawthorne put his name to the biography, it became a powerful document. Whatever the public had thought of Pierce before, he was now regarded as Hawthorne's general.[39]

The period between Pierce's nomination as the Democratic candidate and the national election – July to November 1852 – was a tense one for Hawthorne. He had written a book, though not a very good one, about his old friend. Was his literary career jeopardized now that he had laid his reputation on the line for Pierce? He had no way of knowing, although many people had made their displeasure known to him. But what if Pierce *lost?* He told Bridge of his anxiety and, in so doing, revealed unspoken concern for his own future. "Should he [Pierce] fail, what an extinction it will be!" he said, ". . . in one little month he will fall utterly out of sight and never come up again."[40] But defeat was not in the cards for Franklin Pierce. In the popular vote he received 1.6 million ballots to 1.3 million for the unfortunate Scott. The all-important electoral vote was even more one-sided: 254 to 42.

Most presidential inauguration are happy affairs with balls, dinners, and other social events arranged to celebrate the beginning of a new administration. The Pierce inauguration on March 4, 1853, by contrast, was a sad, sombre affair, for only two months before, the president-elect's only surviving son, Benjamin (aged eleven), was killed in a train accident in which Franklin and Jane Pierce escaped without injury. To the grieving Mrs. Pierce this loss seemed yet one more needless sacrifice for her husband's career. She was in no condition to be festive by March 4 and out of respect to her and the President, the traditional inauguration ball was cancelled.

When Pierce began to select his Cabinet, he confounded his Whig opponents by naming a staunch Southerner, Jefferson Davis, as Secretary of War. Davis, a West Point graduate who was to become the only president of the Confederate States of America, assured Pierce of support from the South during the stormy four years to come. To appease Northerners who were appalled at the inclusion of Davis, Pierce named New York's William L. Marcy as Secretary of State. Marcy was noted for his strong Unionist views and Pierce hoped that by choosing him he had achieved a balance in his Cabinet.

Marcy was sixty-six when he assumed office and had already retired once from public life. He served with distinction in the War of 1812, was a United States Senator from New York, had been thrice elected governor of his state, and was Secretary of War under President James K. Polk. Now, as director of Pierce's foreign policy, Marcy was to distinguish himself as Secretary of State and particularly by his adroit handling of difficult issues involving Mexico, Canada, and Great Britain. One Marcy initiative, however, was not well received in European capitals: his 1853 State Department circular requiring American diplomats to appear on formal occasions attired in the dress of an ordinary American citizen.

While Pierce was busy assigning important posts in government to his friends, Hawthorne was obliged to come face to face with the reality of accepting patronage from his old classmate. By this time he had put aside his former resolve never to depend on Uncle Sam again for a living. But what kind of appointment should he seek?

His significant contribution to Pierce's victory left him in a position to demand any job within the president's gift. At least on one occasion he toyed with the notion of becoming a United States Minister. "Do make some enquiries about Portugal," he wrote his co-publisher, James T. Fields, "as, for instance, in what part of the world it lies, and whether it is an empire, a kingdom, or a republic. Also, and more particularly, the expenses of living there, and whether the Minister would be likely to be much pestered with his own countrymen."[41]

The spoils system profoundly affected the U.S. State Department in the first half of the nineteenth century, partly because of the large number of unnecessary consulships that were created to accommodate the political appointees, and partly because many of the appointees possessed precisely the opposite qualities required of an official sent to represent his country abroad. In 1826 there were 110 consuls; by the end of President Andrew Jackson's first term (1833) the number had soared to 152.[42]

In the first century of America's independence six men who served as diplomats became President of the United States. All six served at the time when a successful diplomatic career was regarded by the public as a natural stepping stone to the White House. For men of letters the case could be slightly different. A prominent author, even a wealthy one, might regard a ministerial appointment abroad as national recognition for his literary achievement.

But for the vast majority of writers the holding of public office was a sure way of supplementing income. Perhaps more than half of American writers during the period 1800–1875 who had attained truly national status either sought or held public office at the local, state or national level. As one observer noted, holding office was the answer to a writer's dilemma: "It offered financial security, leisure to create as one could, and freedom to say what one pleased rather than what the public demanded. It was a kind of republican patronage, similar to the monarchial variety, but better."[43]

Thus, some consuls in Hawthorne's day cared little for the prestige of their position, and everything for the fees they pocketed. Heading the list of lucrative American consulates was Havana where the occupant could count on fees in excess of $9,000 – most of which he could keep. Hawthorne, however, had no interest in Cuba, and instead concentrated his efforts on landing the consulship at Liverpool. The fees there, he may have reasoned, would be almost as great as at Havana, but the port was also the gateway to England – that enchanting land from whence his ancestors had come.

Franklin Pierce, occupied with more urgent business, was slow in acting on the Liverpool assignment. The delay was maddening to the impecunious Hawthorne. When, on February 16 he had heard nothing about the position, he asked William Ticknor to approach the President. But ten days went by and there was no word, and he again appealed to Ticknor. His letter hinted at his personal tragedy should Pierce not name him to the Liverpool post. "The General means well," he said, "but it would be a great pity if he should be led into doing a wrong thing as regards that consulship.[44]

But Pierce, the Bowdoin College classmate, had not forgotten Hawthorne. Eleven days after his inauguration, the President proposed Hawthorne in the United States Senate as the next American Consul in Liverpool. There was to be a slight delay before he was confirmed, and a longer one before he could actually take up the position. Meanwhile, he sent Ticknor the manuscript of *Tanglewood Tales*, asking him to rush it into print immediately, and do the illustrations afterwards, "otherwise, I may not be able to correct the proofs."[45] The wheels of government at last began to turn, and on March 26 the nomination was confirmed. The New York *Home Journal* was ecstatic:

> "Honor and glory Mr. Hawthorne has already in abundance. No office whatever could increase his fame or elevate his position. Money, on the contrary, is the precise commodity of which he stands in need, and money therefore, has been placed within his reach. To a literary man, pecuniary independence is a blessing beyond estimate. It bestows upon him that leisure in which alone immortal books can be composed, and that freedom from care which he, beyond all other men, requires, for the cheerful elaboration of his works."[46]

Massachusetts' Senator Charles Sumner conveyed the sentiment of many:

My Dear Hawthorne:

> "Good! Good!" I exclaimed aloud on the floor of the Senate as your nomination was announced.

"Good! Good!" I now write to you, on its confirmation. Nothing could be more grateful to me. Before you go, I hope to see you.

Ever yours
CHARLES SUMNER[47]

Politicians and editors may have considered it perfectly proper for Hawthorne to accept patronage in return for his biography of Pierce, but not all literary men did. Henry David Thoreau left no doubt of his feelings. If the choice had been up to him, he said acidly, he would prefer to go cranberrying in his native New England than to go as consul to Liverpool. One had a special flavour, he added; the other did not.[48]

Sophia was thrilled that Nathaniel's confirmation by the Senate was now fact. The doubt about obtaining the Liverpool post were gone. But a new problem now presented itself; could she bear to leave the United States and live for an unknown period in a strange land? Would her aged father rejoice in Nathaniel's confirmation – or would he be saddened at the prospect of Sophia's departure? She tried to bolster his spirits by predicting he would be "more glad than sorry at the turning up of our wheel of fortune," and added that she hoped to return to the United States for a visit before her husband's assignment had run its full course. She also pointed out how quickly ships could now traverse the Atlantic and how that much-heralded marvel – the telegraph – should shortly make communication between the old world and the new almost instantaneous. She reminded her father that it was Franklin Pierce, the President of the United States, who had offered her husband the Liverpool consulship. "It was a very noble act . . .," she told Dr. Peabody, "for the office is second in dignity only to the Embassy in London and is more sought for than any other, and is nearly the most lucrative . . .."[49] As it happened, Sophia's concern for her father was fully justified; she was not to see him again after leaving the shores of the United States.

Hawthorne, impatient to embark for Liverpool, was obliged to cool his heels for the incumbent did not wish to quit the consulate until August. While this delay no doubt aided the consul's financial position, it did nothing for Hawthorne's own critical situation. He resigned himself to waiting and set about to undertake all those details which face a family about to proceed overseas for extended residence. But there was also a need for him to make one last journey within the United States – to Washington. If the bee-hive of the nation's politicians had never before attracted him, it did now, for his old Bowdoin friend and patron, Franklin Pierce, ruled over them all from the White House. Plans were accordingly made for the trip with William Ticknor agreeing to accompany him. Then he remembered the sad state of his wardrobe. In eager anticipation, he wrote Ticknor in Boston: "My best dress coat is rather shabby (befitting an author much more than a man of consular rank), so when you next smoke a cigar with our friend Driscoll, I wish you would tell him to put another suit on the stocks for me – a black dress coat and pantaloons, and he may select the cloth."[50]

# IV
# Mr. Hawthorne Sails for Liverpool

Hawthorne was elated. "I mean to go to Washington (for the first time in my life) in about a fortnight," he told his friend John O'Sullivan. In the same letter he commiserated with O'Sullivan over lack of news from Washington about his own patronage job. "It vexes me," Hawthorne said, "that you are not yet appointed to some most desirable office or other."[1] He need not have worried, for O'Sullivan, the former editor of the *Democratic Review*, was eventually named United States Minister to Portugal, the post which Hawthorne had half-jokingly enquired about.

Two weeks later, as planned, William Ticknor and Hawthorne left for the nation's capital. Sophia rushed to take up paper and pen and tell her mother. "My husband," she said, "went off in a dark rain this morning, on his way to Washington."[2] She was soon reminded that the days of the family's happy sojourn at The Wayside were numbered. During Hawthorne's absence she noted "some documents came this morning from the State Department, relating to the Consulate at Liverpool."[3] Meanwhile, the enforced separation was enlivened by such domestic dramas as Rose's doll falling into a jug of molasses and Julian's excitement over discovering wild sweet-brier which was duly transplanted beneath his bedroom window.

Hawthorne reached New York on April 14 and was immediately caught up in a flurry of activity arising out of his friendship with Pierce. Some people wanted to see the author who had helped put his friend into the White House; others sought his influence with Pierce. Hawthorne's letter to Sophia reveals how much he missed the family, but it nonetheless was light-hearted enough to permit a pun at the expense of a lady's name.

New York, Sunday morning, April 17th, 1853

Dearest,

I arrived here in good condition Thursday night at $\frac{1}{2}$ past 12. Every moment of my time has been so taken up with calls and engagements that I really could not put pen to paper until now, when I am writing before going down to breakfast.

I do wish I could be let alone, to follow my own ideas of what is agreeable. Today, I am to dine with a college professor of mathematics, to meet Miss Lynch!! Why did I ever leave thee, my own dearest wife? Now, thou seest, I am to be lynched.

We have an ugly storm here today. I intend to leave New York for Philadelphia tomorrow, and shall probably reach Washington on Wednesday.

I am homesick for thee. The children, too, seem very good and beautiful. I hope Una will be very kind and sweet. As for Julian, let Ellen make him a pandowdy. Does Rosebud still remember me? It seems an age since I left home.

No words can tell how I love thee. I will write again as soon as possible.

THINE OWNEST HUSBAND[4]

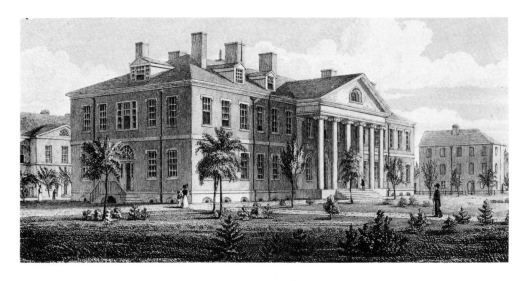

**THE STATE DEPARTMENT IN HAWTHORNE'S TIME**
"I feel rather inclined . . . [to go] to Washington," Hawthorne told his friend
William Ticknor after Franklin Pierce had been inaugurated as president. Ticknor
agreed to accompany his old friend and was instrumental in having Manchester
added to Hawthorne's consular territory. Shown here is the Northeast Executive
Building, home of the State Department from 1819 to 1866.

In Washington, Hawthorne was the toast of the town. Ticknor was less busy, and found
time to write Mrs. Ticknor about their capital adventures: "We have just taken a walk
around the White House. It far exceeds . . . expectations. Tomorrow at nine he [Haw-
thorne] sees the President."[5] Two days later Ticknor reported on his own visit with
Franklin Pierce. "I called upon the President this morning," he said, "He is looking well
and in my judgment is doing well. He was very cordial and I think bears his honors with
becoming modesty, and yet with proper dignity." Then, in a reference slightly tinged with
envy, he added: "Hawthorne is quite a lion here. Much attention is shown, and yet it
annoys him very much. He is to take tea with the President tonight."[6]
   Ticknor was irritated because Hawthorne's Washington stay was stretching from one
day to another with no discernible end. "I fully expected to have left this morning," he told
Mrs. Ticknor, "but the President wished Hawthorne to remain [until] Saturday, and
although he would not urge me to wait for him, I felt he would be disappointed if I left
him." But this was not the end of the affair. Hawthorne, with other friends, took an excursion boat to Mount Vernon to see George Washington's home without letting Ticknor
know. ". . . had I been informed in regard to the 'Boat'," he said to his wife, ". . . I should
have gone also."[7]
   Aside from seeing Pierce and the sights of Washington, Hawthorne gained one
noteworthy monetary advantage during his stay in the national capital. Manchester was a
growing port and could have been operated as a separate consulate, but thanks to Ticknor's

**JULIAN AND UNA**
In 1853, before leaving for England with their parents, Julian and Una posed for this daguerreotype. Julian was seven and Una nine at the time of sailing.

and Hawthorne's intervention, the town was added to the Liverpool consulate's territory. This astute move not only eliminated Manchester as a rival consulate, but resulted in a welcome addition to Hawthorne's income from its fees. "This he would have lost," Ticknor pointed out, "if he had not come on [to Washington]. I am glad for his sake."[8]

Hawthorne sent Sophia a brief note to let her know he had arrived safely in Washington, but it was a week before he could find time to send a fuller report:

> Washington, April 28th, Thursday, 1853
>
> Dearest,
>
> The President has asked me to remain in the city a few days longer, for particular reasons, but I think I shall be free to leave by Saturday. It is very queer how much I have done for other people and myself since my arrival here. . . . Ticknor stands by me manfully, and will not quit me until we see Boston again.
>
> I went to Mount Vernon yesterday with the ladies of the President's family. Thou never sawst such a beautiful and blossoming Spring as we have here.
>
> Expect me early in next week. How I long to be in thy arms is impossible to tell. Tell the children I love them all.
>
> THINEST.[9]

His letter to Sophia reflected satisfaction at having obtained the agency for Manchester for himself, as well as positions for others for whom he may have given endorsements to President Pierce and his staff. Nonetheless he was bound to have been disappointed at not having done anything for his friend, Herman Melville. Aside from this one misgiving, he seemed content with the reception he had received in the capital.

However enjoyable the Washington visit had been, Hawthorne was pleased to rejoin the family circle at The Wayside. Sophia, basking in the euphoria of her husband's consular appointment, proudly relayed to her father just how busy Hawthorne had been in the capital. "He received fifty letters while there," she said, "I forget how many telegraphic despatches, and a vast number of cards, and was introduced to everybody of any note."[10] With the official arrangements now complete, Hawthorne turned to the pressing problem of when and how he should take the family to Liverpool. In Washington he had been told he would take over the consulate on August 1; this being so, he considered it wise to sail from Boston in early July.

The choice of shipping lines lay between the two "C" companies – Collins, the American firm, and Cunard, the British line. The two were then engaged in a fierce struggle for the highly profitable transatlantic passenger trade with Collins ships calling mainly at New York and Cunard's at Boston. The Collins vessels were generally faster, but – their critics maintained – dangerously overpowered. The firm enjoyed substantial support from the U.S. Government and one might have expected Hawthorne, now officially designated as the next U.S. Consul at Liverpool, to embark his family from New York. However, Boston was undoubtedly more convenient. There may have been another reason why he chose to travel on a Cunard vessel. As part of their standing instructions, consuls are required to obtain maritime intelligence – especially when the shipping interests of one's country are affected. Hawthorne may have reasoned that a crossing of the Atlantic in a Cunard ship would give him first-hand knowledge of the accommodation and service aboard a ship operated by Collins' arch rival of the seas. Hawthorne revealed his plans to a friend in early June. He had, he said, "sent Mrs. Hawthorne to look at one of the Cunard steamers and, on her recommendation, I have engaged two staterooms aboard the *Niagara* to sail from Boston on the 6th July."[11]

Booking the family's passage was but the first of many items on the family's list of preparations for the forthcoming adventure. There was clothing to be fitted, articles to buy, children's toys and books to choose, and all those seemingly inconsequential things which families feel they must take with them overseas to remind them of home. Sophia was especially concerned about the lack of clothing for Rose. "It is hardly eight weeks before we sail to England . . .," she told her father, 'poor little Rosebud has nothing of her wardrobe – scarcely begun except a few little skirts."[12]

Hawthorne's self-esteem received a sudden boost when he learned that he would be entitled to a Special Passport because of his consular title. He applied for the passport on June 29, but it arrived in time for his departure a week later. The application for the document had been countersigned by Secretary of State Marcy, the man to whom the Liverpool consul shortly would be sending his dispatches.[13]

When Hawthorne's relatives and friends learned the family was sailing on the *Niagara*, the news would have elicited pleasant surprise for the ship was perhaps the best known on the Atlantic run at the time. No doubt some of her fame derived from reports of passengers singing her praise, but the *Niagara*'s greatest notoriety came from pure coincidence. In 1848 a young Scot, Francis Bennoch (who was to become one of Hawthorne's closest friends) voyaged to the United States aboard the *Niagara*. So impressed was he with the ship that he composed in mid-ocean a poem, "Our Ship."[14] The words were lively and led a fellow passenger, John L. Hatton (1809–66), to set them to music. After arriving in the United States, Hatton sang the song with great success during his concert tour. The *Niagara* is not mentioned by name, but Hatton, a Liverpool native, would have missed an excellent chance to promote the ship if he did not cite the *Niagara* each time he introduced the melody. The last verse of the rollicking tune shows why "Our Ship" was a great favourite of mid-nineteenth century American music halls:

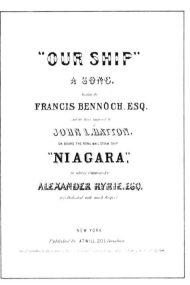

**SONG OF A SHIP**

Crossing the Atlantic in the *Niagara* in 1848, Francis Bennoch was inspired to praise the vessel by verse. "Our Ship," as it was called, was promptly put to music and became a great hit in the United States. Bennoch was later to become the Hawthornes' closest friend in Britain.

With a dip and a rise, like a bird she flies,
    And we fear not the storm or squall;
For faithful officers rule the helm,
    and Heaven protects us all.
Then a ho and a hip to the gallant ship
    That carries us o'er the sea
Through storm and foam, to a western home,
    The home of the brave and free.[15]

The Hawthornes' friends wanted to say farewell, but time was too short and much had to be done before the *Niagara* sailed. Many were disappointed not to have the chance of seeing the family before its departure, but Longfellow was pleased that Hawthorne agreed to attend a dinner at Craigie House three weeks before leaving America's shores. Among those present were Ralph Waldo Emerson, James Russell Lowell, and Charles Eliot Norton. When the dinner was over, the men of letters gathered on the piazza of Longfellow's home for warm conversation. The day after, Longfellow wrote in his journal: "The memory of yesterday sweetens today. It was a delightful farewell to my old friend. He seems much cheered by the prospect before him, and is very lively and in good spirits."[16]

The day of embarkation drew nearer and the Hawthorne household devoted all its energies to packing. William Manning, who had so conscientiously watched Nathaniel's progress since his Bowdoin College days, planned to visit his nephew in Concord before he sailed from Boston as the next United States Consul to Liverpool. He was to be disappointed by the last-minute panic. "Mrs. Hawthorne wishes me to say," wrote Nathaniel only four days before sailing date, "that she hopes you will not do this [come to Concord] because she will not be able to make you so comfortable as she would wish. Our heavy luggage will be ready to send off tomorrow, and we shall have other preparations to make before starting. We have no spare bed, having packed up all our bedclothes, and now sleeping in our borrowed sheets. It will give us great pleasure to see you in Boston on the forenoon of Wednesday . . . ."[17]

July 6 dawned and the intending passengers converged on Boston. Accompanying the Hawthornes were the Hearne sisters, Mary and Ellen, who were going to Liverpool as their servants. Both Hawthorne and his wife were relieved that their friend, William Ticknor, was also accompanying them on their first venture abroad. Ticknor's gesture for Hawthorne's welfare and happiness was but one of many acts of kindness which were to make him an indispensable ally in the coming years. Hawthorne's other co-publisher, James T. Fields, was unable to go to England, but did come to the docks to see the author embark. So, too, did Mrs. Hawthorne's father and other relatives and friends.

The *Niagara* was one of the finest vessels afloat, and her captain, John Leitch, was a much respected and experienced master. The ship could accommodate up to about 140 passengers, of whom the great majority would board at Boston and a much smaller number at Halifax. Among the hundred-plus who embarked at Boston were several well-known personalities of the period, including Enoch Train, the American shipowner and merchant; John Sandfield Macdonald, Speaker of the Canadian House of Parliament; Field Talfourd, the English artist; and two senior diplomats, Senor Pacheo, Mexico's Minister to France, and John F. T. Crampton, Great Britain's Minister to the United States.[18] Captain John Leitch may not have followed the rules of protocol strictly when he assigned guests to his table, but his Cunard superiors would have entirely approved of his business acumen. The two ministers, by virtue of their identical rank, should have flanked Leitch at his "Captain's Table," but the master kept in mind the country from which came the vast majority of his passengers.[19] Thus Hawthorne found himself seated on one side of Leitch, and his wife on the other.

John Leitch was one of the most popular of the great Cunard commanders in the middle of the nineteenth century when the fight for passengers on the Atlantic run reached fever height. Born in Scotland in 1817, he gained his master's certificate at thirty and a year later commanded the *Caledonia* on the Liverpool–New York service. Before he was thirty-five he had been – at one time or another – captain of Cunard's *Cambria*, *America*, and *Niagara*. He went on to command almost every major vessel in the Cunard fleet, and was Commodore of the fleet at the time of his death in 1883.[20] In Britain's build-up for the Crimean War, Leitch took a contingent of British troops to the Mediterranean in the *Niagara*. Suddenly the compass went awry by several degrees and he was obliged to navigate by calculating amplitudes and azimuths. His skill was cited as an example for other commanders to emulate.[21] But his abilities were not limited to seamanship; he possessed tact and was a most personable man. "His smile is charming," said Sophia, "and his voice fine."[22]

When the last farewells were said and Captain Leitch was satisfied the *Niagara* was prepared for the voyage to Halifax, he gave the order for the ship to edge away from the Boston docks. It was precisely twelve noon, the advertised time for sailing. As the vessel got under way, a round of shots from the ship's guns signalled to all within earshot that a prominent United States government official – none other than the country's next consul to the port of Liverpool – was aboard. Sophia hastened to record the event for her father. ". . . came the cannonade, which was very long. And, why," she asked, "do you suppose it was so long? Mr. Ticknor says that always they give a salute of two guns, but that yesterday so many were thundered off because Mr. Hawthorne, the distinguished United States Consul and author, was leaving the shore, and honoring her Majesty's steamship with his presence."[23]

Sophia was not the only member of Hawthorne's party to take advantage of the chance to drop off letters when the *Niagara* reached Halifax. William Ticknor, able to relax now that Hawthorne and his family were now safely on board, brought Mrs. Ticknor up to date. "My dear wife," he wrote, "As we shall have an opportunity to mail letters at Halifax you will not be sorry to receive even a short note. . . . Yesterday it was excessively hot. The Captain says he has never experienced a hotter day at sea. Today is quite cool but very pleasant. The sea is smooth and the steamer moving with very little tossing. I believe there are a good many sick. I have not come to that point yet . . ."[24] Sophia, too, spoke of the calm voyage: ". . . we were moving magically over a sea like a vast pearl, almost white with peace. I never saw anything so fair and lovely . . . ."[25]

Young Julian had other notions. Now a strapping lad of seven, he was more concerned about the geography of the voyage. On the port side of the ship was the coast of New England, on the starboard, the ocean. At one stage of the Halifax run, the land extended close to the ship, and Julian voiced his impression to his mother. "That, I suppose, is the end of America!" As an afterthought, he added: "I don't think America reaches very far!"[26]

The spectacle of the ship surging across the vast expanse of the Atlantic was enough to hold the attention of most passengers. For the Hawthornes – and especially Nathaniel and Sophia – the vessel's attraction lay in its passengers, and in their own new-found prestige. Sophia never hesitated to strike up an acquaintance if she felt the subject of her choice might prove interesting. Even on the short run from Boston to Halifax she had put her boldness to test, but with a startling result. "I heard that the British Minister [Crampton] was on board, and I searched round to find him out," she said. "I decided upon a fine-looking elderly gentlemen who was asleep near the helmhouse. Afterwards the mail-agent came to Mr. Hawthorne and said the Minister wished to make his acquaintance, and behold, here was my minister . . . ."[27] Sophia was captivated by the British diplomat, whom she found to be "a stately, handsome person," a man "with an air noble," and one having "great simplicity and charm of manner." Most of all she was struck with the Minister's speech. "The enunciation of Mr. Crampton," she said, ". . . is . . . wonderfully fine."[28]

Diplomat that he was, Crampton did not miss the opportunity to impress Sophia with Captain Leitch's excellent record which he knew also amounted to praise of the Cunard line. He told her: "Captain Leitch is remarkable among the best."[29] Julian remembered the captain as being "very courtly to my mother, and pranksome with my two sisters and myself." Leitch he characterized as a 'small, active man with bright eyes and very thick black whiskers – a genial, debonair, entertaining little gentleman" who was at his most impressive when astride the paddle-box "with his neat dark blue suit, his gilt buttons, with the old and the young."[30]

The *Niagara* reached Halifax at eleven in the evening under perfect skies. Several passengers disembarked, among them Minister Crampton. There was a three-hour lay-over and Hawthorne quickly decided this was enough time for Sophia and himself to see something of the port, then a thriving town of 20,000 people. "Behold!" Sophia said, "my husband pressed on to the pier, and on and on into the streets of Halifax, till I was quite alarmed, and feared we should not get back. But I have really been to Halifax now."[31]

In the present era of huge passenger liners, it is difficult to understand how a vessel of the *Niagara*'s size and construction could have transported so many people in such relative comfort. Completed in 1848 by Robert Steel and Sons at Greenock, the *Niagara* was only 250 feet long and had a gross tonnage of just 1,800. Like her sister ships, the *America* and the *Canada*, she was a three-masted bark with a cargo capacity of about 450 tons. The distinctive features of these ships were giant paddle-wheels situated on either side. The wheels were powered by 2,000 h.p. steam engines producing a cruising speed of over 10 knots and top speeds which reached 13 knots. By 1852 the crossing time on the New York–Liverpool route was already under ten days.[32]

The *Niagara*, with her giant paddle-wheels encased in a huge "box," was an impressive sight to behold, but her interior arrangements are best described as ingenious. Instead of wasting space with numerous small tables, the dining saloon was efficiently arranged with two long tables, parallel to each other, running its entire length. "At tea," said Sophia, "[the tables] looked very pretty with long rows of silver candlesticks and wax candles, lighting up the glass and silver (or what looks like silver) up and down the long extent."[33]

Sophia was struck by Captain Leitch's attention to detail. "We have a bountiful table and plenty of ice, and admirable attendance," she wrote her father. "The captain said he . . . never knew it so hot out of the time. He quickly sent for the joiner to take the saloon doors off the hinges that Mr. Hawthorne who sat against them might have more air." But she was less pleased when she discovered the milk had been mixed with water. "This contrivance," she said, "does not please Rosebud, and she refused to drink alloyed milk. I told the servant that the milk might well be diluted for the whole of the ship's company, but that I *must* have pure milk for my baby, as that was her whole food." Sophia need not have worried. "The Captain," she added, "had given orders that I should have everything just as I wished for the children."[34]

The *Niagara*'s all-wooden construction meant that the ship's carpenter was a key member of the crew. His tiny shop, only eight by five feet, was strategically placed on the deck where he could be within easy range of Captain Leitch's voice. This accessibility also made him a favourite of the passengers, and Julian struck up a close friendship for the duration of the voyage. "The most engaging friend of the small people was the carpenter," he recalled later, ". . . from whom I acquired that passion for the profession which every normal boy ought to have, and from the practice of which I derived deep enjoyment and many bloody thumbs and fingers for ten years afterwards." Una, when not reading an advance copy of *Tanglewood Tales*, accompanied Julian about the ship. The catering arrangements aboard the *Niagara* particularly intrigued Julian who wondered how all those passengers could enjoy fresh milk and meat during a ten-day voyage. He soon discovered the ship's cow, who seemed totally unaware of her important role, and simply gazed contentedly out of her window. With the vessel's source of milk revealed, Julian soon learned that much of the meat served the passengers came from the coops of chickens he discovered. While he may have been chagrined to see the number of birds gradually decrease during the voyage, he was pleased to note – as the *Niagara* neared the end of her voyage – that "there were still left alive and pecking contentedly about their coops a number of fowls, after we had eaten all of their brethren at the ten dinners that were served during the voyage."[35]

Living arrangements aboard the *Niagara* were austere. The elegant appointments which later became such a cherished feature of transatlantic travel, were almost unknown in the 1850s. Nonetheless the Hawthornes expressed no displeasure over their staterooms which, Julian said, were no larger than "the cases in which upright pianos are packed."[36] There was no water in the staterooms and, Julian added, no such thing as a bath on the entire ship. For those who wished to read, the ship provided a small library of volumes appropriately bound in Cunard's favourite colour – red.

Fine weather prevailed during most of the crossing and the family took advantage of it by remaining above deck. Here the great attraction was the pair of great box-like guards built above the paddle-wheels. When the *Niagara* was in port, Captain Leitch used them for his bridge, marching one way and then the other, while giving instructions. But when the vessel was at sea, these areas became the favourite haunts of passengers. It was while propped up against one of the boxes, "close against the vast scarlet cylinder of scalding hot steam," that

**THE HAWTHORNE FAMILY ABOARD THE *NIAGARA***
In this artist's impression Hawthorne is engaged in conversation with a fellow passenger to the right of the lifeboat. Seated against the box of the paddle wheel are Sophia (writing) and Una (reading), while Julian and Rose are being regaled by the stories of the ship's carpenter in front of his workshop. The Niagara's captain, John Leitch, surveys the horizon from his vantage point astride the port paddle wheel. (Original watercolour by Stuart Beck, R.S.M.A.)

Sophia wrote her letters.[37] Neither she nor any other member of the family commented on the *Niagara*'s safety features, if indeed, there were any. Little imagination is needed, however, to foresee the perils that would haunt an all-wooden vessel with sixteen furnaces consuming sixty tons of coal a day.[38] (Yet the *Niagara* served her owners well in all the seven seas, ending her days as a sailing ship in the Australian trade; she was wrecked, without loss of life, on June 6, 1875.)[39]

Thus passed the ten days at sea – days in which Hawthorne had no worry or responsibility. Sophia took the two girls in hand and Julian was content with the run of the ship. Good conversationalists were there for the effort of making oneself known, and William Ticknor was always within hailing distance to lend a hand, or to offer advice about any problem. Seldom had Hawthorne known such a period of order and contentment, and it would be a long time before he was again at such ease.

Sophia confessed to enjoying the attention shown her by the captain and the crew. "It is very convenient," she wrote her father, "to have rank with these English people. It commands good service."[40] Julian, viewing the eastward crossing many years later, said "these must have been blessed hours for them both. Behind them lay nearly eleven years of married life, spent in narrow outward circumstances, lightened only towards the last by the promise of some relaxation from strain . . . . They had filled their minds with knowledge concerning the beauties and interests of foreign lands, with but slender expectation of ever beholding them with bodily sight . . . . And now, suddenly, it had arrived, and they were on their way to the regions of their dreams, with the prospect of comparative affluence added."[41]

Sophia was artistically inclined and longed to see Italy's art treasures; it seems probable that Hawthorne promised her to visit Italy when his consular tour ended. It came as a pleasant surprise, therefore – after Minister Crampton left the ship at Halifax – that she discovered on board one of the leading British artists of the day, Field Talfourd. She discussed art and architecture with him at length, comparing the status of the several arts in the United States, Britain, and elsewhere. As a man, Talfourd was "irresistibly attractive."[42]

Two days out of Liverpool the *Niagara* ran into the only spell of rough weather during the Atlantic crossing. The wind suddenly changed and a gale tossed the little vessel about for the next thirty-six hours. "As we had enjoyed the luxury of the table in profusion," Ticknor reported to his wife, "this coming upon us so suddenly, nearly all were in more or less trouble! I had a slight touch, but not enough to avoid my dinner."[43] But the voyage was nearly over and the knowledge that the *Niagara* would shortly be sailing into the Irish Sea was enough to cheer up the passengers until the storm abated.

Not until they were on the high seas did Hawthorne and his wife have time to take a close look at the Special Passport which had arrived for the consul-designate just before the family embarked at Boston. Now, in the more relaxed surroundings of the *Niagara*, they examined it together. Sophia was much amused by the wording, and pleased by the privilege it conveyed. "I forgot to tell you," she wrote her father, "that Mr. Hawthorne's passport from the Secretary of State demands that Mr. Hawthorne should 'pass without let or molestation' – which means that our luggage is not to be looked over." Her husband, she added, "laughed inextinguishably at this solemn appeal."[44]

Early on the morning of Sunday, July 17, the ship entered the River Mersey and dropped anchor off Liverpool. "Wet tugboats with salty whistles were plashing in the brown wavelets manned by British mariners with burly, foggy voices, uttering strange dialects," recalled Julian. "Everything was delightfully incomprehensible, for a child, being free from responsibilities, can enjoy unhindered the pleasure of seeing, hearing, and being borne hither and thither without understanding anything." Presently a lighter was brought alongside the *Niagara*, and the ship began to disgorge her passengers and cargo. Julian was concerned about the "bearded or whiskered persons with official caps" who set to work examining the baggage. "I was shocked," he said, "to see them thrust their hands into these private receptacles and sometimes actually rummage in them, but I was pleased to note that our own little mountain got by undesecrated – indeed, with polite smiles and gestures." This first demonstration of consular privilege was no doubt facilitated by some sharp-eyed official who would have pointed out the Hawthorne baggage to Her Majesty's customs officials. But seven-year old Julian was oblivious to the time-honoured courtesies accorded diplomats, and ascribed a completely different reason to the polite processing of the family's possessions. "I knew my father was the greatest man in the world," he said, "but I didn't know that they knew it."[45]

Thomas Crittenden, Hawthorne's predecessor in Liverpool, was not due to relinquish his position until August 1, and thus Nathaniel had much looked forward to the respite of another two weeks before assuming his official duties. But immediately they were confronted with a change in plans – and a threat to Hawthorne's thin purse. The Hawthornes thought they had firmly booked rooms in the favourite haunt of American seaman, Mrs. Blodget's boarding house, but because of a misunderstanding Mrs. Blodget could not accommodate them for another week or so. Meanwhile, the family would be obliged, and at considerable expense, to stay in a Liverpool hotel. So Hawthorne huddled Sophia and the children into a cab, placed the baggage on the roof, and clattered off across the cobblestones to the Waterloo Hotel. Julian retained a vivid memory of the eventful trip from the pier to the hotel. The jogging over the uneven stones caused Hawthorne to smile amusedly, for the family was "tossed about on land as never before on the Atlantic." Victorian Liverpool on a rainy day was not the best introduction to "Our Old Home," as Hawthorne came to call England. "Grey stone edifices lined the sombre streets, their severity hardly relieved by shop windows," Julian recalled. "People in dun-coloured clothes forged this way and that, most of them not spreading umbrellas against the grey drizzle."[46]

Finally, the cab stopped before an imposing grey stone structure, the Waterloo Hotel, where they were to spend their first days in England. Within minutes the weary travellers were shown to a room "with tinkling glass candelabras with candles, and a small fireplace with a grate full of black coal lumps, to which one of the attendants applied a sulphur match." When the attendants had been dismissed, the family sighed with relief now that the long voyage from The Wayside was over, and their new life abroad was about to begin. Julian recalled the family's spontaneous reaction:

"'Liverpool!' we congratulated one another, exchanging pregnant glances."[47]

# V
# The Consul's "Parish"

Their unexpected confinement in the Waterloo Hotel no doubt caused the Hawthornes to ponder more deeply their homesickness and anxieties. Here they were, not in Mrs. Blodget's friendly boarding house – as they had planned – but in a hotel where even kindness and attention by the staff could not compensate for their disappointment. But this temporary frustration with living arrangements was only symptomatic of the overriding question: would the family be content on Merseyside? Happily, Julian, Una and Rose were blissfully unaware of these concerns and set about to explore their temporary home, the Waterloo Hotel.

The Waterloo was not Liverpool's first hotel, but it shared honours for the second best with the Queen's. If the Hawthornes had consulted a Liverpool guide of the period they would have found the Waterloo described in most complimentary terms:

> WATERLOO HOTEL. – Very fashionable, and frequented chiefly by Americans. It is quite luxurious. The civic banquets at the Town Hall are under the direction of Mr. Lynn, whose reputation is very high.[1]

William Lynn's culinary fame, as well as that of James Radley of Liverpool's leading hotel, The Adelphi, were firmly established. These two gentlemen so excelled at the preparation of a common speciality – *tortue claire* – that *London at Dinner; or, Where to Dine*, insisted the London gourmet would have no other.[2] This renowned turtle soup was not cheap; at fifteen shillings a quart it cost several times what a visitor would pay for his room. No doubt one of the secrets of the Waterloo Hotel's high standing among connoisseurs of food was its superb kitchen – which the Hawthorne children promptly set out to reconnoitre. The prize attraction was the hotel's twin tubs for holding the live turtles – huge monsters they were. "The only turtles we had known were the little creatures that crawled beside the brook at the foot of the meadow in Concord, sometimes no higher than a finger-nail," said Julian. "But these Brobdingnags? They were to become soup . . .. They floated in their tubs, their flat feet paddling continuously at the sides, just the toes of them appearing beyond the rim of the great carapaces. Soup! Meanwhile, they were Publicity."[3]

Sophia was flattered by the attention shown the family, as is revealed by several passages of a letter to her father. "The head of the Waterloo House, Mr. Lynn, is a venerable-looking person," she said, "resembling one's idea of an ancient duke, – dressing with elaborate elegance, and with the finest ruffled bosoms. Out of peculiar respect to the Consul of the United States, he comes in at the serving of the soup, and holds each plate while I pour the soup, and then, with great state, presents it to the waiter to place before each person. After this ceremony he retires with graceful obeisance. This homage diverts Mr. Hawthorne so much that I am afraid he will smile one day." The gravity of the servants she termed "imperturbable," and one in particular, was referred to by Hawthorne as "our Methodist preacher."[4]

Although Hawthorne was not installed in the consulate, the Liverpool commercial community still awaited word that Her Majesty's Government had accepted the appointment.

## THE WATERLOO HOTEL (LEFT) AND THE LYCEUM

When Mrs. Blodget was unable to take the family into her crowded boarding house, the Hawthornes were obliged to stay at the Waterloo Hotel. Here Hawthorne was amused at the gravity of the waiter and here, from an upstairs room, the children saw their first Punch and Judy show. The Lyceum survives, but the hotel has long since vanished.

On August 5, they read in the local press the assurance they had been seeking:

> The Queen has been pleased to approve the appointment of Mr. Nathaniel Hawthorne as consul at this port for the United States of America.[5]

One person who did not stand on ceremony and wasted no time in calling on the family at the Waterloo Hotel was Henry Bright, a brilliant twenty-four year old Liverpudlian whom Hawthorne had met briefly in the United States. Bright had been educated at Cambridge, but had not then been eligible for a degree because of his Unitarian (nonconformist) faith. His family was prominent in Liverpool's shipping circle, but young Henry's interests were more literary than commercial. He and Hawthorne, despite their great difference in age, became close friends. While the family was still confined to the hotel Henry persuaded his parents to invite them to Sandheys, West Derby, for tea. It was but the first of many occasions when Bright brought cheer to the Hawthornes. Sophia was full of praise for him. "Young Henry Bright," she said, "is a very enthusiastic young gentleman, full of life and emotion, and he very politely brought me from his gardens a radiant bouquet of flowers, among which the heliotrope and moss-roses and all other roses and mignonette make delicious fragrance."[6] Bright, aware that a single invitation to tea would not undo the languishing homesickness of the Hawthornes, came a week later with his family to take the newly arrived consul and his wife to the theatre.

The years of living in conditions near to poverty made Sophia appreciative of the smallest perquisites that accrued from her husband's consulship. ". . . the joyful news," she told her father in an early letter from Liverpool "[is] that all our letters can go to America free of charge in the ministerial budget [bag] – and all letters can be sent to me free of charge, if Nat will deposit them in cover to the Despatch Agent in Boston ... Is not this nice? Therefore I take this thick paper instead of gossamer ..."[7]

Children frequently are more resilient than their parents in adapting to strange situations and young Julian seems to have been so blessed. During one of those miserable days when he was captive in the Waterloo Hotel, a great commotion suddenly erupted in the street. Instantly he forgot his confinement and his longing for America. The chambermaid rushed with him to the window, and below they saw a strange oblong object made of canvas. "... the thing walked on two human legs, in a slanting position," he recalled. "... Figures of misshapen dwarfs were painted on the canvas sides of the structure. ... 'It's just Punch, dear,' explained the chambermaid, who was holding up my hand in her rough palm ... 'They'll stop here – you'll see! Yes, they stopped ... and for the next twenty minutes I experienced the sensation of my life."[8] But this happy episode and the discovery of the hotel's turtles were rare moments of pleasure for the Hawthorne children as the family waited impatiently for Mrs. Blodget to find them rooms.

Had Mrs. Blodget been able to receive the family then, Hawthorne would have kept to his original intention of seeing London with William Ticknor before tackling his consular duties in earnest. But the hotel stay was prolonged and, despite the cheery efforts of the staff, the morale of the family continued to sag.

Ticknor told his wife about the delay, saying that he remained with Hawthorne four days, "arranging his business as well as I could ..." He added that Col. Thomas L. Crittenden, the outgoing consul, "is very civil to him and will give him all needed instructions as to the practical duties of his office." The publisher did not think much of Hawthorne's consular territory. "In Liverpool," he said, "there is not much to be seen except the Docks and their commercial buildings. I would have not remained for twelve hours, but for Hawthorne. He wished me to stay by him as long as possible."[9]

But Liverpool, like it or not, was Hawthorne's chosen arena, and he was obliged to make the most of it. A home for his family he had not found, but at least he could start learning something about the district in which the consulate was located – Brunswick Street and its environs. The street, opened only in 1790, is a short one and terminates on the Liverpool waterfront. The American Consul was thus easily accessible to incoming and departing American captains and crews. But waterfront districts rarely show off a seaport to best advantage, and Brunswick Street was no exception in the 1850s. Hawthorne's very first entry in his journal records his dismal impression. "My office," he noted, "consists of two rooms in an edifice called Washington Buildings ... It is near the docks ... and from my window, across the narrow street, I have a view of a tall, dismal, smoke-blackened, ugly brick warehouse, – uglier than any building I ever saw in America ... There is a continual rumble of heavy wheels, which makes conversation rather difficult, although I am gradually getting accustomed to it."[10]

To a friend in the United States he was more explicit. "Liverpool," he said, "is a most detestable place as a residence that ever my lot was cast in – smoky, noisy, dirty, pestilential; and the consulate is situated in the most detestable part of the city. The streets swarm with beggars by day and by night. You never saw the like, and I pray that you may never see it in America." To the same friend he described his family's unhappiness since landing on English soil: "Myself and my family have suffered very much from the elements. There has not been what we should call a fair day since our arrival, nor a rain, but you are pretty sure to get a sprinkling if you go out without an umbrella. Except by the fireside I have not been as warm as I should like to be, but the Englishmen call it a sultry day whenever the thermometer rises above 60 degrees."[11]

Five minutes walk from the consulate was Tithebarn Street, a narrow and grimy thoroughfare. Hawthorne visited the short, bustling street during his lunch hour not long after assuming office. "I never saw . . . nor imagined," he said, "from any description, what squalor there is in the inhabitants of these streets as seen along the sidewalks. Women with young figures, but old and wrinkled countenances; young girls without any maiden neatness and trimness, barefooted, with dirty legs. Women of all ages, even elderly, go along with great, bare, ugly feet, many have baskets and other burthens on their heads. All along the street, with their wares at the edge of the sidewalk and their own seats fairly in the carriageway, you see women with fruit to sell, or combs and cheap jewelry, or coarse crockery, or oysters, or the devil knows what, and sometimes the woman is sewing meanwhile."[12]

If the populace which thronged Tithebarn Street was wretchedly poor, the same could be said for the miserable shops they were obliged to patronize. "Pawnbrokers' establishments," he said, ". . . were conveniently accessible, though what personal property these wretched people could possess . . . so as to afford the basis for a loan, was a problem that still perplexes me. Old clothesmen, likewise, dwelt hard by and hung out ancient garments to dangle in the wind. There were butchers' shops, too, presenting . . . bits and gobbets of lean meat, selvages snipped off from steaks, tough and stringy morsels, bare bones smitten away from joints by the cleaver; tripe, liver, bullock's feet, or whatever else was cheapest and divisible into the smallest lots."[13] Hawthorne surmised that even these snippets found their way into the homes of the poorest only at Christmas. In other shop windows he saw eggs "looking so dingily antique that your imagination smelt them," segments of "hungry cheese" and "fly-specked biscuits."[14]

Liverpool's depressed districts, it is true, were among the worst in the kingdom, but there was a brighter picture of the town for those who cared to look for it. Two years before Hawthorne arrived in the city another American, writing anonymously in *The Working Man's Friend, and Family Instructor*, made some surprising comparisons between the old world and the new. "The general appearance of Liverpool," he said, "was more inviting than I had supposed. Its streets, though not so wide or regular as those of New York, are much cleaner, and better paved. The buildings are not generally as lofty (except the warehouses, which are seven or eight storeys), but more relieved by architectural ornaments, heavy cornices, paneling and pediments." Liverpool's magnificent docks also captivated the visiting American; they are, he said, "the greatest 'lions' of Liverpool. They are constructed in the side of the bank of the river, and are on a most stupendous scale: wet and dry and graving docks, connected with wide and commodious quays, and immense warehouses!"[15]

The American traveller also disagreed with Hawthorne's view of Liverpool people, although it is possible he based his judgment mainly on the merchant class, whereas Hawthorne was almost always concerned with the town's poorer inhabitants. "I was struck with the marked difference in the appearance of people I met in the streets from those I had been accustomed to see at home," the visitor said. "The people here are heartier, fuller-faced, ruddier, carry their heads higher, and project their chests more, their lips are more parted, as if breathing more freely, and they are more leisurely in their gait. They have more of the vivacity and buoyancy of youth, their tones of voice are higher and more varied, and, to use a common English expression, they look more 'jolly' than our New York merchants, driving along Wall-street, as if hurrying for dear life, with stooping shoulders, compressed lips, pale faces, and anxious looks."[16]

But perhaps these views of Liverpool and Liverpudlians, offered by Americans through glasses of contrasting tints, are not so valid as opinions expressed by the town's own citizens. A leading guide of the period, *The Royal Picturesque Handbook*, explained why Liverpool was unique in some respects. "Owing to the rapid rise of Liverpool, its population consists, in a great degree, of adventurers, not merely from all parts of the United Kingdom, but of the world, attracted to it in the expectation, which, in many instances, has not been disappointed, of making a fortune," the guide said. ". . . It would be idle in such a place to look for that polish, and careful avoidance of debatable and irritating topics that distinguish more aristocratic societies, but, on the other hand, it is free from the sameness and insipidity which characterize the latter."[17]

Commerce, thus, was the theme which dominated life in mid-nineteenth century Liverpool. "Every house . . .," said *The Royal Picturesque Handbook*, "is either a counting-house, a warehouse, a shop, or a house that, in one way or other, is either an instrument, or the result of trade. The great buildings and institutions of the town are either directly or indirectly serviceable to commerce, and the inhabitants are nearly to a man traders or the servants of traders."[18] It was this same commerce with its bounteous consular fees that brought Hawthorne to Liverpool. In whatever direction he turned on leaving the consulate in Brunswick Street, he saw visible proof of the stamp made by shipping upon the city. Only five minutes away was the pride of Liverpool's waterfront, the elegant Albert Dock and its warehouse complex. Opened in the previous decade by Albert the Prince Consort, the massive buildings were erected at a cost of over £500,000. "With its well-adapted fire-proof warehouses surrounding the sheet of water, stored with goods of surprising value and variety, and its hydraulic cranes," said *The Stranger's Vade Mecum*, "the Albert Dock is a model dock, and should by all means be visited by every stranger."[19] The crowning feature of the structure was its entrance, or office façade, a sight Hawthorne would have frequently admired while on his waterfront rambles. The façade was adorned with massive Doric columns cast in iron – an aspect which still remains as a reminder of the city's dockland charm. Hawthorne's friend, Herman Melville, had been in Liverpool several years before, and captured some of its commercial flavour in his book, *Redburn*. New York's dirty wooden piers, he wrote, were nothing when compared with Liverpool's stone and iron docks which, he added, surely must have been the world's finest.

Within sight of the Albert Dock was one of Liverpool's most striking buildings and the nerve-centre of its shipping activity – the Custom House. An American viewing it while arriving in the port by sea would have rubbed his eyes in disbelief, for the building vaguely resembled the national capitol in Washington or, for that matter, any number of the state capitol buildings. On closer inspection, however, the Liverpool Custom House could be seen to have serious deficiencies: its central dome bore no statue or other adornment; also the cupola was bereft of columns to break up the monotony of the design, and the general appearance of the building was of classical heaviness. Hawthorne had much business with the Custom House, whose premises also embraced the Excise Office, the Dock Office, and the Post Office.

A short walk in another direction brought Hawthorne to the Liverpool Town Hall, the second of the town's great domed buildings. Unlike the massive bare dome of the Custom House, that atop the Town Hall was graceful with columns supporting the main structure. Appropriately for this great port, a statue of Britannia adorned the summit. Liverpool's

**THE LIVERPOOL CUSTOM HOUSE, A TEMPLE TO COMMERCE**
Hawthorne frequently visited the Custom House and its complex of other agencies, among them the post office, the dock office and the excise office. The building was damaged by enemy action in May, 1941, and eventually demolished in 1947.

town council elected a new mayor annually from among its own members. Thus it happened that Consul Hawthorne was invited to gala dinners in the Town Hall during all the years he served in the consulate.

The banquet room for these elaborate affairs was on the upper floor and, in Hawthorne's day, was lighted by superb glass chandeliers. An extensive refurbishing of all the major apartments of the Town Hall was undertaken at great cost in 1851, prior to the visit by Queen Victoria to the town in that year. Hawthorne was much impressed by the civic dinners offered by Liverpool mayors, for there never seemed to be a shortage of funds for presenting the guests with the finest of food and drink. The City Treasurer's accounts show that, during Hawthorne's first year in Liverpool, the mayor received an allowance of £1,300 for general expenses and another £700 for carriages and servants. But this was not all; a sum of £190 was allotted for the Sword-bearer and Keeper of the Wine, fifty pounds for the mayor's servant, £164 for upkeep of the mayor's stables, £896 for the maintenance of his carriages, and £751 for replenishing the Town Hall's wine cellar.[20]

Noble as the Custom House and Town Hall were, they did not compare with the city's grandest edifice – St. George's Hall. Begun in 1839 and not completed until the year after Hawthorne arrived, St. George's was acclaimed by some as the finest neo-classical building in Europe. The building was sufficiently advanced to be visited by Queen Victoria in 1851, and in the same year the law courts convened there. Aside from the apartments used for the several courts, judges, jurors, sheriff, and law library, there was a spacious and majestic hall whose floor was laid with Minton tiles.

Opposite St. George's Hall is Liverpool's Lime Street station from which Hawthorne departed on his many train journeys to London and points south. In a sense, St. George's Hall was the city's temple of culture and Lime Street station its temple of communication.

Only a few steps away from Lime Street station was Radley's Adelphi Hotel, the precursor of the hotel which bears the same name today. James Radley had worked hard to make the Adelphi one of the great hotels of Europe. Not only had he absorbed adjacent

## LIVERPOOL'S FAMED ADELPHI HOTEL AND ITS PROPRIETOR

James Radley (right) amassed a fortune while making the Adelphi one of the world's great hotels. James Buchanan and Charles Dickens stayed there and parliamentary candidates spoke from its portico. Radley's turtle soup was the envy of Londoners.

buildings into the hotel's complex, always with exquisite taste and elegance; he had, in addition, imbued his staff with his own zeal for perfection and efficiency. No wonder *The Stranger's Vade Mecum* praised the hostelry in such glowing terms:

> ADELPHI HOTEL, *Ranelagh Place.* – This is the most fashionable hotel in Liverpool, and is a magnificent one. It is greatly frequented by the nobility, distinguished foreigners, and wealthy gentry. Its comfort, quiet, and orderly management, are above all praise. It is specially celebrated for its clear turtle, and we may add, its well-selected wines; but for *tortue claire* no place can surpass the Adelphi. From the elegant balcony in front, our M.P.s are wont to address their constituents, and we have witnessed every inch of ground contested, every window filled, and even the house tops occupied![21]

A decade before Hawthorne arrived in Liverpool, Charles Dickens made his celebrated trip to the United States which resulted in the publication of his *American Notes*. It was early in January, 1842 when he came to Liverpool to board the Cunard paddle steamer, *Britannia*, for Boston. Dickens passed his last night ashore at the Adelphi, and on this occasion he pondered which of the excellent choice of food and drink offered by "my faultless friend, Mr. Radley" would be most likely to combat sea-sickness.[22]

Liverpool is one of those ancient English cities in which any of the older streets is an encapsulation of the city's history. No street can portray Liverpool's commercial past better than Duke Street, a thoroughfare Hawthorne was to know well. It was here that Mrs. Blodget's boarding house was located, an establishment that was to be their temporary home on more than one occasion. For anyone connected with Liverpool's maritime interests Duke Street was the ideal place to live. Its lower end near the waterfront was convenient for those who worked in the port area. The street was residential and sufficiently

## ST. GEORGE'S HALL IN HAWTHORNE'S DAY
One of the finest neo-classical buildings in Europe, St. George's Hall was completed shortly after Hawthorne arrived in Liverpool. It was here that he gave an address during the dedication of the town's new public library.

removed from the docks to be free of the unpleasantness arising from the movement of cargoes, passengers, and their associated hurly-burly.

The street was already in decline when Hawthorne arrived in Liverpool, but previously it was the "correct" place to live for the prosperous merchant, retired sea captain, professional man, or anyone directly or indirectly connected with ocean commerce. At least eight mayors of Liverpool had Duke Street addresses between 1714 and 1820. John Howard, the noted penal reformer, stayed in Duke Street when compiling his definitive work about English prison conditions. At 32 Duke Street was born Felicia Dorothea Browne, the poetess who became Mrs. Hemans. But Duke Street's most notorious resident undoubtedly was John Bellingham, a quiet, respected citizen who – like many of his neighbours – was a merchant-broker. He became involved in a doubtful trading enterprise which led to his detention in Russia. When his appeals to the British government for intervention seemingly fell upon deaf ears, he became embittered and determined to gain revenge. On his return to Britain he went to the House of Commons where, on May 11, 1812, he drew a pistol and killed the Prime Minister, Spencer Perceval.

Besides its notorious residents, Duke Street was renowned for several landmarks. Before Hawthorne's time it boasted "Ladies Walk," a graceful arrangement of four rows of trees with walks between them. Then, one day, the earth where the trees stood was discovered to be high quality clay and commercial interests put an end to this cherished avenue. The walk was converted in a short time into a brickyard which, citizens claimed, produced the finest bricks manufactured anywhere. Another interesting feature of Duke Street was the Union News Room (named to commemorate the union with Ireland in 1800) where anyone could have access to the latest news only for the effort of reading it. "The London morning papers arrived early the following morning," wrote a local historian, "and the evening papers the following evening, thus suiting the *habitués* in their way to and from town, and especially the select circle inhabiting the region of Duke Street."[23] The year before Hawthorne arrived in Liverpool the newsroom became the town's first free public library.

Duke Street also had one of the most ingenious cemeteries ever conceived by man, St. James. Originally an ugly stone quarry, the site was landscaped and converted into a striking cemetery. Hawthorne visited the cemetery soon after his arrival in the city and was much impressed. "I walked through St. James'. . . yesterday," he noted in his journal entry of September 14, 1853. "It is a very pretty place, dug out of the rock, having formerly, I believe, been a stone quarry. It is now a deep and spacious valley, with graves and monuments on its level and grassy floor, through which run gravel-paths, and where grows luxuriant shrubbery. It was a warm and sunny day, and the cemetery really had a most agreeable aspect. I saw several grave-stones of Americans; but what struck me most was one line of an epitaph on an English woman – 'Here rests in *pease* a virtuous wife'."[24] But it was not Duke Street's unusual cemetery, its other noted landmarks, or its associations with the city's great and near-great that was to make the thoroughfare so attractive to Hawthorne. His primary interest in the ancient street was Mary Blodget's boarding house, a notable institution talked about by seamen on both sides of the Atlantic.

Duke Street, however, did not hold the same fascination for Hawthorne as the area adjacent to his offices in Brunswick Street. In particular, Goree Piazza – just around the corner from the American Consulate – was in a sense the microcosm of Liverpool's entire waterfront district. Goree's warehouses and offices overlooked the harbour itself, with its forest of ships' masts. The intervening piazza was a bee-hive of activity, and had been since 1780 when the gigantic warehouse and office complex was erected. During the era of the infamous slave trade, Goree Piazza became the unofficial headquarters for shipping tens of thousands of African natives to the new world. In the half-century before Hawthorne's arrival, Goree Piazza and its adjacent buildings suffered two great fires. The first, in 1802, was perhaps the largest Liverpool knew before the bombing raids of the Second World War. The writer, Thomas De Quincey, was then resident in the city and said that sparks from the fire landed as far away as Warrington – fifteen miles distant. Ignited cotton from the southern states of America was a principal cause for the conflagration spreading out of control. Eventual losses were estimated at over £300,000, a catastrophe that caused a leading Liverpool insurance company to fail. In 1840 two warehouses in Back Goree Street, which sided onto the building housing the American Consulate, were destroyed with a loss of £65,000. The smoke from this fire probably accounted for the blackened walls which made Hawthorne's view from his office so depressing. One feature of the waterfront warehouses which attracted young Julian were the ingenious hoists or "jiggers" used to raise and lower goods. Some were the conventional rope-and-tackle device, but others employed great sheets of sailcloth.

A favourite haunt of Hawthorne's in Castle Street was Henry Young's bookshop. Bountifully stocked with leather-bound books at attractive prices, the shop was sometimes the meeting place of Hawthorne and his friend, Henry Bright. In time, the nook where the two met came to be known as "Hawthorne's Corner." The shop's proprietor, Henry Young, retained a vivid memory of the Consul's first visit. ". . . [This] dark-haired, remarkably quiet, gentlemanly looking man . . . walked into my shop," he said, "and, without saying a word to any person or any person speaking to him, proceeded to investigate the books. In a little time he took from the shelf a uncut copy of *Don Quixote* in two volumes, illustrated by Tony Johannot, asked me the price, paid me the money and requested me to send the book to Mr. Hawthorne at the American Consulate. . . . After a

**HAWTHORNE'S CORNER**
This nook in Henry Young's bookshop was a favourite meeting place for Hawthorne and Henry Bright. On his first visit the consul bought a copy of *Don Quixote*.

while he became more familiar and would ask about some of the rarer books, but more for information than purchase."[25]

Although Hawthorne accepted the hospitality of Liverpool's merchants and a succession of mayors, he chose to spend a great part of his leisure time in observing the town's less fortunate citizens. "Almost every day," he confided in his journal, "I take walks about Liverpool preferring the darker and dingier streets inhabited by the poorer classes. The scenes there are very picturesque in their way ... [some people] filthy in clothes and persons, ragged, pale often afflicted with humors; women, nursing their babies at dirty bosoms; men, haggard, drunken, care-worn, hopeless, but with a kind of patience, as if all this were the rule of their life; groups stand or sit talking together, around the door-steps, or in the descent of a cellar." Hawthorne explained the magic attraction of what he was seeing: "... there is a bustle, a sense of being in the midst of life, and of having got hold of something real, which I do not find in the better streets of the city."[26] Thus Tithebarn Street came to be a favourite haunt of Hawthorne's. "In the drama of low life," he said, "the street might fairly and truly be the scene where everything should take place – court- ship, quarrels, plot and counterplot, and whatnot besides. My God, what dirty, dirty children! And the grownup people are the flowers of these buds, physically and morally. At every ten steps, too, are 'Spirit Vaults,' and often 'Beds' are advertised on a placard in con- nection with the liquor-trade. Little children are often seen taking care of little children, and it seems to me that they take good and faithful care of them. Today I heard a dirty mother laughing and priding herself on the pretty ways of her dirty infant ... I must study this street-life more, and think of it more deeply."[27]

Beggars were a new experience to Hawthorne and in the vicinity of Brunswick Street he

## "JIGGER" AT WORK ON LIVERPOOL WATERFRONT

A few minutes walk from Hawthorne's office was Strand Street with its busy enterprises, mostly concerned with shipping. Warehouses employed huge sailcloths to hoist cargo.

was to see many. One in particular was such a monster that he vowed he would walk a mile to avoid him. ". . . the hardest to encounter," he said, "is a man without any legs, and if I mistake not, likewise deficient in arms. You see him before you all at once, as if he had sprouted half-way out of the earth, and would sink down and reappear in some other place the moment he had done with you. His countenance is large, fresh, and intelligent, but his great power lies in his fixed gaze, which is inconceivably difficult to bear." This man, Hawthorne added, never once removed his eyes from his subject "till you are quite past his range; and you feel it all the same, although you do not meet his glance. He is perfectly respectful, but the intentness and directness of his silent appeal is far worse than any impudence."[28]

There was novelty, too, in Liverpool's ever-changing waterfront activity. One day, shortly after Hawthorne began his consular duties, the steamer *Great Britain* anchored in the Mersey just off the Rock Ferry landing opposite the city. The impressive vessel, owned by the Great Western Steam Navigation Company and the first iron screw steamer to enter the Atlantic trade, dwarfed the nearby ferries and tug-boats, as Hawthorne, with boyish delight, noted in his diary.[29] There were other memorable scenes – "old hulks of ships of war, dismantled, roofed over, and anchored in the river, formerly for quarantine purposes, but now used chiefly or solely as homes for old seamen, whose light labor it is to take care of these condemned ships. . . . the immense multitude of ships . . . ensconced in the dock where their masts make an intricate forest for miles up and down the Liverpool shore. . . . The Mersey has the color of a mud-puddle, and no atmospheric effect, so far as I have seen, ever gives it a more agreeable tinge."[30]

Hawthorne's inclination to dwell on Liverpool's squalidness in his writing did not, quite understandably, go down well with the town's inhabitants. This emphasis was sometimes construed to indicate he was not appreciative of the attention shown him by Liverpool's leading citizens. Sir James Picton, in his *Memorials of Liverpool*, put it bluntly: "It is to be regretted that in his *Notes on England* he [Hawthorne] has indulged in a cynical spirit, rather bitter in expression, respecting a circle in which he never met with anything but the utmost kindness and consideration."[31] Nonetheless, Picton himself described Liverpool's climate as "murky and moist" and other authorities asserted that the city's rapid growth, at a time when emigration was at its peak, had left the town with enormous problems. The mortality rate in 1853, the year Hawthorne arrived in Liverpool, was over 400 for each 10,000 children born in the poorer districts, and less than half that figure for the more prosperous areas.[32] Population growth for Liverpool was near its all-time peak during Hawthorne's four years as consul. In 1801 the inhabitants numbered 77,000; by 1853 the figure was just short of 400,000.

A leading Liverpool guidebook of the period speculated that the town's unfortunate reputation as a place "celebrated for the unhealthiness of its densely populated streets, and the occupancy of unsuitable abodes" derived from its position upon a series of hills. "A crowded portion of the town," the work continues, "below rather than above the level of the tide when flowing, naturally suffering from the pent-up filth, the inundation of the lowest floors, and the back flow of deadly gases, became on that account inimical to health."[33]

Hawthorne's much-criticized impressions of Liverpool's poor districts are also supported by a contemporary observer, the Rev. Abraham Hume. Liverpool's poor were obliged to live in hovels fit only for animals, and many were crowded into cellars despite a vigorous campaign to eliminate these dark and damp places as living quarters. "In many cases," Hume said, "the letter of the law has been evaded, and cellars are used not only for domestic or mechanical operations, but also as sleeping places."

The town was also a violent place during Hawthorne's consular tour. In 1857, for example, 18% of deaths were due to injuries received in and around the waterfront. Records at St. Anne's Dispensary for 1853, the year of Hawthorne's arrival, indicated the average age of those who died there was only 14 years and 11 months. Drink was the greatest problem of all, and much of the dock area's misery stemmed from it. Hume reported 1,485 public houses in Liverpool during Hawthorne's time, or one for every 307 inhabitants; in the port area the concentration was even heavier.[34]

"Gin-shops, or what the English call spirit-vaults, are numerous in the vicinity of these poor streets," Hawthorne said, "and are set off with the magnificence of gilded door-posts, tarnished by contact with the unclean customers who haunt them. Ragged children come thither with old shaving mugs, or broken-nosed teapots, or any such makeshift receptacle, to get a little poison or madness for their parents . . . Inconceivably sluttish women enter at noonday and stand at the counter among boon-companions of both sexes, stirring up misery and jollity in a bumper together, and quaffing off the mixture with relish. As for the men, they lounge there continually, drinking till they are drunken, – drinking as long as they have a halfpenny left, – and then, as it seemed to me, waiting for a sixpenny miracle to be wrought in their pockets so as to enable them to be drunken again."[35]

In fairness to the town's reputation, it should be pointed out that many of the public houses catered exclusively to seamen with their ready money. Shipping was unmistakably the lifeblood of Liverpool and the growth of emigration to the new world and the spawning of the textile industry in Manchester and Yorkshire made the River Mersey the most frequented waterway at the British end of the Atlantic trade route. In 1851, a thousand ships sailed from Liverpool to ports in the United States. New York was the destination for the largest number – 435, but the port of New Orleans was in second place well ahead of Boston and Philadelphia. Indeed, the Manchester textile mills consumed so much cotton that the smaller Southern ports – Charleston, Mobile, and Savannah – also did a thriving business with Liverpool. So great was commerce with the United States in 1851 that £93,000 of a total of £235,000 in Liverpool dock fees resulted from American shipping.[36]

**SCENE IN A VICTORIAN GIN-SHOP**
"At every ten steps," Hawthorne wrote of Liverpool's waterfront area, "there are 'spirit vaults'." There were nearly 1,500 public houses in Liverpool during the consul's time there, or one for every 300 people.

Whatever were Liverpool's faults and the reasons that lay behind them, there was escape for any willing to make the effort. The escape route was across the Mersey, the same stream which brought the city its mixed bag of blessings and troubles. From the town's heights lovely Cheshire villages and the open countryside were visible on the opposite shore. No less than seven ferry services operated across the Mersey in Hawthorne's time, none charging more than a penny or two. The poor were content to take a weekly outing, if they could afford it, while the rich made their home in newly developed Rock Park. The ferry crossings were not without peril; a few years before Hawthorne arrived fifty people lost their lives when two boats, returning from a prize fight in Rock Ferry, capsized.

Perilous or not, the prospect of temporary escape from the Waterloo Hotel to the green fields of Cheshire seemed just the right antidote for the homesickness and culture shock which affected Sophia. In a letter to a relative, she announced her determination to do something about it. "The children," she said, "have suffered very much from confinement within doors and bad air without, and almost 'ever-during' rain . . . We find it will not do to remain in the city any longer, and tomorrow we go across the Mersey to Rockferry, a fine watering-place, twenty minutes off by steam, where the air is pure and healthy."[37]

# VI
# The Consul's Open Door

". . . the dusty and stifled chamber in which I spent wearily a considerable portion of more than four good years of my existence" – such was Nathaniel Hawthorne's terse description of the American Consulate premises in Liverpool.[1]

A consul assigned to a seaport expects most of his business to come from seamen, and their problems. Hawthorne sometimes encountered the characters who generated these problems even before setting foot in his office. On entering the Washington Buildings he mounted the poorly lit stairway to the next floor where he turned down a passageway, also with little illumination. Both the staircase and the hall were frequently packed with "beggarly and piratical-looking scoundrels" who had a common objective – Uncle Sam's Consul. The only barrier to their entry was a wooden door above which was implanted that symbol which is familiar to any wandering Yankee – the official seal of the United States, but jokingly referred to at that time as the Goose and Gridiron. Before he could reach his door, Hawthorne was obliged to push aside, step over or jump past the "Liverpool Blackballers and the scum of every maritime nation on earth" who blocked his way.[2] They frequently shouted abuse or demanded redress for their varied injustices, some real and others imagined. Some were ship-wrecked and in genuine need of assistance, some were invalids wanting permits to enter hospital, some came complaining of mistreatment by ship's officers, some were outright vagabonds in search of a hand-out, and inevitably there was a contingent of drunks.

A visitor to the consulate, if he succeeded in elbowing his way past these ruffians, found more of the same species inside the door detailing their respective woes to the vice-consul and the clerks. Fortunately Hawthorne was seated in the next room, the one which looked out on the warehouse wall, and thus escaped at least a portion of the characters who daily besieged the place. The consul's office was roughly fifteen feet square, painted in imitation oak, and lit only by the two windows overlooking the warehouse. The walls of the chamber represent an interesting commentary on what consuls had considered essential to give the place an official flavour, and at the same time, one that was distinctly American. A large but out-dated map of the United States hung on one side, as well as one of Great Britain. In case the British had forgotten, there were also engravings of American naval victories in the War of 1812. Seamen from the state of Tennessee would have been pleased at two mementos from their homeland, an engraving of the Tennessee State House in Nashville (no doubt in compliment to the late President Polk who was once the state's governor), and a "fierce and terrible bust of General Andrew Jackson." The bust of Jackson stood on a bookcase, a vantage point – according to Hawthorne – which allowed the old general to frown forth "immitigably at any Englishman who might happen to cross the threshold."[3] For all the general's fierceness, the effect was lost on most Englishmen who enquired who the gentleman was. The younger generation, Hawthorne found, had never heard of the Battle of New Orleans, their elders had forgotten it, or – worse still – had twisted the event into an English victory. There was also a print of the American steamship, the *Empire State*, one or two engraved portraits, and a representation of the American eagle spread over the words "E Pluribus Unum," painted on wood above the mantelpiece.

Hawthorne considered removing some of these adornments, particularly those which

## A "DUSTY AND STIFLED CHAMBER"
This artist's sketch, made while the American Consulate was intact, shows some of the features that Hawthorne describes – including the out-dated map of the United States above the mantlepiece, and below it, the motto "E PLURIBUS UNUM" which is just visible.

were now badly outdated or somewhat irrelevant, but on second thought changed his mind: ". . . my patriotism forbade me to take down either the bust or the pictures, both because it seemed no more than right that an American Consulate (being a little patch of our nationality imbedded into the soil and institutions of England) should fairly represent the American taste in the fine arts, and because these decorations reminded me so delightfully of an old-fashioned American barber shop."[4]

There was one purely English object in the room – a very necessary one for anyone living in Liverpool – a barometer. Hawthorne said it generally indicated one degree or another of bad weather, and so rarely pointed to Fair that he considered that part of the dial unnecessary. The sole means of heating the consul's chamber was a grate fire fed with bituminous coal. The chill temperature and the exclusion of sunlight by the warehouse sometimes compelled Hawthorne to make a fire in midsummer and light his gas lamp at noon. The "library" of the consulate, if it may be called that, consisted of miscellaneous volumes of American statutes. Filing cabinets did not exist, but correspondence between previous consuls and their Secretaries of State was stuffed in pigeon holes. One other object

**LIVERPOOL CONSULATE**
An X marks the location of
Hawthorne's office. From the
windows the blackened walls of
the warehouse opposite could be
seen. The building was
demolished as part of a road
improvement plan.

was of prime importance, for it was the means of solemnizing much consular business – a battered copy of the New Testament. It was bound in black morocco which was slick and grubby from so much use. Other items of the consulate inventory included the official seal of the United States and its press for stamping documents, and the American flag and its flagpole.

Seedy though the chamber was, it did not appear so to young Julian, who frequently accompanied his father either from normal boyish curiosity or out of necessity when Sophia was away from Liverpool. On those occasions he took great interest in the sight of cotton bales being raised or lowered at the warehouse next door. Secretly he hoped one would be dropped, but he never saw it happen. He always sat on the other side of the office from his father, scribbling, drawing pictures, and asking questions. He recalled Hawthorne complaining of the endless questions, but he said his father always answered them, even when there were no proper answers.

Sometimes Julian was party to gory stories of mutiny and assault proclaimed by pugnacious old captains who would not depart without having their say. Hawthorne had to make a judgment as to the truth of these allegations and send a report to Washington. Julian listened silently during these occasions and when the evidence was completed and his father had given his verdict, he would say to himself, "That's right!" He retained a precise picture of one particular American captain who stormed into the consul's office alleging he had been assaulted. Pointing to his hat which had a jagged hole in it, he said, "First, there's my hat!" Then with a flourish he swept off his hat and pointed to his bare head, saying "There's my head!" Julian saw, but Hawthorne preferred not to see, the nasty gash in the man's scalp – as yet unhealed. It bothered Julian that his father had said "Yes" at this point, as if he had actually seen the wound when really he had looked away.[5]

The highlight of Julian's visits with his father came at noon when appetites were hearty. Not far from the consulate was a baker's shop which was their favourite haunt. The shop was long and narrow with a counter running its full length. Customers stood on one side, the baker on the other. The counter consisted of a single wide plank, always scrubbed white, on which stood a column of fresh butter three to four feet high. Nearby was a great pile of rolls, hot and crisp from the oven. There was nothing else, for the idea was to eat as many rolls and as much butter as one could for twopence. Simple fare, but one which young Julian relished. Hawthorne's other children spent less time at the consulate, for its business was scarcely congenial to girls. Sophia had other things to do, but her letters home leave no doubt what she thought of the office. She regarded her husband as being a virtual prisoner, harnessed, and tied to "the terrors of the old Consulate."[6]

Terrors or not, Hawthorne was determined to do a creditable job, for his consuming ambition was to save enough money to forget about security for the rest of his days. He took over the consulate from Colonel Thomas Crittenden on August 1. Crittenden, a Kentuckian, should have relinquished his post shortly after Franklin Pierce was inaugurated in March, but he asked to stay on several months more. By remaining on until August he enriched his personal wealth by several thousand dollars from fees that might have gone to his successor. The first entry in Hawthorne's English journal is for August 4, in which he stated the pleasantest moment of the day was when the vice-consul (Mr. Pearce) came in with the account books and the day's receipts. On this particular day the takings were almost nine pounds – "a pretty fair day's work, though not more than the average should be."[7] Colonel Crittenden said that he had taken as much as £50 in a single day, but such windfalls were rare and Hawthorne was content to set his sights on lesser sums.

Although he was plainly elated with his consular cornucopia, Hawthorne was determined not to forget the generosity of those in America who, through George Hillard, had come to his rescue with a gift of money at a time of great need. He had aimed to repay this sum as soon as he had saved enough from the consular fees, and on December 9, 1853, wrote this moving letter:

> DEAR HILLARD, – I herewith send you a draft on Ticknor for the sum (with interest included) which was so kindly given me by unknown friends, through you, about four years ago.
>
> I have always hoped and intended to do this, from the first moment when I made up my mind to accept the money. It would not have been right to speak of this purpose before it was in my power to accomplish it, but it has never been out of my mind for a single day, nor hardly, I think, for a single working hour. I am most happy that this loan (as I may fairly call it, at this moment) can now be repaid without the risk on my part of leaving my wife and children utterly destitute. I should have done it sooner, but I felt it would be selfish to purchase the great satisfaction for myself, at any fresh risk to them. We are not rich, nor are we ever likely to be; but the miserable pinch is over.[8]

Hawthorne had a small staff to assist him with the consular duties. The senior assistant was Samuel Pearce, the Vice-Consul. An Englishman who had seen American Consuls come and go, Pearce long since had lost his enthusiasm. Hawthorne tolerated him, but would have been just as pleased to see him go – especially as he had to be paid £200 annually. The second clerk, Henry Wilding, a younger and more energetic man, was more

**TENNESSEE IN BRITAIN**
One of the incongruous adornments of the consul's office was an engraving of the Tennessee state capitol. Hawthorne refused to remove it, or the other mementoes, saying they reminded him of an old-fashioned American barber shop.

to Hawthorne's liking; his pay was £150. Two less important staff members were a third clerk and a messenger, who sometimes lent a hand at routine writing; their combined wages probably came to no more than £160. Whatever their limitations, these men were "honest and capable" and Hawthorne was sure no American would take their jobs for double the pay.[9] The consular agency in Manchester was left vacant for as long as Hawthorne dared; an agent would have to be paid, but no agent meant that the entire fees went to the Liverpool consul. At one time Hawthorne hoped to have his old Salem Custom House friend, William Pike, take the Manchester agency, but this plan did not materialize. Another agency of the Liverpool consulate was at Bangor in North Wales, where a trickle of slate exports went to America. A retired American, Cyrno Morrall, handled the consular business there, and for his efforts received £10 ($50) annually.

The economics of the consulate mattered very much to Hawthorne. He confided to his old friend, Pike, that he hoped "to bag from $5,000 to $7,000 clear per annum," but to succeed he would be obliged to go without many things. Crittenden, who had no children and lived with his wife at Mrs. Blodget's, had spent around $4,000 a year. Hawthorne took Crittenden's yearly expenditure as his own yardstick, but realized he would have to reside outside of Liverpool to live so cheaply with a family of five. But the burning question Hawthorne kept asking himself was, *how much* could he save during his four years of President Pierce's administration? In previous years Liverpool consuls received fees ranging from about $8,000 to $12,000 per year; however, by Hawthorne's time they began to increase. Nonetheless, the consul had to deduct from his fees the wages for his staff and other office expenses, as well as the cost of maintaining his family. It did not take Hawthorne long to realize that he must constantly practise thriftiness.

Between his previous experience in two United States customs houses and what he may have learned from other sources, Hawthorne undoubtedly arrived in Liverpool knowing a great deal more about his duties than the average consul of his period. He already had dealt with sea captains and their cargoes, and was intimately acquainted with ships' manifests and other forms of marine documentation from which he would derive his fees.

What Hawthorne could only guess at was the cunning of ships' captains who sometimes sought to flatter consuls in the hope they would not assess the full amount of fees normally due. In the same year that Hawthorne sailed from the United States to become U.S. Consul in Liverpool a former American Consul in Genoa, Charles Edwards Lester, published a two-volume account of his adventures in the Italian port a decade earlier. This work, *My Consulship*, was preceded by an article on the same subject in one of the popular journals of the day, *Hunt's Magazine*. If Hawthorne perchanced to read Lester's article, he would have gained some insight into the wiles practised by captains bent on dodging payment of fees. One excerpt reveals how a captain might ensnare the consul:

> Now and then . . . a generous captain comes along – "Consul, I'm going up," says he, "tomorrow, to take some of your grub." "Well done, captain, come on." You give him a good dinner, he's a generous fellow; before he sails, you and it may be, your wife, are invited aboard; the ship's boat is at the pier for you, before the time – there's a cushion in it, too, and it's all nice and clean; there is a very nice little piece of bunting, too, hanging over the tiller, with thirteen red and white stripes . . . .. Well, the dinner is plain but good cheer, such as hungry men call good; the captain is a gallant for the hour . . .. We are again in the boat, captain at the tiller this time – "What you got there, Captain?" "Oh, there's a half a dozen smoked hams and a keg of molasses and a barrel of buck-wheat flour . . . and I shall be much obliged to you, if you'll let my men take [them] up to your house." But out again with the truth. The chance is, that the captain asks you if you'll have the goodness to send the bill of port charges and consular fees on board. . . . Well more than once my vice-consul has received just as much of the bill as the captain pleased to pay and then been told to leave the deck and tell the consul . . . he would pay him under the bowsprit.[10]

Hawthorne put his signature to official documents of many types, the charge for which was usually two dollars (slightly less than ten shillings). Cargo documents of a single vessel could be numerous, much to Hawthorne's delight. "Heaven prosper the trade between America and Liverpool!" he exclaimed.[22] This trade, indeed, did prosper, as an item from a local newspaper in October, 1853, attests:

> Last week an unusually large number of vessels sailed from this port. In one day there were 81 ships. . . . Twelve of those vessels to the United States, com-prised a tonnage of 12,476 while thirty-one vessels to European ports did not extend beyond 4,554, [proof of] the enormous size of the vessels engaged in transatlantic traffic as compared with the craft which load for European ports.[12]

In 1855 a uniform table of fees was circulated to American consuls. The basic one, for authenticating documents of most types, remained at two dollars. Others included half a cent for each registered ton of a vessel processed through the consul's office; a dollar for every seaman discharged or shipped; five per cent of the gross amount of the estates of Americans dying in a consul's territory, when that officer *totally* administered the estate; twenty-five cents for administering an oath; one to two dollars for noting a protest, depend-ing on its length and whether it might be continued beyond the original document; fifty cents for recording any document; five dollars for preparing a power of attorney; and three to five dollars for valuing goods.

These services were performed regularly and provided the bulk of Hawthorne's income. But there were other services, rendered less frequently and usually as the result of violence aboard ships, deaths, and disasters at sea, which produced additional fees for the consul. Had the scale of fees remained intact and all revenue gained from them gone to Hawthorne, there is no doubt but that he could have saved up to $10,000 during each of his four years in Liverpool. But, unknown to him at the time of his appointment, devotees of reform in the

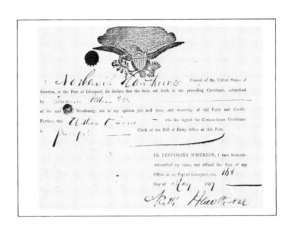

### $2 PER SIGNATURE
The consul's fee for signing documents was usually $2. "The autograph of a living author has seldom been so much in request at so respectable a price," said Hawthorne.

consular service were hard at work drafting proposals which, if enacted, would deprive consuls of all their fees, except for purely clerical work, and place them on salaries.

Hawthorne was content to let Pearce and Wilding prepare much of the routine paperwork in the consulate, but he – unlike Crittenden – either drafted or prepared in his own handwriting every dispatch sent to the State Department.[13] Pearce had actually written, and signed several dispatches during Consul Crittenden's time. Hawthorne's dispatches bear the hallmarks of his writings – perception, analysis, and faultless phrasing. Preparing copies of dispatches involved the ingenious letterpress technique whereby the original was written in iron-based ink and placed on top of a blank sheet of wet paper. After being inserted in the letterpress and left to dry, the pages were separated, providing an original and a copy. The State Department received the original and the copy remained in Liverpool for reference.

No diplomat has ever come up with a solution for dealing with visiting fellow countrymen who simply want to see their country's representative abroad, and Hawthorne fared no better than most. This strange phenomenon has afflicted the foreign service of every nation since the beginning of diplomacy; particularly vulnerable are ambassadors and ministers in capital cities, and consuls who usually are the sole representatives of their countries in seaports. Diplomats are sent abroad ostensibly to assure that their countries' national interests are understood and preserved. But some tourists feel that their ambassador, minister or consul should drop his official business and chat at length on any subject whatever and even undertake to wine and dine them. The consul is particularly open to exploitation because he, more than any other diplomat, is required to help fellow-citizens with their concerns – whether personal or commercial. But this unfortunate officer has no way of distinguishing between callers who have genuine concerns and those who have merely dropped by for idle chat. So he must listen sympathetically to all.

On a typical day, Hawthorne saw a steady procession of callers. The largest number were visiting Americans, many of whom wanted to satisfy their ego by having an audience with their man in Liverpool. Some, indeed, had valid reasons for seeing Hawthorne – a piece of shipping intelligence worthy of being passed back to Washington, complaints of unjust British commercial practices, or opportunities for selling American ships or goods in Britain. But others had no such purpose. One brazen ship's captain was honest enough to tell Hawthorne that he "had never, in his heretofore voyages, been able to get a sight of the American Consul."[14] Hawthorne saw to it that this deficiency was rectified.

## A DIPLOMAT'S PRIVILEGE: MEETING IMPORTANT PEOPLE

As consul, Hawthorne was obliged to meet every visiting American. Some had official business but others were pests. Among the prominent visitors who called on Hawthorne were Orson Pratt, the Mormon apostle (left); Stephen A. Douglas, the American presidential hopeful (centre); and Commodore Matthew C. Perry who negotiated the "open-door" treaty with Japan.

But there are occasional compensations for the weary foreign service officer who takes pains to greet everyone who turns up at his open door. Invariably a number of very prominent figures – Americans and foreigners – seek out the consul; thus Hawthorne met many such whom he would never have known had he remained resident in the United States. One was Orson Pratt, the noted Mormon and one of that church's original twelve apostles. Pratt was forty-five when he called on Hawthorne at the consulate, "a short, dark-haired, dark complexioned man ... [with] a shrewd, intelligent, but unrefined countenance." He had been on several missions to England already, and was to continue his visits long after Hawthorne's death. Hawthorne correctly regarded Pratt as one with little formal education but immense potential. Pratt's request to Hawthorne was for a letter of introduction to the British Museum, but the consul – in a rare moment of "buck-passing" – advised him to apply to Minister Dallas in London, "the proper person for his purpose."[15]

Another prominent caller at the Liverpool consulate was "one of the Potentates of the Earth" – J. J. Roberts of Liberia. He had been President of his country from 1847 to 1855, and would again serve as chief executive from 1871 to 1876. He visited Hawthorne to deliver a note from Mrs. O'Sullivan whom he had met in Madeira. A woolly-haired mulatto, Roberts made a striking impression on the consul. He was shy and reserved, but – in Hawthorne's view – possessed of great intelligence, discretion, and tact.[16]

U.S. Senator Stephen A. Douglas, the "boy-wonder" of American politics who had sought the Democratic Party's candidacy for president in 1852 at the tender age of thirty-nine, was another visitor to Hawthorne's Brunswick Street office. The consul sized up Douglas as having an "uncommon dignity of manner, without seeming to aim at it, being free and simple in manners. . . . When I last saw him [Douglas] in Washington," recalled Hawthorne, "he had on a very dirty shirt collar. I believe it was clean, yesterday."[17]

Hawthorne's literary fame was probably the reason why a world-renowned American called at the consulate towards the end of 1854. He was Commodore Matthew C. Perry who signed the treaty with Japan in March of the same year. Perry was aware of his epoch-making mission and hoped Hawthorne could suggest someone to help him put it into writing. "I seldom meet with a man who puts himself more immediately on conversible [sic] terms than the Commodore," Hawthorne said. "He was good enough to say that he had fixed upon me [to assist him], but that my public duties would of course prevent me from engaging in it."[18]

Apostle Pratt, President Roberts, Senator Douglas and Commodore Perry may have had good reason to see Consul Hawthorne, but this did not apply to all visitors. "They often came to the Consulate in parties of half a dozen or more, on no business whatever, but merely to subject their public servant to a rigid examination, and see how he was getting on with his duties," Hawthorne said. He also suspected that many of these group visits were far from being the casual affairs their members would have him believe. "It is my firm belief," he said, "that these fellow-citizens, possessing a native tendency to organization, generally halted outside of the door, to elect a speaker, chairman, or moderator, and thus approached me with all the formalities of a deputation from the American people."[19]

No consul can serve for long without encountering characters whose life stories – even when true – makes fiction puny by comparison. It is in this realm, whatever may be the drawbacks of his office, that he has the edge over the average diplomat. Hawthorne came to know such characters and described some of them in *Our Old Home*, published a year before his death. One was a ragged, pitiful old fellow who in each visit to Hawthorne's office had only one thing to say: "I want to get home to Ninety-Second Street, Philadelphia." He had been in England for twenty-seven years, unable to raise the fare, but never losing sight of his old address in Philadelphia. Each visit to the Consulate ended the same way, as Hawthorne recounted: ". . . I contented myself with giving him alms, which he thankfully accepted, and went away with bent shoulders and an aspect of gentle forlornness."[20]

Then there was the case of the New England shop-keeper who, having named one child for Queen Victoria and another for Prince Albert, advised their Royal Majesties of the honour bestowed upon them. Back came a courteous note from Buckingham Palace, on the strength of which the man sold up his business, boarded a ship, and presented himself to Hawthorne. Having long held a fantasy that he was the rightful descendant of a large English estate, the New Englander hoped to use the note as a means of seeing the Queen and enlisting her aid in his cause. Hawthorne refused to give him the fare to London, but did offer to assist him with his passage home. The man was crest-fallen. "Finally," Hawthorne said, "he disappeared altogether and whither he had wandered and whether he ever saw the Queen or wasted quite away in the endeavor, I never knew, but I remember unfolding the "Times" about that period with a daily dread of reading an account of a ragged Yankee's attempt to steal into Buckingham Palace, and how he smiled tearfully at his captors, and besought them to introduce him to her Majesty."[21]

But it was neither the American nor the Briton whose plight caused Hawthorne the most heartache. "The men, whose appeals to the consul's charity are the hardest to be denied," he said, "are those who have no country – Hungarians, Poles, Cubans, Spanish Americans, French republicans. All exiles for liberty come to me, as if the representative of America were their representative. Yesterday came an old French soldier, and showed his wounds; today, a Spaniard . . . bringing his little daughter with him. He said he was starving, and looked so. The little girl was in good case enough, and decently dressed."[22]

The notorious "spoils system' that permitted Hawthorne to be named United States Consul also opened the way for small town politicans being named to these posts. Some turned out to be the worst possible representatives of the United States; Hawthorne saw several during his consular years. At least two had money troubles and called upon him for help. He wrote Ticknor about one: "I enclose a little due bill from the late consul at Beyroot who finds himself short on his way home. He seems to be an honest man, and I think will call and pay it. He belongs in Concord, N.H."[23] Some consuls, during the era when party patronage dominated American politics, were not content with the rather generous fees they earned, but insisted on remunerative sidelines as well. One such man, assigned to a port on the east coast of South America, called on Hawthorne and proudly announced he was taking along a thousand pounds of tobacco for speculation. He was to prove financially unreliable, but it was his behaviour that most shocked Hawthorne. The visitor, Hawthorne said, was "a very unfavorable specimen of American manners – an outrageous tobacco-chewer, and atrocious spitter on carpets."[24]

Consuls must assume the burdens of their fellow-countrymen, however awesome and distasteful they are. Thus Hawthorne found himself turning up frequently in police court, seeing unfortunate Americans in hospital or the lunatic asylum, and attending their funerals. Having had little to do with such affairs before coming to Liverpool, he did not find this aspect of his consular duty attractive. Once, after having gone with his clerk to take the inventory of a dead sea captain's chattels, Hawthorne was asked by the lady of the house if he would like to view the corpse in the room nearby. "But," he said, "never having seen him during his lifetime, I declined to commence his acquaintance now."[25]

Occasionally a consulate visitor admitted to a most unusual profession, as happened one day during Hawthorne's first winter in Liverpool. A nattily dressed man of about fifty, of an aggressive manner, entered the office. "He announced himself as an eradicator of corns," Hawthorne said, "and produced two thick quarto volumes of testimonials from innumerable persons, among which were many distinguished Americans . . . Many of these were fortified with the wax-seals as well as signatures of the writers. He wished to know if I myself had any corns for him to operate upon, or if Madame, my lady, had any, and failing of these, he desired the addresses of any Americans' houses in Liverpool – which I did not give him." Hawthorne sized up the caller as a "vulgar humbug," but admitted that the man, "who takes out any number of corns out of a foot, at half a dollar a-piece . . . never fails to find an abundant harvest."[26]

No ambassador or consul can serve a country effectively without a circle of acquaintances who can instantly provide information on any subject. Such contacts are particularly valuable to a consul who must report to Washington on developments in commerce and shipping that might affect the interests of the United States. Besides this continuing requirement, the State Department sometimes initiated lengthy questionnaires, the answers to which no consul could hope to supply without consulting local experts. Hawthorne was fortunate in that Liverpool possessed both a vigorous American Chamber of Commerce and a community of local merchants friendly to him and the United States.

The American Chamber of Commerce was formed in 1801 and boasted from twenty to forty members, depending on circumstances of war and trade. Its members were mainly Americans who operated out of Liverpool or managed branches of parent American firms, and English merchants who dealt with the United States extensively. Its influence was great, given its relatively small membership. It did not, so long as American commerce was healthy, suffer from under-financing; in Hawthorne's last year as consul (1857) its assets exceeded £4,000. A perusal of the Chamber's minute books, which survive in the Liverpool Record Office, reveals the wide-ranging interests of the body. Five days after Hawthorne assumed his consular duties the Chamber met and passed a resolution "that the President

**JULY 4TH DINNER**
This is Hawthorne's invitation to a Fourth of July dinner given by Liverpool's American community.

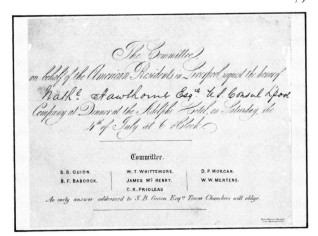

and Members do forthwith wait upon Mr. Hawthorne and congratulate him on his appointment as Consul for the Port of Liverpool and its dependencies."[27] Nor did the group confine its interest to Liverpool; on August 30, 1853, when William Brown (Member of Parliament and benefactor of the Liverpool public library) was in the chair, the Chamber resolved "that the Hon. James Buchanan [the U.S. Minister in London] be requested to name a day which will suit his convenience to honor the Chamber with his attendance at a banquet."[28] Buchanan was unable to attend such an occasion, but wrote Brown a courteous reply giving his reasons for declining the honour.

Decimal coinage did not come to Great Britain until 1971, but in the 1850s a determined effort was made by many people – especially those engaged in business – to adopt a decimal system. Model coins were actually prepared to show how simple such a system would be. Liverpool's American Chamber of Commerce worked hard to promote decimal coinage in its area. In January 1854, it passed a resolution favouring the decimal system; later that year, and again in 1856, it appropriated £100 for a lecturer to promote decimal coinage.[29] When Minister Buchanan eventually came to Liverpool and when his successor, George M. Dallas, arrived there from the United States, a committee from the Chamber called on them – in each case at the Adelphi Hotel. Hawthorne was much concerned about the brutal treatment of seamen aboard American vessels; in this cause he found a staunch ally in the American Chamber of Commerce. In March of 1857 the Chamber took the unusual step of alerting chambers of commerce in American ports and masters of American ships of its concern for the welfare of the seamen.[30]

One enthusiastic member of the American Chamber of Commerce was Liverpool's William Rathbone, Jr. The seventh in his family to bear the name of William, he also was destined to be the greatest. Most of his ancestors had been Quakers, but in the nineteenth century they – in common with many merchants – became Unitarians. William, Jr.'s father, a friend of John James Audubon, visited Lousiana in 1829, being much interested in opossums which he hoped to capture. The elder Rathbone's adventures are cited in Audubon's journals, in particular how Audubon's collection of twenty-five opossums (caught for shipment to England) dwindled to only sixteen after the older males devoured the young ones. These ties with Audubon, and other Americans, made the Rathbones good friends of the United States.

William Rathbone, Sr., was already sixty-six when Hawthorne arrived in Liverpool, and effectively had handed over his business to his son. William, Jr., whom Hawthorne saw socially and sometimes called upon for information in responding to State Department queries. He became a Member of Parliament for Liverpool, a strong proponent of training schools for nurses, and a founder of the University of Liverpool. Throughout the long succession of William Rathbones, the family was noted for its philanthropic and social interests.

Deep involvement in other people's problems has a debilitating effect on most men; Hawthorne found himself similarly afflicted by his consular woes. ". . . a weary life it is," he said, "and one that leaves little of profit behind it. I am sick to death of my office – brutal captains and brutish sailors – continual complaints of mutual wrong, which I have no power to set right, and which, indeed, seem to have no right on either side – calls of idleness or ceremony from my travelling countrymen, who seldom know what they are in search of, at the commencement of their tour, and never have attained any desirable end, at the close of it – beggars, cheats, simpletons, unfortunates, so mixed up that it is impossible to distinguish one from another, and so, in self defence, the consul distrusts them all. I see many specimens of mankind, but come to the conclusion that there is but little variety among them, after all."[31]

Hawthorne plodded resolutely to his Brunswick Street office, day after day. In time he came to develop his own yardstick of what a good consul should be. The essential qualities, he concluded, ought to be common sense, an acquaintance with his country's statutes, insight into character, general knowledge of the world, and "a reasonable but not too inveterately decided preference for his own will and judgement over those of interested people . . ." Although he was himself a political appointee, Hawthorne deplored the system of tying consular assignments to a President's term of office, and then removing them to make way for favourites of the new President. "It is not too much to say (of course allowing for a brilliant exception here and there)," he said, "that an American never is thoroughly qualified for a foreign post, nor has time to make himself so, before the revolution of the political wheel discards him from his office. Our country wrongs itself by permitting such a system of unsuitable appointments, and still more, of removals for no cause, just when the incumbent might be beginning to ripen into usefulness."[32]

# VII
# Of Shipwrecks and Bureaucracy

"As to shipwrecked sailors," wrote Sophia to her family in America, "there seems no end of them . . . in the history of the world, it is said, there were never so many shipwrecks as there have been this last winter. The coasts of Great Britain seem to have been nothing but stumbling blocks in the way of every ship."[1]

Sophia was referring to her husband's first winter (1853–4) as U.S. Consul when she wrote the passage above, but, in fact, the coasts of Britain took a heavy toll of ships in each of the winters during Hawthorne's consulship. Each disaster brought additional revenue for the consul because of the special certificates required to document the loss of crews and cargoes. Hawthorne could not resist telling his friend Ticknor of his macabre reaction to the news of each new shipwreck. "I wish nobody any harm," he said, "but failures, shipwrecks and all sorts of commercial disaster would have a direct tendency to fill my pockets . . ."[2]

Hawthorne had been consul only twelve days when he was initiated into the first of many cases involving wrecked American vessels and destitute seamen. This incident involved the New York vessel *Iz*, which caught fire at sea. A Norwegian schooner, the *Ebenezer*, happened to be in the vicinity, saw the *Iz*'s distress signal, and went to her rescue. Captain Claussen of the *Ebenezer* stood by in case the ship could be saved, but when he saw it would be totally destroyed by fire, he took the captain and crew of the *Iz* aboard his tiny vessel. As the *Ebenezer* was incapable of accommodating such a large influx of newcomers, Captain Claussen, a practical and humane man, took the only course open to him. He threw overboard enough deck cargo (thirty-three barrels of tar), to make room for an improvised house. When Claussen arrived in Liverpool he made no claim for feeding the *Iz*'s survivors, but asked only that he receive compensation for the lost tar (about $150). Hawthorne, impressed with Claussen's gallantry and refusal to seek reimbursement for subsistence – normal in such cases – told the State Department that the captain would be unable to claim insurance for the value of the tar. At the same time, Hawthorne knew there was no provision in consular regulations for reimbursing a ship's master for this rather unusual expenditure.[3]

The wheels of bureaucracy grind slowly, and despite Hawthorne's doubts over the outcome of his appeal, he was bound to have been pleased by Washington's action. Captain Claussen's generosity had been reported to President Pierce who was so moved that he directed that a gold chronometer, as well as £30 be presented the master. The carpenter of the *Ebenezer*, who had broken his right arm during the rescue operations, was also given a gold watch and a cash award.[4] The Norwegian captain's gallantry, and that of other foreign ship masters, so impressed the State Department that a circular was issued late in 1854 directing all consuls to report the name of any master of a foreign vessel who had rescued seamen or citizens of the United States.[5]

Hawthorne was almost immediately involved in bringing to Washington's attention another deserving case of foreign assistance to an American ship. The bark *Pilgrim* sailed from Baltimore in January, 1855, but soon encountered heavy gales which left it in a sinking state. The British bark *Ellen* luckily arrived and removed the crew of thirteen.[6] Hawthorne reported the circumstances in graphic detail, and in May he was told by the

State Department that "the President, immediately after being made acquainted with the facts, directed that a silver speaking trumpet be presented to Captain Bosdet [of the *Ellen*] in token of the appreciation entertained by the Government of the United States of the humane and gallant conduct exhibited by him on the occasion."[7]

Commendable though was the State Department's and the President's interest in seeing that masters of foreign vessels received some token of appreciation for their humane acts, such recognition did not always take into account the differing personal circumstances of the recipients. Thus, Hawthorne felt impelled in early 1856 to stay Washington's hand in sending another watch, trumpet, or medal when he knew – in the latest such rescue – that another form of reward was desirable. The case centred around a Captain Ferguson of the British bark *Emperor*, a poor man, who had rescued twelve crew members from the sinking American bark, *Olivia*. "The master of the *Emperor*," explained Hawthorne to the State Department, "is a very old man, and from enquiries I have made I believe he has been unfortunate and is very poor, so that I suspect any recognition of his service in this matter would be most acceptable in money."[8] The consul could only have been gratified when the Department wrote back saying the substance of his report had been given to President Pierce who had directed that Captain Ferguson receive a check for £50.[9]

During the winter of 1856–1857 Hawthorne was confronted with an embarrassing situation. Local pilots, in harbours the world over, were required to steer vessels in and out of their ports. Great respect usually accrued to those pilots who, however narrow and difficult the shipping lanes, managed to deliver the vessels safely – even in adverse weather. But the reputation of Liverpool pilots was dealt a staggering blow on November 12, 1856, when three large American ships, all in the hands of pilots, were wrecked when outward bound from the harbour. "The fact of three large vessels being wrecked within so short a time of leaving port, so near together and within the same hour, with steamers towing and pilots in charge, is very remarkable," reported Hawthorne to Washington. He added that the occurrence was unprecedented in the history of the port of Liverpool and that an inquiry was underway, although "no blame is attributed to anyone."[10] Happily, there was no loss of life, and a goodly part of the cargoes was saved.

Ten weeks later there was quite a different event to report to Washington. The American ship, *Confederation*, was lost while moving into the port with a local pilot at the helm. This time the ship's master and two other crew members lost their lives, and Hawthorne did not hesitate to put the general view on record. "Shipmasters," he said, "generally attributed the wreck to the carelessness of the pilot, and Captain Corning [of the *Confederation*] had been heard to express himself to the same effect."[11]

"Ghost ships" turn up on the high seas from time to time, and Hawthorne, in March of 1855, was concerned with one surrounded by bewildering circumstances. The American vessel, *James Cheston*, was spotted drifting in mid-Atlantic by members of the crew of the British ship, *Marathon*. Not a soul was on board and there was no evidence of fire or damage. "There is nothing about the vessel denoting that she has experienced hard weather," reported Hawthorne, "[and] on the contrary, with the exception of a leak now very slight, she is in perfectly good order in hull, spars, and rigging." What was Hawthorne's theory about what had happened? He suggested a mutiny and added that some shipmasters believed that the officers of the *James Cheston* had been killed.[12]

But the officers of the ship later turned up in the United States where they were charged with abandoning the vessel. Hawthorne tried in vain to persuade crew members of the *Marathon* to return to the United States and give testimony, but they were more interested

**GETTING READY FOR THE VOYAGE ACROSS THE ATLANTIC**
By shopping around, a would-be emigrant could obtain passage to America for very little. The medical inspection often was a joke, with emigrants passing out of the examination office almost as quickly as they had entered. Nonetheless, Hawthorne found British passenger ship requirements more stringent than those of the United States.

in giving their views to the British Admiralty which eventually granted them a salvage award of £16,000.[13]

Navigation was a precarious business in the 1850s, given the relatively small size of vessels and the dearth of safety devices then in use. Thus, when Hawthorne learned of hazards to navigation he dutifully reported them to the State Department so the facts could receive world-wide dissemination. One of his reports dealt with an obstruction in the busy Gulf Stream. Already charted and known as Orion Rock, the hazard was actually some forty miles to the east of the spot indicated on navigational charts. Hawthorne noted the apparent discrepancy and quoted an American captain's view that "May not the rock I saw and the Orion Rock be one and the same."[14] On other occasions Hawthorne informed Washington about mysterious compass deviations aboard American ships in the Irish sea, and how American – and *only* American vessels – seemed to be wrecked on treacherous banks of this sea. The consul was not content merely to report the facts of these varying maritime disasters (as, indeed, he was required to do), but frequently offered his opinion about the causes. Thus, in one dispatch, he concluded there had to be some connection between the manner of stowing cargo and the resulting compass deviations.[15]

Emigration to the United States was at a high level in the 1850s and conditions aboard American emigrant ships were generally deplorable. The State Department, aware of these deficiencies, sent circulars to its consuls asking for copies of passenger ship requirements of the major maritime nations. Hawthorne, in forwarding the British regulations, pointedly informed the Department that "the British Act's provisions generally are of a more stringent character than those of our own Passenger Act . . .."[16]

The eagle-eyed Hawthorne also kept a sharp look-out for opportunities for American business firms in Britain. In October of 1856 he called the State Department's attention to an advertisement which appeared in leading British newspapers about a competition open to architects of all nations for a Whitehall government-building complex. Again Hawthorne felt compelled to write an accompanying dispatch setting forth his views. In this instance he urged the State Department to give publicity to the competition in the United States, adding that "the premiums will no doubt be handsome enough to be worth competing for, and competition for a building of such magnitude cannot fail to have a highly improving effect on the competitors and tend to advance the art of architecture in America."[17]

Before the United States posted agricultural attachés abroad, consuls were required to send to Washington samples of seed likely to produce new crops in the United States. In 1856 there was considerable excitement in Britain over the prospect of growing sweet sorghum, which had been introduced from Italy. Hawthorne obtained sorghum seed and sent it to Washington with his own prognosis of the British experiments: "it is all but certain they will fail."[18] Although sweet sorghum had been brought to the United States three years earlier from France, Hawthorne had no way of knowing this when he forwarded his seed to the Department.

A fascinating picture of Victorian England – and in particular, of Liverpool – emerges from Hawthorne's response to a massive State Department questionnaire. The long list of questions was sent to consuls in October of 1853, but Hawthorne did not submit his reply until the following July. The delay was undoubtedly due to his newness in office and unfamiliarity with the great range of subjects to which he had to respond. When his reply was received in Washington, State Department officials must have been agreeably surprised, for the response amounted to a miniature library of maritime and commercial intelligence.

In replying to a question about the extent of shipbuilding in Liverpool, Hawthorne gave an insight to early trade unionism. Few ships, he said, were constructed in the port because of "the exorbitant rate of wages resulting from combination among the operative shipbuilders." He then explained how the system worked. "These operatives," he said, "are banded together into a Society, or Trade Union, called the Carpenter's Club. One of their objects is to limit the supply of labor by preventing the introduction of strange workmen, and it is their rule not to accept employment where any individual, not a member of their Society, may be engaged. . . . The effect is to prevent the building of vessels here . . ."[19]

Another reply to the long circular questionnaire dealt with the types of wood used in ship construction, with special regard to any preference for American species. Hawthorne discovered that English oak was the favoured material for ships built in England, and that the timber usually came from the large landed estates. Pine was not held in high esteem by British shipbuilders, with the exception of American red pine which enjoyed a reputation of great durability.[20]

Hawthorne stumbled upon an unusual occupation of Britain's poorer classes in his

## EMIGRANTS EMBARK FROM WATERLOO DOCKS FOR AMERICA
While working at the Boston custom house, Hawthorne had seen immigrants arriving to settle in New England. Now at Waterloo Docks, not far from his consulate office, he saw the start of the process. Over 19 million immigrants arrived in the United States during the reign of Queen Victoria, and the largest number of English-speaking ones left from the port of Liverpool.

research on the caulking material, oakum. This material, he found, "is made from old rope by the occupants of prisons and workhouses, and by poor people from whom it is collected by dealers. The ship chandlers likewise employ women to pick old rope into oakum at their own homes, at the price of three halfpence per pound." Another product much used in shipping was hemp, and Hawthorne suggested if due attention were bestowed on quality, American hemp could invade the English market with success.[32]

The 1850s saw the zenith of the great clipper ships which had captured the public imagination by their graceful styling and fantastic speed. In time they were to give way to steamships, but in 1854 — when Hawthorne was compiling the response to the State Department's questionnaire — they were still the elite of sea-going vessels. Although American-made clippers commanded wide respect among ship owners, clippers were increasingly being constructed in Britain. Hawthorne reported that Liverpool's yards had produced no clippers, but nearby Workington had built thirteen in 1853 alone. "American vessels," he told Washington, "are saleable here at remunerative prices," but — he cautioned — American shipbuilders should send "none but carefully and faithfully constructed vessels."[22]

Hawthorne's dispatches and journal notes contain many prophecies of things to come, of which some have proved to be correct. One predicted that the United States one day would become a leading producer of newsprint and paper. He cited Britain's high consumption of paper as being a potentially lucrative market and enclosed an advertisement by the proprietors of a leading British newspaper offering £1,000 reward to the person inventing a cheap substitute for the conventional paper-making process which relied mainly on linen and cotton. Hawthorne asked if the rich soil and varied climate of the United States would not permit production of paper which would defy European competition. "Should such be the case," he pointed out, "a new field of agricultural industry and commercial wealth would at once be opened to us."[23]

The port of Liverpool owed its prosperity largely to trade between Britain and the United States and it was hardly surprising that the city's merchants advocated free trade. Hawthorne was inclined to agree with their liberal views and put their case as strongly as he dared to Washington. "Whether we can obtain any advantages . . . by placing the leading articles of British manufacture on the lower schedules of our tariff," he said, "or by removing the restrictions on the sale of British ships in the United States, is not for me to determine." But he raised the possibility, "by concession or diplomacy," that the United States might obtain a reduction in the excessive duties on tobacco imported into Britain. Hawthorne was careful to emphasize that these liberal views were not his, but those "of all English merchants, so far as I am conversant with them."[24]

Sending regular reports to one's own country is an important duty of any diplomat. Among consuls this responsibility can be especially arduous with the arrival or departure of ships, especially if violence and disasters are involved and these require the taking of numerous affidavits. Hawthorne, unlike his predecessor, Thomas Crittenden, drafted virtually all of the one hundred dispatches sent to Washington during his consulship, and even wrote two in his own hand. The original note cards used in preparing some of these reports are in the National Archives; they confirm, as do the dispatches prepared from them, that Hawthorne was a conscientious drafter who was not afraid to use the first-person style to make a point.[25]

If Hawthorne could analyze, synthesize and write clearly about business and technical subjects, he could also bring his literary powers to bear on a cause about which he had particularly strong feelings. He was impatient with the Treasury Department's insistence that strict accounting rather than a humane approach be applied to emergency situations such as shipwrecks. Once, when a shipwreck occurred some distance from Liverpool, he was obliged to visit the scene and render what assistance he could to the distressed seamen. Itemizing each article of clothing purchased and obtaining the name of the man to whom it was supplied seemed to him secondary to the primary mission of providing relief. On his return to Liverpool from the shipwreck, Hawthorne informed Washington that he had been obliged to reclothe thirty-seven men, pay for their subsistence, and arrange for them to be brought to Liverpool.

The Treasury Department, to whom Hawthorne was obliged to refer all fiscal matters, was unimpressed with the humane aspects of the consul's assistance. "It is the rule of this office," the Department told him, ". . . to determine the amount paid for the relief of each seaman and the particular articles furnished each. This we find almost impossible to do from the manner in which your account is rendered."[26]

One truism in diplomacy is that a foreign service officer always experiences more difficulty in dealing with his own government than with that of the country to which he is accredited. Hawthorne had few clashes with British officials (mainly over articles passing through the Liverpool customs), but he had a running battle with the U.S. Treasury Department about the manner in which he submitted his accounts, and with John Addison

Thomas, the Assistant Secretary of State, about a small allowance which came under scrutiny.

The allowance, £100 ($500) annually, had been paid to Liverpool consuls for their trouble and expense in receiving and forwarding dispatch bags at the port. While this arrangement had nothing to do with the consul's normal duties, it nonetheless was an essential link in the Washington–London–Washington diplomatic mail route. Looking after these bags on incoming and departing steamers must have been an irksome chore for every American Consul since the system was inaugurated. No doubt each consul gladly would have passed up the allowance to be free of the responsibility. Hawthorne was annoyed, and understandably so, in late 1855 when he received a letter from Secretary Marcy stating that, "the circumstances attending the [dispatch bag] business have . . . so much changed of late that doubts may be entertained whether the charge . . . should continue to be allowed."[27]

When Hawthorne did not reply promptly to Marcy's letter asking Hawthorne to justify the payment, Assistant Secretary Thomas followed up with a letter over his signature in January, 1856. He began by saying Marcy's original letter must "have miscarried," so he was sending another copy. Then he pointed out that incoming dispatch bags sometimes reached London later then ordinary mail from the same ship and he suggested a plan to remedy the situation. "The easiest way of accomplishing that object," he said, "would perhaps be for you to be on the alert for the arrivals of the steamers, and board them at once, so that the person in whose custody the bag is sent may experience no difficulty or delay in delivering it to you."[28]

Hawthorne, at the time he received Thomas' letter, had not tendered his resignation, and the boldness of his reply is surprising. He began by agreeing with Thomas that circumstances had changed: "the consul's remuneration has been reduced much below the remuneration of the office at that time [when the arrangement began] . . . [and] business has increased to nearly eight times the amount." These changes, he asserted, suggested an increase in the allowance, rather than its withdrawal. But he made clear that the £100 allowance meant absolutely nothing to him. "So far as I am personally concerned . . .," he said, "I should hail with pleasure its withdrawal . . ." He went on to point out that he had to employ a man, days and nights, to watch out for arriving and departing steameers, and to move the bags between the railway station and ships. There were other costs which, added together, appeared to leave very little, if anything, for the consul.[29]

Hawthorne made his most blunt comment to Thomas' suggestion that he personally board each arriving steamship and remove the dispatch bags. "Your suggestion . . .," said the consul, "would involve a watch on the pier from four to five nights of each week, and I question whether such vigils might not somewhat impair my ability to discharge the important and onerous duties which demand my attention during . . . intervening days. I shall, therefore, unless otherwise directed, employ a trustworthy agent."[30]

Hawthorne added that nothing short of abandoning the existing system of conveying dispatches was likely to solve the problem. Indeed, virtually anyone could take charge of American dispatches aboard an ocean-going vessel; he need not be a responsible person, and there was no requirement that he be an American citizen. Hawthorne suggested to Assistant Secretary Thomas that dispatch bags be confided to pursers of ships who normally were "trustworthy men, of established character and permanent responsibility." He considered remuneration of five pounds a voyage as adequate. Making use of ships' pursers, he added, would be infinitely better than the existing arrangement under which "dispatch bearers have generally no feeling of duty and really care very little whether the dispatches come to hand at all, or when, or how."[31]

Thomas appeared to be mollified when, on March 1, 1856, he informed Hawthorne that he had looked into the history of the £100 compensation. He concluded that Liverpool consuls should regard the payment as reimbursement – not compensation – and directed that future claims be submitted as such. Hawthorne's suggestion that pursers take charge of dispatch bags accorded with State Department thinking, and in April, Secretary Marcy told the consul that Samuel Cunard had arranged for pursers to receive the bags on all Cunard vessels plying the Atlantic. Cunard added he would make no charge. A few days later E. K. Collins agreed to a similar arrangement on his fleet of ships.

Hawthorne no doubt was gratified that the plan for employing pursers had been adopted by the Department, but his confrontation with Thomas was to continue elsewhere. Just what is official and what is not, has always been a contentious issue in determining what foreign service officers may send in a dispatch bag – today known as the diplomatic pouch. In Hawthorne's time, as at present, the State Department attempted to enforce the rule that only official items be transmitted by bag. During the consul's tussle with Thomas over the £100 compensation, the Assistant Secretary informed Hawthorne that the U.S. Dispatch Agent in Boston had received from Hawthorne "a bag containing parcels not addressed to this or any other department of the Government, and it is inferred that even the bag itself was not addressed in that manner."[32] Hawthorne's reply, if any was made, is not known, but he did write William Ticknor about the affair. It would appear that Hawthorne had promised a friend to send his parcels to Secretary Marcy through the dispatch system, and that it was these parcels which the U.S. Dispatch Agent in Boston had found, and questioned. ". . . the Assistant Secretary of State has written to me," said Hawthorne to Ticknor, "laying the blame at my door. The Devil take him . . . and the Government, and everybody connected with it! . . . I shall continue to send the bag, although hereafter I shall certainly decline having anything to do with Col. Lawrence's parcels."[33]

The final round in the Hawthorne-Thomas encounter came in the autumn of 1856 when the Assistant Secretary informed the consul that the system of using pursers to convey dispatch bags did not always work. Again, Thomas put the blame on Hawthorne. The issue centred on what happened to the bag which arrived in Liverpool on the Cunard ship *Persia* in mid-August, the inference being that neither Hawthorne nor his agent was on hand to receive it from the purser. The U.S. Dispatch agent in New York, who had placed the bag in the hands of the Cunard purser, was told by the purser on his next voyage, that he had taken the bag to the Cunard offices in Liverpool after no representative of the American consulate turned up to accept it.

Hawthorne was at first baffled by this allegation, but after making inquiries discovered what had happened. "The *Persia*," he told the Assistant Secretary, "was detained at the bar by the lowness of the water and her mails sent up by a steam tender. The dispatches were sent along with them and received by my messenger on board the tender on her arrival, about 7 o'clock. The ship herself did not arrive for several hours afterwards. The purser must have been misunderstood, or his recollection have failed him."[34]

The consul thus had the last word with the Assistant Secretary, although the vexing problem of how best to convey diplomatic dispatches was not yet solved to anyone's real satisfaction. It was to be several decades before the State Department would institute its present system of entrusting its sensitive documents to the care of full-time couriers – American citizens – in its own employ.

# VIII
## The Hawthornes at Home

"Mr. Hawthorne wishes to escape from too constant invitations to dinner . . . in Liverpool," wrote Sophia to her father from the Royal Rock Hotel in August 1853. ". . . by living here [in Rock Ferry] there will always be a good excuse for refusing when there is really no reason or rhyme in accepting, for the last steamer leaves Liverpool at ten in the evening . . . And I shall have a fair cause for keeping out of all company I do not very much covet."[1]

Rock Ferry was undoubtedly one of the most attractive villages in the Liverpool area and its Rock Park estate was the last word in early Victorian suburban development. Essentially a retreat for wealthy Liverpudlians, the houses in Rock Park were tastefully and sturdily built, and stood in spacious gardens with splendid views of the River Mersey and Liverpool. Their inhabitants were obliged to walk only a few minutes to reach the ferry landing and yet enjoyed complete privacy. Lodge gates prevented the curious from entering, but the envious on-looker had no difficulty in seeing the sweeping serpentine drives and the elegant villas within.[2]

Hawthorne had no desire for ostentation, but was determined that his family should not be exposed to unhealthy conditions which at that time affected much of Liverpool's low-lying waterfront area. Having the River Mersey between himself and the city's hectic social life was another advantage for settling in Rock Ferry. Thus firmly resolved to find a house in the area, he moved his family into the Royal Rock Hotel – within sight of the ferry landing – pending the time when a suitable abode might become available.

The family had been living in the hotel only a few days when an important event occurred. This was the arrival of James Buchanan, President Pierce's Minister to Great Britain. His voyage aboard the *Atlantic* had been anything but pleasant. It lasted, as he wrote his niece back in the United States, "10 days, 16 hours" and he was seasick most of the time.[3] From her vantage point in the Royal Rock Hotel Sophia saw the disembarkation of passengers. "We heard the announcing cannons," she told her father, "and presently the huge ship came in sight, very majestically moving up the river till it stopped exactly opposite our hotel. With the spyglass I could see every person on board. Two tugs went alongside and into one all the passengers crowded and into the other all the luggage was stowed. . . . Many dignitaries came – among them at last Mr. Buchanan, our Minister to England . . ."[4]

The sojourn in the hotel lasted a month, but it produced the desired result – finding a furnished twelve-room villa in the Rock Park estate. Hawthorne was elated over the privacy the house afforded. "There being a toll," he said, "it precludes all unnecessary passage of carriages; and there never were more noiseless streets than those that give access to these pretty residences."[5] Julian was particularly impressed with the lodgekeeper whose command post was a stone hut at the park entrance. "He may have been formidable to gipsies and vagrants from without," he said, "but to us within he was genial and indulgent."[6] Moving-day was September 1st and, as luck would have it, the rain pelted down. Between showers the family dashed into the house; Hawthorne wrapped Rose in his cloak, pressed her to his chest, and sprinted through the downpour. But the rain outside did not affect the spirits of those inside who had waited so long for a place of their own. Within

**THE HAWTHORNES' TEMPORARY HOME IN ROCK FERRY**
For nearly a month in the autumn of 1853 the Hawthornes took rooms in the Royal
Rock Hotel, shown above. Eventually they found a home in the adjacent Rock Park
estate (to the left of the hotel). Hawthorne commuted daily to Liverpool by ferry (see
passengers boarding at pier). The hotel no longer exists.

twenty-four hours the family had made the villa habitable. The day after moving in
Hawthorne felt sufficiently settled to invite Ticknor to stay at Rock Park. "You must not
think of going anywhere else than to our house," Hawthorne wrote his old friend. "We got
into it yesterday, and are just as well established as if we had been there a year."[7]

Sophia, now installed as queen of her "castle," was enraptured over the house at 26 Rock
Park. She lost no time in telling her father the good news, listing the several varieties of
flowers in the garden – among them geraniums, fuchsias, carnations, pansies, and, of
course, roses. "The children," she added, "are delighted with the aspect of things, and with
the house, which they think very stately and elegant."[8] Each of the children was given a
patch in the back garden. Julian promptly began clearing his of pebbles. The more he
tossed aside the more he was tempted to remove the soil as well. Before he knew it, he was
heaving away the earth. ". . . my garden was a cavity," he said, "and still going down."[9] It
was perhaps just as well that Julian was assigned to one specific plot, for the flowers and
shrubbery in the elaborate gardens of the Rock Park villas were not intended for youthful
hands. The previous occupant – a widow, Mrs. Campbell – had planted many rare
specimens and had so varied them that blooms appeared in some corner the year round.

If the garden was nicer than those the Hawthornes had known previously, the house was
even more so. It dwarfed all others the family had inhabited. On the ground floor were
three public rooms, as well as the kitchen and larder. Each of the other three stories contained bedrooms. Fortunately, Sophia and Nathaniel did not have to furnish the house, or
they could not have afforded it. Even so, Hawthorne was not happy about the annual rent
of £160 ($800). ". . . without furniture," he mused, "[it] probably would have been £100."[10]

The stay at 26 Rock Park was to be the high point of Nathaniel's and Sophia's living style. Never again would they live in such a commodious house surrounded by beautiful gardens, nor would they ever again have such an army of servants. Yet, Hawthorne had mixed feelings at the end of the first day when he sat, no doubt exhausted by the move, before the coal fire in the living room. His mind went back to all the places in New England and Old England where he had led his family since Sophia had become his bride. Now the family was installed in Rock Park – its eighth home in just eleven years. Sadly Hawthorne noted his thoughts in his journal: "As I sit in this English house, with the chill, rainy English twilight brooding over the lawn, and a coal fire to keep me comfortable on the first evening of September, and the picture of a stranger (the dead husband of Mrs. Campbell) gazing down at me from above the mantel-piece, I felt that I never should be quite at home here."[11]

Nonetheless 26 Rock Park was home in the sense that the Hawthornes, for the first time in their lives, had both the space and the means to receive friends. Many were to make their way there over the following year and a half, but the person whom the entire family most wanted to see was William Ticknor. The faithful Ticknor, who had accompanied Hawthorne first to Washington and then to Liverpool aboard the *Niagara*, had several times planned to embark for Boston, but one business matter or another delayed him.

Toward the end of September he eventually arrived, bearing gifts for each member of the family. Sophia received a case of Sheffield scissors with her name engraved on each blade as well as a book on flowers. For Hawthorne, Ticknor chose another Sheffield product – a pair of fine razors – again personalized with "N. Hawthorne" engraved on the ivory handles. Baby Rose got a waxen doll, Julian a country year-book with over a hundred fine engravings, and Una a green and gold portfolio on which her name was engraved in gilt letters. In tribute to his closest friend, Hawthorne took time off to accompany him to Chester. The two old cronies thoroughly enjoyed the ancient cathedral city. Hawthorne noted in his journal: "It is quite an indescribable old town, and I feel, at last, as if I had had a glimpse of Old England."[12] A few days later Ticknor sailed on the *Canada*; for the first time since their friendship blossomed the two were now separated by an ocean. "His departure," said Hawthorne, "seems to make me feel more abroad – more dissevered from my native country – than before."[13]

During the many moves in her married life and the accompanying vicissitudes of her husband's literary career Sophia had never ceased to keep her father abreast of family news. She dearly longed to give her ailing parent in America comforting news about Hawthorne's consular position and the family's improved financial status. Thus, she took great pleasure, following the move to Rock Park, in telling her father that the family at last had ceased living out of suitcases and was happily installed in a large and attractive villa.

But old Nathaniel Peabody misunderstood Sophia's meaning and took her description of the new home as outright boasting that the Hawthornes were living in grand style. She hastened to correct the impression. ". . . oh, no dear father," she said, "we do not 'live in grand style,' neither do we intend to have much company. We could not afford it, for though so many persons at home, who might be supposed to know, account the consular income here to be so great and the arrival of ships so abundant, they are sadly mistaken." She went on to explain that her husband had to put aside a good part of his income, "or we shall return ruined, not benefited, by this office, for he cannot write . . .." The cost of living in England, she added, was much more than in Massachusetts: "meat [here is] never below fourteen cents, and some kinds twenty cents, potatoes thirty cents a peck, no tea below a dollar a pound, grapes are a penny apiece, and fruit here is not good. England cannot grow fruit with the sun crying its eyes out every day."[14]

Hawthorne's House.

**THE HOME IN ROCK PARK**
The happiest days of the Hawthorne's stay in England were spent at their 26 Rock Park residence in Rock Ferry, pictured above by an unknown artist.

As it was unreasonable to expect guests to cross the River Mersey twice in the same evening, Hawthorne effectively prevented most of his Liverpool acquaintances from being entertained at dinner. Nonetheless, Sophia was host to several prominent American visitors, some of whom stayed overnight, and to Hawthorne's English friends, Henry Bright and Francis Bennoch.

It was during the last week in September, when the family had been installed in Rock Park only three weeks, that she mustered enough confidence to invite Bright to dinner. To her father she proudly reported the outcome: "My dinner-party on Wednesday went off quite elegantly. When the gentlemen joined me in the drawing room, I had tea ready for them, and Una requested to be the Hebe of the banquet. Mr. Bright thought it lovely to have such an attendant."[15]

Sophia wrote her father enthusiastically about the English fireplace. "Coal is comparatively cheap," she said, "and it blazes delightfully and we can really sit round a glowing hearth. Mr. Hawthorne truly enjoys it. It is what he always wanted."[16] But Hawthorne was not at first able to master its intricacies. His London friend, Francis Bennoch, came upon him one winter's day, sitting disconsolately in a chair and poking away furiously at the black coals without producing the slightest effect. "Give me the poker, my dear sir!" exclaimed Bennoch, "and I'll give you a lesson." Whereupon he grabbed the poker, thrust it deep into the smouldering heap, and instantly produced a blazing fire. Bennoch seized the moment to drive home to Hawthorne a truth about understanding English people. "That's the way to get warmth out of an English fire," he said, "and that's

**HENRY BRIGHT**
Member of a prominent shipping family, Henry Bright was Hawthorne's closest friend in Liverpool. In later life he became an authority on gardening.

the way to get warmth out of an English heart, too! Treat us like that, my dear sir, and you'll find us all good fellows!"[17]

Rose retained a fond memory of her mother's almost child-like excitement over being able to entertain so elegantly at Rock Park. "The delightful novelty to my small self of a peep at the glitter of little dinner parties," she said, "was . . . surprising . . . [for] its contrast to all the former simplicity of my parents' life. Down the damask trooped the splendid silver covers, entrancingly catching a hundred reflections from candle-flame and cut-glass, and my own face as I hovered for a moment upon the scene while the butler was gliding hither and thither to complete his artistic arrangements." Rose also remembered the moment when she first saw her mother splendidly robed. "I was supposed to be fast asleep," she said, "and she had come to look at me before going out to some social function, as she told me she never failed to do when leaving the house for a party. Her superb brocade, pale-tinted, low-necked and short sleeved, her happy, airy manner, her glowing though pale face, her dancing eyes, her ever-hovering smile of perfect kindness, all flashed upon me in the sudden light as I roused myself. I insisted upon gazing and admiring, yet I ended by indignantly weeping to find that my gentle little mother could be so splendid and wear so triumphant an expression."[18]

Another early visitor to Rock Park who gave the Hawthornes much pleasure was the American actress, Charlotte Cushman. She dined and stayed the night on December 29, 1853, much to the delight of the younger generation. "The children liked her prodigiously," said Sophia, "and Rose was never weary of the treasures attached to her watch-chain." Well might the tiniest Hawthorne be enchanted, for there was everything on Miss Cushman's watch-chain to keep a small child spell-bound: "a fairy tiny gold palette, with all the colors arranged; a tiny easel with a colored landscape, quarter of an inch wide; a tragic and comic mask, just big enough for a gnome; a cross of the Legion of Honor; a wallet, opening with a spring . . .; a dagger for a pigmy; two minute daguerreotypes of friends . . .; an opera glass; Faith, Hope and Charity represented by a golden heart and anchor, and I forget what."[19]

The visits by Henry Bright, Francis Bennoch and Charlotte Cushman were the

**FRANCIS BENNOCH**
Although based in London, Bennoch did a great deal to make the Hawthornes feel at ease during their entire residence in Britain. Hawthorne regarded Bennoch as his best friend in Britain.

highlights of the Hawthornes' first months in residence at Rock Park. Enjoyable as they were, they were costly pleasures, and Sophia was determined to cut down on the expenses of maintaining the Rock Park villa and its staff. Rose, in later life, recalled that her mother refused to permit herself even momentary extravagances, for there was always the dread of the unknown future and the expense of rearing three children.[20] There were occasions when friendship or protocol demanded that costs be cast aside, as when Minister James Buchanan and the American Minister to Portugal (and friend of Hawthorne's from the *Democratic Review* days), John L. O'Sullivan, came to stay.

Sophia's housekeeping accounts were kept in a ledger which still survives.[21] The book reveals the ups and downs of the family during its residence in England and sheds light on the Hawthornes' mode of living. Perhaps the most interesting entries refer to the family's eating habits and the expenditures on the children. Beef and mutton do not appear in the ledger during the Rock Park period, but there were frequent purchases of rabbits, cheese, and chicken. Milk, butter and eggs were consumed in quantity, as were the traditional English vegetables (potatoes, peas, cabbage, broccoli and cauliflower) and fruits (gooseberries, apples, strawberries, rhubarb, and plums). The family's "sweet tooth" was soothed by copious quantities of marmalade, jam, jelly, preserves, and honey – much of it no doubt accompanied by the home-made bread baked by Emily, the cook and maid. Pastries were bought from the baker, for the account book shows purchases of such English favourites as sponge cake and tea cakes. Although the house was furnished, Sophia was obliged to buy many household items, including silver plate and kitchen utensils. Wages made a big dent in the family's annual budget.

Expenses for the children form a fascinating pattern in Sophia's account book. In the first month of occupancy at Rock Park, Una had to have a tooth extracted (the cost: two shillings, sixpence); this is followed by an entry of a doll for her at 7s. 6d – the soothing agent having cost more than the extraction. The following month Sophia spent 4s. on hoops, a top, and soldiers, and in November a shilling for "Punch and Judy." In the same month "baby" was presented with an expensive gift, a harmonica costing 9s. At Christmas the two older children were given special allowances, apparently determined by their ages: Una received nine shillings, Julian only five. In January 1854, there are two entries suggesting a

**THE CUSHMAN SISTERS**
Charlotte Cushman (left, with her sister Susan, in *Romeo and Juliet*) visited the Hawthornes at Rock Park. Little Rose was intrigued by the many charms on Charlotte's watch-chain.

minor family feud: on the 23rd one jumping rope was purchased – for which child, is unspecified; two days later, following what seems to have been a juvenile rebellion, there is the further entry: "2 jumping ropes." Una's music lessons involved an initial outlay of £50 ($250) for a piano, then a further £24 ($120) for lessons and books.

Ticknor had now returned to Boston. He and Hawthorne resumed their correspondence, and it was to continue throughout the author's consulship and afterwards. Hawthorne's letters were mainly concerned with official business, but they usually contained family news as well. Sophia once sent Ticknor an English cheese; Hawthorne followed up by suggesting to his other co-publisher, James T. Fields, that the cheese be distributed daily around noon with crackers and something to drink, to destitute authors. Ticknor must have been pleased with the cheese, for he reciprocated by dispatching an entire barrel of American apples to the Hawthornes.

Una, a precocious girl of ten, reported her own impressions of England in letters sent to the United States. An early one gives a child's view of the happy family circle. "Rose," she wrote, "is sitting on papa's knee and through her golden hair I can see her little contented face. Julian has been dancing round with the heat, for he thought dancing round would keep him cool. Rose is sitting in mama's lap now and she looks so jolly. She is very sharp and she has a great deal of fun in her. She has learnt 'Hark, the lark,' 'The Cuckoo,' and 'Where the bee sucks, there suck I.' She says them very prettily and she has a sweet, simple way of saying what she knows."[22]

Although some twenty families lived in Rock Park, the Hawthornes came to know only a few. One neighbouring family had two young boys and they promptly introduced Julian to the game of cricket. Another family with whom the Hawthornes became intimate was the Squareys. Mr. Squarey was an erect, military-like man whose stiff bearing belied his affable nature. Mrs. Squarey was short and stout. "My father," recalled Julian, "was wont to refer to her in the privacy of domestic intercourse as Mrs. Roundey."[23]

However, over-solicitous the Squareys may have been on occasion, they helped the Hawthornes to adapt to their new surroundings and, in particular, enabled them to observe English law in action. On a memorable occasion Mrs. Squarey, whose husband was a member of the bar in Liverpool, invited Sophia to attend a session of court in St. George's Hall, a building Sophia described as "the most magnificent . . . I ever saw." Because of Mr. Squarey's connection with the bar, Mrs. Squarey and Sophia were permitted to sit in the sheriff's box. This vantage point may have been the best for witnessing the court proceedings, but it also had an effect which caught Sophia by surprise. "I was rather startled," she said, "to find myself the object of thousands of eyes . . ."[24]

The parents usually were in accord over how to deal with the children's interests and problems, but there was one memorable occasion on which Sophia disagreed sharply with her husband's handling of a particularly sensitive situation regarding Julian. The incident started when Julian asked Hawthorne for an expensive toy. Hawthorne turned down the request, explaining that business was not so good at the consulate just then. He added that Julian should avoid asking for everything that struck his fancy. "Julian said no more," Sophia recalled, "and when he went to bed he expressed great condolence, and said he would not ask his father for anything if he were so poor, but that he would give him all his money (amounting to five-pence halfpenny)." With his mind thus made up, Julian was a different boy. "When he lay down," Sophia said, "his face shone with a splendour of joy that he was able thus to make his father's affairs assume a brighter aspect." Julian's decision was heart-rending, for he had saved up his money to buy a Christmas present for baby Rose or Una. "In the morning," Sophia said, "he took the opportunity when I was not looking to go behind his father, and silently handed him the five-pence halfpenny over his shoulder. My attention was first attracted by hearing Mr. Hawthorne say, 'No, I thank you my boy; when I am starving I will apply to you!' I turned round and Julian's face was deep red and his lips were quivering as he took back the money. I was sorry his father did not keep it . . ."[25]

Sophia need not have worried that Julain would be hurt by the money incident, for love between father and son ran deep. Together they were to explore the country lanes and villages of Cheshire with nearby Eastham and Bebbington being particular favourites. On one occasion the pair visited Liverpool's Zoological Gardens where Julian had his daguerreotype taken for three shillings. One Sunday the Hawthornes decided to visit Chester Cathedral in the company of their neighbours, the Squareys. Julian's presence almost turned the visit into disaster. In the middle of the service, Sophia explained in a letter to her father, "Julian inadvertently gaped aloud, which so startled Mr. Hawthorne that he exclaimed, '*Good God!*' thus making the matter much worse . . ."[26]

Neither Una nor Julian attended a conventional English school during Hawthorne's consulship, but both took private lessons. Perhaps more important than these lessons was the extensive reading that took place in the home. Both parents read aloud, and the children also were fond of reading. In later life Julian remembered the rather heavy literary fare his father served up during evening reading; among the titles were Macaulay's *Lays of Ancient*

*Rome*, Scott's poems and novels, Maria Edgeworth's *Moral Tales*, and Thomas de Quincey's *Klosterheim*.

The schooling that took place within the home was organized by Sophia with strict adherence to a timetable. Outlining the schedule to her father, she said: "At ten we commence and the children study two hours and at twelve I take them to walk till luncheon at $\frac{1}{2}$ past one. After luncheon they study again until four when we all go upstairs to the gymnasium and practise half an hour, when we dress to receive Papa. With him by firelight we have a sociable time till dinner (his dinner –our tea). After that we have games of bagatelle till Rosebud bids us goodnight."[27]

When guests were present, life at Rock Park was orderly and formal. The dinners, Julian observed, were certainly rather elaborate compared with the simple repasts of Salem and Concord. But when visitors were not around, or if the weather was too bad to venture outside, Hawthorne threw his usual reserve to the winds and entered with great hilarity into the family frolicking. He was, on those occasions, "the youngest and merriest person in the room," Rose recalled. On Sundays, just as dusk fell, the family halted all other activities for the event of the week – a rollicking game of blind man's buff with Hawthorne permanently in the role of groper. ". . . between five and six," Rose said, "we spread butterfly wings again . . . We ran around the large centre-table and made this gambol most tempestuously merry. If anything had been left upon the table before we began, it was removed with rapidity before we finished. There was a distinct understanding that our blindfolded father must not be permitted to touch any of us, or else we should be reduced forthwith to our original dust. . . . My father's gentle laughter and happy-looking lips were a revelation during these bouts."[28]

Although Hawthorne was no church-goer, he did acquiesce in the Victorian tradition of home prayers. In these, members of the family and servants attended. At 26 Rock Park the custom was observed in simple fashion with everyone grouped in a semicircle. Hawthorne would begin the service by reading a passage from the Bible. This completed, he then picked up a standard collection of prepared religious addresses from which he proceeded to read. Afterwards, as Julian remembered, everyone would kneel down – with eyes closed or covered with their hands – until the final "Amen" was said, after which all would rise to their feet and the servants would file out of the room. These family services seem to have been virtually the whole of Hawthorne's involvement in religious practice, for no amount of persuasion could induce him to attend church service regularly. He did hear a few sermons in cathedrals, but he had come in the first place to study the buildings and their histories. When his friend Henry Bright composed his brief parody on *Hiawatha*, entitling it *Song of Consul Hawthorne*, he included a verse calling attention to Hawthorne's laxity in religious matters:

> Do you ask me, 'Tell me further
> Of this Consul, of this Hawthorne?'
> I would say, 'He is a sinner, –
> Never goes inside a chapel,
> Only sees outsides of chapels,
> Says his prayers without a chapel! '[29]

Sophia, however, was deeply religious. She was overjoyed to learn, while the family lived at 26 Rock Park, that a prominent American Unitarian – Dr. William H. Channing of

## THE REVEREND CHANNING AND THE RENSHAW STREET CHAPEL

Sophia was ecstatic when she learned that Channing, a Boston Unitarian, was coming to Liverpool's Renshaw Street Chapel as guest minister. Channing, she said after hearing a sermon, "brought out my dearest, inmost doctrines and faith."

Boston – had agreed to become minister of Liverpool's Renshaw Street Church. In accepting the invitation the Reverend Channing left no doubt that it was Sophia who was his reliable friend in Liverpool.

"I intend writing to my friend, Mrs. Hawthorne, by this week's steamer," he informed his Liverpool correspondent, "requesting her to engage rooms for us at the Rock Ferry House, where I understand, Mr. and Mrs. Hawthorne resided for a time. I shall also ask her to keep an eye on any rooms or house, which she thinks might be suitable for us.[30] Channing reached Liverpool in the autumn of 1854, and was well received. After hearing him, Sophia was ecstatic in the next letter to her father: "In his sermon before the last, Mr. Channing brought out my dearest, inmost doctrines and faith: the sovereignty of good, the unfallen ideal in man, the impossibility of God's ever for one moment turning from man, or being averse to him . . ."[31] Several of Hawthorne's associates in Liverpool were staunch Unitarians, among them the Brights and the Rathbones. When Dr. Channing left Liverpool after three years' service with the Renshaw Street Unitarian Church, the congregation collected one hundred guineas as a parting gift. Among the donors were eight members of the Bright family and six Rathbones.[32]

If religious occasions found Nathaniel and Sophia separated, national holidays did not. Coming from that part of the United States where the Thanksgiving custom originated, the Hawthornes were determined not to let the holiday pass without according it proper observance. Sophia, in a letter to her father, outlined a plan which would allow the family to celebrate Thanksgiving and, at the same time, pay homage to one of Hawthorne's best friends. "Tomorrow is Thanksgiving Day," she said, "We are going to observe it in memory of the fatherland. Mr. [Henry] Bright will dine with us by his own invitation, not knowing it was a festival day with us."[33] Sophia's account book confirms that the traditional turkey was bought for the great day; whether she managed to prepare a pumpkin pie

**VIEW OF LIVERPOOL FROM ROCK FERRY AT LOW TIDE**
This is the aspect of the Mersey and Liverpool that Hawthorne would have seen
each morning as he walked to the Rock Ferry pier to take the ferry. On cold days
intending passengers crowded into the tiny waiting room at the pier gate.

is not recorded. Hawthorne afterwards reported to Ticknor: "We kept the New England
Thanksgiving, as descendants of the old Puritans should, and we shall likewise keep
Christmas, as everybody in England does."[34]

For the Hawthornes, the two Christmases at Rock Ferry were happy affairs with Sophia
doing her utmost to provide the atmosphere to which the family had been accustomed.
Although Albert, the Prince Consort, had already introduced the Christmas tree to
England, the custom had not yet gained widespread public acceptance and the Hawthornes
were to be without this symbol. If there could be no Christmas tree, Sophia reasoned, then
there would at least be a Christmas table. Accordingly, she made the drawing room table
the centre of the holiday festivities, adorning it with a vase from which a banner proclaimed
"A Merry Christmas to all!" On one Christmas there was a rosary for Una from Mrs.
O'Sullivan and an illustrated edition of *This is the House that Jack Built* from Henry Bright.
Julian received a flag from nurse Fanny Wrigley, and Rose was given a miniature watch for
her footman, "Pompey," by Una. But it was to be the sounds of Christmas in England that
Sophia would recall most vividly when she sat down to pen her impressions to her father.
"On Christmas night," she said, "the bells chimed in the dawn, beginning at twelve and
continuing till daybreak. . . . I waked before light and thought I heard some ineffable music.
I thought of the song of the angels on that blessed morn, but while listening, through a
sudden opening in the air or breeze blowing towards us, I found it was not the angels, but
the bells of Liverpool."[35]

Christmas of 1854 was a memorable one for Hawthorne. The children had found wall-
flowers, pansies, and "pinks" in the garden, and the nearby Rock Ferry Hotel had provided
a rose – all grown outdoors. Then, given his frequent criticism of English weather, he made

a startling admission: "I think I have been happier, this Christmas, than ever before – by my own fireside, and with my wife and children about me. More content to enjoy what I had; less anxious for anything beyond it, in this life."[36]

During his sojourn at Rock Park, Hawthorne travelled nearly 500 miles by ferry. He may have dreaded this form of commuting, especially during the fog-enshrouded days of winter, but to his observant eye the crossings were never dull events. Intending passengers always assembled in the little ferry huts, sometimes heated by small fires. In his second month at Rock Ferry Hawthorne came upon a poor Irish family huddled together in front of the fire. Instantly they offered him a place, but he refused their kind gesture. They explained their difficulties in trying to earn a livelihood in England and how, with all hope gone and no resources except their few worldly possessions in a pack, they were about to cross over to Liverpool and return to the old country. They did not beg or make a display of poverty, but Hawthorne gave the little girl of the family sixpence, which she readily accepted. He was particularly struck by the quiet dignity of the family, especially the thin, pale-faced woman who, despite the seemingly hopeless circumstances, exuded grace and decency. The sight of the plucky family moved Hawthorne deeply. "It made me understand," he said, ". . . how poor people feel, wandering about in such destitute circumstances, and how they suffer . . . and how family love goes along with them."[37]

With the coming of cold weather, the little waiting room at Rock Ferry was more crowded than ever. Hawthorne suspected that some people crept in merely because they had no warmth at home, for a few remained close to the little fire for a good part of the day. Once the prize position nearest the fire was taken by a proud beggar who would yield his cozy place to no one. "He was smoking a pipe of vile tobacco," Hawthorne said, "but, after all, this was fortunate, because the man himself was not personally fragrant."[38]

Although some Mersey ferries had operated for centuries between Liverpool and the Cheshire coast, that connecting the city and Rock Ferry had started only in 1820. By 1836 the Royal Rock Ferry Steam Packet Company was operating a small fleet of ferry-boats which were easily recognized by the large star adorning the masts.[39] In Hawthorne's day the boats plied the two-mile distance at thirty-minute intervals during the peak working hours. Each of the little vessels had a charming name and long after he had made his last crossing in one of them, Julian remembered his favourite – the *Bee*. Others in service at the time of the family's residence at Rock Park included the *Ant*, the *Sylph I*, the *Royal Tar*, and the *Nymph* – all names that would have delighted the young Hawthornes.

Once, on a ferry during mid-winter, Hawthorne was approached by a young man – "the leanest poor-devil I ever saw" – who wanted to sell him a copy of *The Times*. The man obviously was not an authorized newspaper seller, for he had only a single copy and it had "an aspect of doubtful newness." Hawthorne managed to refuse the young man in an almost casual manner, but was dismayed when the young man halted in his tracks, gave the consul a grave, bewildered look, and said: "Well, upon my word, Sir, I'm in want of a bit of bread."[40]

Musicians were another feature of the Mersey ferries during the good weather season. Sometimes there was an entire band, after which a collection would be made. Once, after such a performance, a member of the band went round with an old brass bugle, soliciting pennies. The generous Hawthorne tossed in a sixpence which, being smaller than a penny, promptly jammed. To Hawthorne's embarrassment, the annoyed collector set about taking the instrument apart to retrieve the offending coin.

Among the buskers aboard the ferries was a pathetic pair, a little boy with his sister. The boy played the accordion, but his sister never played. Her sole task was to collect copper coins in a shattered timbrel. Hawthorne did not care for the accordion as an instrument, but admitted it became a "tolerable" thing in the boy's hands. The lad was only about ten, but somehow had already mastered the poise, if not the quality, of a musician. "His body and accordion together became one musical instrument on which his soul plays tunes," Hawthorne said, "for he sways and vibrates with the music from head to foot and throughout his frame, half-closing his eyes and uplifting his face, as painters represent Saint Cecilia . . . ."[41]

Most beggars and musicians aboard the Rock Ferry boats were professionals, all experienced in the sly ways of attracting the interest and playing on the consciences of passengers. But among the ordinary folk who daily went to and fro there were some endearing characters who came under Hawthorne's scrutiny. He was intrigued to observe, on one crossing, how a certain passenger could remain perfectly oblivious to others about him and, indeed, assume he had a birthright to be as eccentric as he wished. He best can be described as a man who truly liked oysters. From an apparently bottomless pocket, he brought them out one after the other. After prising them open with his knife, he gulped them down whole and chucked the shells overboard. This routine continued "in interminable succession" until, at last, the man had either eaten them all or had sated his appetite. He then extracted an old clay pipe, filled and lit it, and puffed away contentedly for the rest of the crossing. One might have expected the man to have been aware of his behaviour, but he displayed "a perfect coolness and independence such as no single man can ever feel in America." The incident led Hawthorne to reason that, in England, a man cared little for what others might think of his manner, but instead whether or not it suited his own whim. "It may be," he concluded, "the better way."[42]

Only one event had occurred to mar the record of serenity and bliss at Rock Ferry – the death of Sophia's father on New Year's Day, 1855. As Dr. Peabody's health declined, his daughter sought by written word to give him the strength and will to live. "It gives me unspeakable satisfaction," she wrote, "to know that the drafts Mr. Hawthorne sent contribute to your ease, and supply you with embellishments and luxuries, which in sickness are necessaries. I only wish I could put strength into your limbs, as well as provide you with a stuffed chair to repose them upon." It fell to Hawthorne to break the news of Dr. Peabody's death to Sophia. Just how well he performed this painful task is related in Sophia's letter to her sister, Elizabeth. "If anything could have softened such a blow," she said, "it would have been the divine way in which my husband told me."[43]

Hawthorne never ceased to worry over Sophia's health. Fortunately, she was invited to spend the winter of 1855–56 with Minister and Mrs. John O'Sullivan in Lisbon – a plan, Hawthorne reckoned – that would provide the sunshine and warm days which Sophia so urgently required. The family had been very happy at Rock Park, but the cost of maintaining a large staff and paying the rent was great. During Sophia's absence he decided to give up the house, find a place for himself and Julian in Liverpool, and look for another residence when Sophia returned.

It was mid-June of 1856 when Sophia and the girls arrived back from Portugal, but the moment when Sophia would have to face up again to the climate of the northwest was slightly delayed when the Bennochs offered the Hawthornes their home in Blackheath for the months of July and August.

Francis Bennoch's gesture of friendship, typical of his generous nature, meant that the Hawthornes could quietly consider where and how they should live before the consul's term of office ended on August 1, 1857 – the date he had set for vacating his post. In weighing the pros and cons of their next place of residence, Hawthorne had at least three considerations to ponder: first, Sophia's health; second, the cost; and third, his desire to live far enough from Liverpool to avoid heavy social demands.

Eventually he settled on the seaside resort of Southport, about an hour's journey by rail from Liverpool. Having decided on the place of residence, it became necessary to find a house. In the last week of August he travelled alone to the resort, a ride he found uninteresting and monotonous. The landscape, he wrote in his journal, was the dreariest he had ever seen – "even in Lancashire." When he reached Southport, he found the town equally unimpressive. It was, he said, "a large village – or rather more than a village – which seems to be entirely made up of lodging-houses and . . . has been created by the influx of summer visitors . . ." He noted the town's principal attraction – its glistening sand beach – was complemented by "a whole city of bathing machines" and numerous donkey carriages.[44]

Hawthorne decided to take a house at 15 Brunswick Terrace on Southport's Promenade. It was owned by Jane Bramwell, described as a "shrewd and shabby-looking mistress."[45] About a month after moving in, Hawthorne stayed at home to allow Sophia to visit a friend in Liverpool. He took the occasion to write Ticknor about life in the family's new surroundings. Southport he described simply as "a dull and dreary little watering-place." In an aside, he seemed to endorse Dr. Samuel Johnson's opinion of the capital. "I must confess I sigh for London," he said, "and consider it time mis-spent to live anywhere else."[46] But, as the winter arrived, Hawthorne revised his opinion of Southport sufficiently to remark on its healthful benefits to Sophia. "She has gained much," he said, "and is better now than at any time since crossing the Atlantic."[47]

In Southport Hawthorne had little cause to complain about the cost of living. Jane Bramwell asked half a guinea weekly per bed and fifteen shillings for the parlour. Although the rent was cheap by Liverpool standards, Hawthorne found the lodging house arrangement a burden in other respects. After the elegance of 26 Rock Park the Hawthornes found the parlour of their Southport lodging house a great disappointment. The carpet was old and patched, the sofa soft and shabby, and the six plain chairs in the fifteen-square-foot room were hardly conducive to an atmosphere of coziness. Hawthorne confessed the only thing he liked in the room was a coloured print of Queen Victoria and Prince Albert.

If Southport was lacking in graciousness, it did provide Sophia with a new lease on life after a sharp warning by her doctor against over-exertion. An extract from a letter to her sister cites the medical caution, affords an informal glimpse of life in the sea-side resort, and reveals Sophia's unabashed affection for her husband. "The Doctor," she said, "will not let me walk more than thirty minutes at the time. Here [in Southport] there are no carriages with horses, but with donkeys, sometimes two and three abreast. They will go out to the edge of the deep sea. The donkeys walk, unless they take it into their heads to run a little. One day I mounted Julian and Una on donkeys while Rose and I were in the carriage."[48]

Then Sophia confided to her sister Hawthorne's deep concern for her health. "Mr. Hawthorne," she said, "knows what has been my danger and he is watchful of every breath I draw, and I would not exchange his guardianship for that of any winged angel of the hosts. . . . Mr. Hawthorne, you may be sure, will take care of me. I should think he would suppose you thought he had no interest in the matter, but he thinks of nothing else and would give up the Consulate today if he saw it was best for me."[49]

Southport's beaches frequently were the scenes of pleasant walks for Hawthorne and the children. Except for the sea and its related beach activities, there was little else in Southport to interest Hawthorne. Most of the holiday visitors seemed to be from Manchester or Liverpool. He was amused at the custom of the local newspaper, *The Southport Visiter* (sic), of printing the names of guests in the various hotels and lodging houses. The scheme

**HENRY BRIGHT TOLD OF THE DEATH OF SOPHIA'S FATHER**
On January 20th Hawthorne wrote this letter to his Liverpool friend, Henry Bright, declining an invitation. Sophia was deeply attached to her father, who had died on New Year's Day.

## SOUTHPORT – A PLACE OF BOREDOM, BEACHES AND BURGLARY

Hawthorne found Southport a dull place, but the children never tired of the town's beaches. The quiet seaside resort received a jolt when the Hawthornes' rented house was burgled by two well known thieves.

apparently carried the hope of selling a copy of the paper to each person whose name appeared in print.

The monotonous life in Southport was broken briefly in November, 1856, when Herman Melville arrived in England. Hawthorne was somewhat apprehensive about seeing him and for very good reason. "I felt very awkward at first," he said, "because this is the first time I have met him since my ineffectual attempt to get him a consular appointment from General Pierce. However, I failed only from real lack of power to serve him, so there was no reason to be ashamed, and we soon found ourselves on pretty much our former terms of sociability and confidence."[50] They passed two pleasant days in chatting, smoking cigars, and walking over the wind-swept dunes of Southport's beaches. Later they made a trip to Chester, the city Hawthorne never tired of visiting. Then Melville left as suddenly as he had arrived, leaving behind his trunk at the consulate and taking along a carpetbag allegedly holding only a nightshirt and toothbrush.

The ever-changing sea laid bare many surprises and raised deep mysteries every time it swept across Southport's beaches, and Hawthorne's children were there to savour them. Julian, writing towards the end of his life, still remembered the simple pleasures of an inquisitive boy turned loose in his own littoral empire. Once, after a violent gale, a ship's mast was washed ashore. It was encrusted with barnacles, sea-weed, and – to Julian's delight – sea-anemones. Hawthorne had earlier given Julian a copy of *The Aquarium* by the noted naturalist, Philip Henry Gosse, and the lad, by perusing its pages, was able to identify the marine animal. Removing a dozen or so specimens from the mast, he transferred them to an old wash-basin where, for a while, they prospered. After "blooming" gloriously and even reproducing their young, they suddenly perished. Through boyish neglect, the refilling of the improvised aquarium lapsed; when a servant took over the task and unwittingly put in fresh water, they died.

Julian fared much better at another enterprise – ship-building. Southport's beach was the haven for boys of the town who came in droves to test their exquisite ship-models. Some, of course, were purchased, and among these were superb replicas of cutters and yachts. Julian, bent on a boy's game of one-upmanship, engaged as tutor a local carpenter – "an elderly, shirt-sleeved, gray-bearded man, who under a stern aspect concealed a warm and companionable heart." Under the old man's watchful eye, he spent several days making his *pièce-de-résistance*, finishing it off in bright green and black. The vessel proudly announced its nationality by flying a tiny American flag from her mast. "Thus decorated, and with her sails set," Julian recalled, "she was a splendid object, and the boys with bought models were depressed with envy, especially when I called their attention to the stars and stripes."[51]

To overcome the problem of the children's education in Southport the Hawthornes employed a tutor. Julian, now ten years old, was tall for his age (four feet, eight inches) and was almost the same height as the instructress. Poor Miss Brown, although supposedly qualified in arithmetic, geometry, geography, and English composition, was put into disarray by Julian and his sisters. "She was particularly perplexed by geometry;" Julian said, "she aroused our hilarity by always calling a parallelogram a parallel-O-gram, with a strong emphasis on the penultimate syllable." Julian also recalled Miss Brown's admitted dilemma in rationalizing the rule that the square of the hypotenuse is equal to the sum of the squares of the two legs of a triangle. "What were the legs of a triangle," Miss Brown wondered, "and how, if there were any, could they be square?" The tutor, Julian said, never solved this little enigma; "although we liked Miss Brown very much," he added, "she speedily lost all shadow of control over us; we treated her as a sort of inferior sister, and would never be serious."[52]

The hum-drum life in Southport was shattered during the evening of February 18, 1857, when a dramatic event occurred – the robbery of the Hawthorne house. Two well-known thieves, James and John McDonald, entered the home by breaking a pane of glass at the rear. Once inside they hastily set about their mission. Julian heard unusual noises and called to his mother. The men, thinking they had been detected, fled – but not before grabbing up many articles of value. Sophia assured Julian all was well and the pair returned to their slumber. The next morning, after the servants had discovered the burglary, the police were called in. There was great excitement as the officers interviewed everyone in the household. By the following Sunday Hawthorne was informed that the McDonald brothers had been arrested, and that he would be required to call at the Southport police station to identify the stolen property which had been recovered – some from a pawnbroker, and some from the men themselves.

"The Police Office," Hawthorne wrote in his journal, "is a small, dark room, in the basement-story of the Town Hall of Southport, and over the mantel-piece, hanging one upon another, there are innumerable advertisements of robberies in houses, and on the high-way, – murders, too, I suppose – garrottings, and offences of all sorts, not only in this district, but wide away, and forwarded from other police stations. ... Most of these advertisements were in pen and ink, with minute lists of the articles stolen, but the more important were in print, and there, too, I saw the printed advertisement of our own robbery, not for circulation, but to be handed about privately among police-officers and pawnbrokers. A rogue has a very poor chance in England, the police being so numerous, and their system so well organized."[53]

Indeed, within the course of a single week the thieves were apprehended, the stolen property recovered, and the first hearings conducted. At the examination of witnesses the

Hawthornes attended as spectators, for the police – out of courtesy to the consul – decided to take statements only from the servants. "There were a half-dozen magistrates on the bench, idle old gentlemen of Southport and vicinity, who lounged into the court more as a matter of amusement than anything else, and lounged out again, at their own pleasure," Hawthorne said, "for these magisterial duties are a part of the pastime of the country-gentlemen of England. They wore their hats on the bench. There were one or two of them more active than their fellows, but the real duty was done by the Clerk of the Court. The seats within the bar were occupied by the witnesses, and around the great table sat some of the more respectable people of Southport, and without the bar were the commonalty in great numbers, for this is said to be the first burglary that has occurred here within the memory of man, and and so it has caused a great stir."[54]

The local newspaper, the *Southport Visiter*, at last had something more exciting to report than the names of guests staying in the town's hotels and lodging houses. It gave a detailed record of the trial, including an account by the Hawthornes' maid, Ellen Hearne, about what happened the morning the robbery was discovered.

Hawthorne was uneasy about the burglary and the apprehension of the culprits. The publicity given the incident may have annoyed him, but he was also concerned about the fate of the McDonald brothers. "I rather wished them to escape," he said.[55] His wish was in vain, for in March they were tried at the Liverpool Assizes and found guilty. John was sentenced to penal servitude for life, and James to twelve months with hard labour.

With the coming of warmer weather, Southport once more was filled with temporary residents. Although Hawthorne claimed he "never was more weary of a place in all my life," he admitted that the seaside resort did have a variety of amusements. Besides the usual donkey rides, there was one fascinating contraption – a massive clumsy boat – mounted on wheels and propelled by sails when the wind blew; it was known locally as the "Flying Dutchman." There were the usual seaside attractions, too – bathing houses, hotels with their popular billiard rooms, archery on the beaches, and a theatrical performance every evening. "From morning till night," Hawthorne said, "comes a succession of organ-grinders, playing interminably under your window, and a man with a bassoon, and a monkey, who takes your pennies and pulls off his cap in acknowledgement, and wandering minstrels, with guitar and voice, and a highland bagpiper, squealing out a tangled skein of discord, together with a highland maid who dances a hornpipe."[56]

The consulate at Liverpool had provided Hawthorne with a good income, but he thoroughly detested the town as a place in which to live. Sadly, the residence in Southport had provided the isolation and the economical living he sought, but there was little else to commend it. "Southport," he concluded, "is as stupid a place as ever I lived in, and I cannot but bewail an ill fortune, to have been compelled to spend these many months on these barren sands, when almost every other square yard of England contains something that would have been historically or poetically interesting. Our life here has been a complete blank."[57]

# IX

# The Consul and the Future President

On January 9, 1854, the *New York Daily Times* announced on its front page the loss of the steamship *San Francisco* and an undetermined number of lives. The newly built vessel had sailed from New York three weeks before with 700 passengers, many of whom were members of an American artillery regiment bound for California. Several ships joined in the rescue, some continuing to England and others to New York.

It was toward the end of January before the first reports of the tragedy reached Britain. That the disaster might turn out to be a major one was hinted at in a brief item in *The Times* of London:

> The day before yesterday the country was startled by the announcement that the new steamship *San Francisco* had been seen on the 26th of December in latitude 38.20, longitude 69, by the *Maria Freeman*, with her decks swept, boats gone, and absolutely disabled. ... it is almost incredible that so well-built a steamer should be so completely disabled in mid-ocean and still be left floating; therefore the report is not universally believed, but still the first flash of the news alarmed the country . . .[1]

The report, dated January 7 and written by the *Times'* New York correspondent, reached London only in time for the January 24 issue. British readers who may have been concerned lest the report was true, had not long to wait. The very next issue of *The Times*, in a long article captioned "SHIPWRECK AND LOSS OF LIFE," confirmed the worst fears of the newspaper's New York representative.

For a full week the *San Francisco* was battered, helpless in a fierce storm. On New Year's Day the *Antarctic* took off some survivors, as did also the *Three Bells* and the *Kilby*. The *Antarctic* continued to Liverpool, the others to New York. Before the *Antarctic* reached the Mersey, over fifty *San Francisco* passengers died from exposure and injuries. When the final toll became known the casualties approached 300. Almost all the dead were American servicemen who had been quartered on the vessel's deck.

The arrival of the *Antarctic* caused great confusion in Liverpool. Consul Hawthorne was confronted with the most serious incident of his career and the utmost tact and speed were required to prevent the tragedy becoming even worse. Looking after the sick and injured was the least of the problems. The other survivors, particularly the soldiers, urgently required warm clothing. Hawthorne's tasks seemed simple enough – clothe the men at U.S. Government expense, and charter a ship to return them to the United States. In fact, the solution was not nearly so simple and before the affair ended the consul stood accused of neglect and intransigence.

Sophia's next letter home reveals the impact the disaster made upon her husband. "In the evening," she wrote, "Mr. Hawthorne told me that there were suddenly thrown upon his care two hundred soldiers who had been shipwrecked in the *San Francisco*, and that he must clothe and board them and send them home to the United States. They were picked up somewhere on the sea and brought to Liverpool. Mr. Hawthorne has no official

## *SAN FRANCISCO* TRAGEDY COMMEMORATED BY MEDAL

Nearly 300 passengers, most of them members of an American artillery regiment, perished when the steamship *San Francisco* was lost in December, 1853. Some survivors were brought to Liverpool where Hawthorne's attempt to provide assistance caused an American newspaper to accuse him of negligence. The American Congress authorized the above medal for rescuers.

authority to take care of any but *sailors* in distress. He invited the lieutenant to come and stay here, and he must take care of the soldiers, even if the expense comes out of his own purse."[2] Sophia had presented the situation fairly accurately. Hawthorne, on his own risk, undertook to feed and clothe the men, for this clearly seemed to be a legitimate government obligation. But chartering a ship to return the troops to America was another matter. This would cost thousands of pounds and, on paper, he did not have authority to enter into such a transaction. And it was by no means certain that a vessel could be chartered on short notice. When Hawthorne appealed to Collins, the foremost American line, he got nowhere. Its *Pacific* was due to sail in two days, but the Collins officials in Liverpool said they could not turn away scheduled passengers with so little warning. Fortunately, Cunard then made a tender to transport the men on its *America*.

Cunard's offer came from Charles McIver, a staunch member of the American Chamber of Commerce in Liverpool.[3] Hawthorne and the commander of the troops, Lt. Charles S. Winder, were busily negotiating the charter of the *America* in Liverpool and unaware that an independent effort to find a ship was being made in London. Captain Watkins, the master of the *San Francisco*, had become impatient with Hawthorne and left Liverpool suddenly for London to see Minister Buchanan. But the Minister could do nothing for Watkins, and the captain returned to Liverpool to find that Lieutenant Winder had already signed the contract with Cunard. Within the week the *America* sailed with 176 survivors of the *San Francisco*.

With the troops on their way home, Hawthorne hoped he had heard the last of the *San Francisco* affair. He explained to William Ticknor that he had been enormously busy with the shipwrecked servicemen from the *San Francisco* – "having had to clothe and feed them all on my own responsibility." He added: "Uncle Sam will pay me, I suppose, and he will likewise pay a larger sum for their passage home than all their bodies and souls are worth. I made the bargain myself, so you will readily conclude that it was a poor one. This responsibility, however, rests on the shoulders of the officer commanding [Lt. Winder] – not mine."[4]

But Hawthorne had not heard the last of the *San Francisco* episode, for the tragedy was to make further headlines on both sides of the Atlantic. On February 7 the London *Times*, in a story sent from Liverpool, recounted how a Merchants' Committee had resolved to honour the captains and principal officers of the several ships which had taken part in the rescue effort. The captains of the *Three Bells, Antarctic,* and *Kilby,* were each to receive silver tea sets valued at $2,500. Their first officers were to get $250 in cash and other officers lesser sums in proportion to their rank. Ordinary sailors were to receive $50 each, plus a silver medal. The article concluded: "The subscriptions from all quarters were very liberal."[5]

Such generosity was deserved and no doubt was applauded by Hawthorne, but he was shocked by the next development in the United States. Someone returning aboard the *America* – presumably not Lieutenant Winder or Captain Watkins – put abroad a false story of what happened when the shipwrecked soldiers arrived in Liverpool. A particularly venomous version appeared in the Portsmouth (New Hampshire) *Journal* indicting Hawthorne:

## A "SCARLET" MARK

> We understand that when application was made on behalf of the U.S. troops conveyed to England in the *Antarctic,* from the wreck of the *San Francisco,* to our consul at Liverpool to procure for them passage to the United States, his reply was, – "I know nothing about the matter. I refer you to my clerk." This clerk, who is an *Englishman,* said that the consul was not authorized to send soldiers to the United States, but that if they had been seamen or marines it could be done; to which the author of the life of General Frank Pierce assented, – and it was only by Capt. Watkins proceeding to London to see our Minister there, that any measures could be taken to send them home. Mr. Buchanan, upon Capt. Watkins' application, immediately telegraphed to the Consul at Liverpool to provide a vessel and everything of which the troops stood in need. . . . Should not Mr. Hawthorne have a "scarlet letter" branded on his own forehead?[6]

The *Journal* article incensed Hawthorne and his friends, but what could be done to put the record straight? For one thing, Hawthorne could set forth the facts in his dispatch recording his efforts. This he did on February 3, 1854, taking the utmost care to be objective. Had he wished to criticize Buchanan, here was his opportunity. Had he wanted to chastise the Collins Line for failing to transport the soldiers, he could have done so. He chose to condemn neither, but did take pains to praise Lieutenant Winder for his coolness and judgement in signing a £6,500 contract to charter the *America.*

Hawthorne, in his dispatch to the State Department, dealt first with his approach to Minister Buchanan. "The case being a new one, . . . I placed the requisite supplies at Lieutenant Winder's disposal on my private responsibility, and proceeded to communicate by telegraph with Mr. Buchanan, our Minister, in order to ascertain whether he would assume the direction of what remained to be done," he stated. "Mr. Buchanan informed me that he had no authority in the premises, but he facilitated my operations, as far as lay

**JAMES BUCHANAN**
The future American president was the U.S. Minister to Britain while Hawthorne was consul in Liverpool. Hawthorne liked Buchanan, but their relationship was delicate because of their common friendship with Franklin Pierce.

in his power, by recommending the Messrs. Barings to open a credit with me in behalf of the troops." Hawthorne then expressed his concern about the vulnerability of the troops to British recruiters. "The British recruiting service being very active just at this juncture," he explained, "the men might readily have exchanged one service for another. For these reasons it was necessary to act promptly and the only method of doing so was by accepting the proposal of the agent [Mr. McIver] of the Cunard line . . . to place their extra steamer *America* at the disposal of Lieut. Winder . . ."[7]

Tragedy frequently thrusts up a leader and, in the case of the *San Francisco* disaster, it was Lt. Winder who emerged a hero. Winder, a Marylander, had graduated from West Point in 1850 and seemingly was destined to a slow rise through the officer ranks until he was caught up in the *San Francisco* affair. However, his superiors in Washington – so impressed by his courage at sea and his resourcefulness in bringing his surviving troops home as quickly as possible – promoted him to captain in March, 1855. At 25 he was reputed to be the youngest officer in the United States Army of that rank.

Although the Portsmouth *Journal* misrepresented the facts of the *San Francisco* affair, another New England paper, the Marblehead *Advocate*, carried the correct version. Hawthorne sent Ticknor a copy of the *Advocate*'s article, together with a letter which he urged his friend to publish if the erroneous account received further circulation. This letter was a simple, shortened version of the dispatch. "If nothing further has been said of the affair," Hawthorne cautioned Ticknor, "let it rest. It will not be worthwhile to take up a forgotten slander." Hawthorne concluded by pondering the identity of the author of the malicious version printed by the *Journal*. "Certainly," he said, "it could not have been either Captain Watkins or Lieutenant Winder, from neither of whom did I hear a word of complaint or dissatisfaction, and after parting from me in perfect kindness and with thanks for my services, they are not the men to attack me behind my back on the other side of the Atlantic, and anonymously, through a newspaper."[8] Hawthorne was astute enough not to prolong the issue and in a short while the accusations were forgotten.

Both Buchanan and Hawthorne were fully aware of the delicate game they were playing. While Hawthorne was a loyal friend of Pierce, Buchanan's position was more nearly that of an exiled rival. Pierce and Hawthorne at all times regarded Buchanan as presidential "timber." Buchanan may have been an old man, but he took care to keep open his lines of communication with powerful members of the Democratic Party in the United States. In the nineteenth century the position of Minister was considered as excellent preparation for the presidency. Buchanan already had won public approval as U.S. Minister to Russia (1832–4) where he had been largely responsible for negotiating the first American-Russian commercial treaty. He entertained presidential aspirations as early as 1844, but lost the Democratic nomination to James K. Polk. Because he was a shrewd politician, Buchanan took his failure without rancour and threw his support to Polk during the subsequent campaign. Polk, in turn, made Buchanan his Secretary of State in 1845.

Hawthorne and Buchanan came to Britain in the autumn of 1853 to take up their duties, the consul assuming office on August 1 and the minister on August 23. Buchanan had hardly settled into his office when he received a letter from Hawthorne calling attention to an odd maritime custom. It seemed that the British government could compel the master of a foreign ship to transport British mail to any port on the vessel's itinerary. It seems no other foreign service officer had dared challenge Her Majesty's Government on this point.

Hawthorne became involved when the American clipper ship, *Sovereign of the Seas*, put into Liverpool. Captain Warner, hoping to make an extraordinarily fast voyage to Australia, proposed to take British mail to Melbourne for a fee of $500. He guaranteed delivery in 70 days and agreed to pay a forfeit of $20 a day for each day beyond that period. The British Post Office not only rejected his proposal, but informed the master that he would be *compelled* to take British mail. The captain was further informed that, should he refuse, he would be fined $200. "On first view," Hawthorne wrote Buchanan, "it does seem to me to be a hardship and withal an injustice that the English Government should compel an American vessel to carry mails on such terms as it shall deem fitting to prescribe . . ."[9]

Buchanan lost no time in transmitting a copy of Hawthorne's letter to the British Foreign Secretary, Lord Clarendon. In his accompanying note, dated August 25th, the minister asked whether the Postmaster General believed he had the right to compel foreign masters to receive British mail for delivery abroad. He avoided giving his own opinion, but repeated Hawthorne's urgent note calling attention to the scheduled departure of the *Sovereign of the Seas* on September 3. On August 31 Buchanan advised Hawthorne he had just received a reply from the Foreign Office enclosing a report from the British Post Office. Its terse wording left no doubt where the Post Office stood. ". . . in the opinion of the Solicitor to this Department . . . no master of any vessel, British or Foreign, bound from the Port of Liverpool to Australia could refuse to take a Post letter Bag delivered or tendered to him for conveyance by an officer of the Post Office, without incurring a penalty of £200."[10]

In his reply to Hawthorne, Buchanan attempted to look at the case from the British point of view: "It is presumed that as the British Government have opened their coasting trade to Foreign vessels, they deem it but reasonable that in the enjoyment of this trade those vessels should be subject to the same terms and conditions with British vessels."[11] Nonetheless, Buchanan said he planned to continue his investigation of the matter, and asked Hawthorne if this was the first case of the kind to occur at Liverpool. Then, ever the practical diplomat, Buchanan suggested that Hawthorne advise the captain of the *Sovereign of the Seas* to carry the British mail, but under protest – if he so wished. The ship's master, Captain Warner, agreed with the suggestion, accepted the mail, and filed a protest which Hawthorne duly forwarded to Buchanan.

During a further exchange of notes Hawthorne told Buchanan: "What national or higher interests are involved in the question thus raised you are the better judge of than I can be, but it is desirable that the right in the matter should be settled and understood."[12] Buchanan asked for, and was granted, an interview with the British Foreign Secretary, Lord Clarendon. By this time Clarendon himself was having doubts about the validity of the British Post Office's stand. In his meeting with Lord Clarendon, Buchanan strongly defended Hawthorne's view that the shipping practice was illegal. Then, to underline the gravity with which the United States viewed the arbitrary act of the British Post Office, Buchanan reminded Clarendon that "my Government . . . might then, if they thought proper, provide by law to impose similar Postal duties on British vessels clearing from the ports of the United States."[13] The question was finally resolved in November, 1853, when Lord Clarendon capitulated.

". . . the United States Consul at Liverpool is mistaken in supposing that the practice complained of by the master of the *Sovereign of the Seas* is new," he told Buchanan; "it has existed, on the contrary, from a period extending as far back as we have any records and almost every day's 'Packet List' contains announcements to the effect 'that the Ship letter office will despatch letters under the regulations of the Acts of Parliament' by foreign as well as British Ships." Having thus confirmed that the practice had been going on for years, Clarendon came to the crux of the matter; ". . . after taking the opinion of the law officers of the Crown upon the subject and having conferred with the Postmaster General, it has been considered that the law is not compulsory as respects foreign vessels, and that if captains or owners of such vessels take charge of letter bags, it must be a voluntary act on their part."[14]

The retreat over the protest raised by the United States Consul at Liverpool was a landmark in the field of international postal agreements. After Lord Clarendon's statement, the principle that one nation could impose postal obligations on another was dead. Oddly, there seems to be not a word of tribute from Buchanan or any other American authority to Hawthorne for his initiative in bringing to light the postal practice.

Hawthorne thus was obliged, within a few months of becoming consul, to correspond with his Minister in London on two important matters, the *San Francisco* incident and the British postal issue. In both cases Buchanan showed, by his action and official correspondence, that he respected the consul's judgment. Relations between the two men thus opened amicably.

From time to time the consul was obliged to consult his minister on matters that required judgment Hawthorne considered himself incapable of giving. In his official correspondence Hawthorne went out of his way to demonstrate his respect for Buchanan's authority and person. An excerpt from a hitherto unpublished letter from Hawthorne to Buchanan, written in March of 1854, when Britain's involvement in the Crimea was imminent, demonstrates the finesse with which the consul in Liverpool approached his superior in London. "I have been asked by several American ship masters," wrote Hawthorne, "whether it would be safe for them in the present state of European politics to go from England to Malta with cargoes of coal the property of British subjects? . . . Being unable to answer so intricate and important a question I am requested to submit it to you, as it is of such great importance to American commerce, I deem it my duty to do so, not doubting that your great diplomatic experience will justify your giving an opinion upon it."[15]

Buchanan, at about the same time, was having trouble with his superior, Secretary of State Marcy, who had sent a circular to all American diplomatic missions demanding that foreign service officers forego formal dress and be attired in the dress of the ordinary American citizen when appearing in public. Buchanan, having served previously as U.S. Minister to Russia, was fully aware that protocol in some European nations required attire which was considerably more elegant than that worn by the "ordinary American citizen" – whoever that might be. When the time came for him to be presented to Queen Victoria early in 1854, he at last resolved to put aside his apprehensions and appear dressed precisely as Secretary Marcy had instructed.

**THE QUEEN AND HER LETTER**
Minister Buchanan put Hawthorne in a delicate position by asking what he thought about the style of Queen Victoria's touching letter on Britain's war-wounded. Hawthorne replied, saying the Queen had "a perfect right to do what she pleases with her *own English.*"

He described the presentation in a letter to his niece, Harriet Lane. "I appeared," he said, "at the [Queen's] levee on Wednesday last, in just such a dress as I have worn at the President one hundred times. . . . As I approached the Queen, an arch but benevolent smile lit up her countenance; – as much as to say, you are the first man who ever appeared before me at Court in such a dress. I must confess that I never felt more proud of being an American than when I stood in that brilliant circle 'in the simple dress of an ordinary American.' I have no doubt the Circular [of Marcy's] is popular with a majority of the people of England."[16]

In April of 1854 the Hawthornes had an opportunity to welcome the American Minister in their Rock Park home. Buchanan's prolonged visit was unexpected, but it provided each person a chance to know the other better. The minister, a bachelor, needed someone to manage his London residence and to accompany him to the capital's social events. He had asked his 23-year old niece, Harriet Lane – an orphan for whom he was guardian – if she would take on the responsibility. Harriet accepted the challenge and promptly boarded a Collins Line ship for Liverpool. The vessel was late in arriving, thus giving the Hawthornes the unexpected pleasure of playing host. "Mr. Buchanan has been here since Tuesday," Hawthorne wrote Ticknor, "in expectation of his niece who is supposed to be on board the steamer. I had the old fellow to dine with me, and liked him better than I expected, so I hope you have not found it necessary to publish my letter on the *San Francisco* business, for though I made it bear lightly on him, it would undoubtedly have provoked a feud between us. But he takes his wine like a true man, loves a good cigar, and is doubtless as honest as nine diplomatists out of ten."[17]

A year later Buchanan paid a second visit to Liverpool and again it was Harriet Lane who provided the excuse. When she was asked to be bridesmaid at the wedding of an American girl in Liverpool, Buchanan seized the opportunity to come along himself. While in Liverpool this time he stayed with William Brown, Member of Parliament, merchant and donor of the town's public library. Brown gave an elaborate dinner for his American guest as a gesture of their long friendship. The two had first met in May of 1832 when

Buchanan was passing through Liverpool en route to St. Petersburg to take up his post as United States Minister to Russia. On that occasion Brown had also feted Buchanan with a dinner. Now, more than two decades later, Brown was repeating his hospitality and Hawthorne was among the guests present. ". . . [Buchanan] cannot be called gentlemanly in his manners," he said, "there being a sort of rusticity about him; – moreover, a habit of squinting one eye, and an awkward carriage of his head, but withal, a dignity in his large, white-headed person, and a consciousness of high position and importance, which gives him ease and freedom."[18]

During the course of the evening someone brought up the subject of Queen Victoria's "autograph letter" – a personal letter from the Queen enquiring about the welfare of British servicemen in the Crimean campaign. The brief message was addressed to Sidney Herbert, with the request that it be passed on to Florence Nightingale or her co-worker, Mrs. Bracebridge. It read:

Windsor Castle, Dec. 6, 1854

Would you tell Mrs. Herbert that I begged she would *let me see frequently* the accounts she receives from Miss Nightingale or Mrs. Bracebridge, as *I hear no details of the wounded*, tho' I see so many from officers, &c., about the battle-field, and naturally the former must interest me more than anyone.

Let Mrs. Herbert also know that I wish Miss Nightingale and the ladies would tell their poor noble wounded and sick men that NO ONE *takes* a warmer interest, or feels *more* for their sufferings, or admires their courage and heroism *MORE* than their Queen. Day and night she thinks of her beloved troops. So does the Prince.

Beg Mrs. Herbert to communicate those my words to the ladies, as I know that our sympathy is much valued by these noble fellows.

VICTORIA[19]

The Queen had obviously written the letter without consulting anyone. Although composed from patriotic motives, the letter contained several embarrassing elements. It inferred her ministers did not keep her informed about casualties, and her style of writing left much to be desired. The letter was published throughout Britain, usually accompanied by favourable comment from editors. Buchanan and Hawthorne should have counted themselves fortunate being Americans when the letter was being discussed, for any honest comment by them was bound to be distasteful. Hawthorne thus was appalled when he was addressed – not by an Englishman – but Buchanan. Sophia said her husband "was much perplexed by Mr. Buchanan's asking him, before the whole company at dinner, 'what he thought of the Queen's letter.'" Holding his ground, Hawthorne replied simply that the letter showed very kind feeling by the Queen. Sophia continues: "No," persisted the wicked Ambassador; 'but what do you think of the *style*?'" She then reveals how her husband squelched the minister: "Mr. Hawthorne was equal to him, or rather, conquered him . . ., for he said, 'The Queen has a perfect right to do what she pleases with her *own English*.'"[20]

While in Liverpool Buchanan called on Hawthorne at the consulate, and the two men chatted for nearly two hours on various subjects – himself, other people in public life, and of affairs in Britain and the United States. He told Hawthorne of his intention to return to America in October of the following year (1856) when he hoped to retire from political life

**BUCHANAN WITH HIS NIECE, HARRIET LANE**
A bachelor, Buchanan asked Harriet to assist with the social demands first, at his ministerial post in London and, later at the White House. Despite her extreme youth, she accomplished both tasks successfully. Hawthorne was smitten by the lovely Harriet who, he said, was both "sweet and simple in aspect."

and settle down to writing his memoirs. "I suggested a doubt," said Hawthorne, "whether the people would permit him to retire, and he immediately responded to my hint as regards his prospects for the Presidency. He said that his mind was fully made up, and that he would never be a candidate, and that he had expressed this intention to his friends in such a way as to put out of his own power to change it." Hawthorne took Buchanan to be sincere in his statement, but when his conversation with him was over, he pondered why the minister had been so frank in disavowing his presidential ambitions. "I wonder," Hawthorne said, "whether he can have had any object in saying all this to me. He might see that it would be perfectly natural for me to tell it to General Pierce."[21]

If Hawthorne had doubts about Buchanan's motives, he had none about the charms of Harriet Lane, who must have stolen the show from her uncle during their Liverpool stay. Hawthorne thought her extremely attractive, entirely self-possessed, well-poised, and without affectation but nonetheless quietly conscious of her rank. "Her gown," he added, "was terribly low across the shoulders. I should judge her to be twenty-five or thereabouts. I talked with her a little and found her sensible, sufficiently vivacious, and seemingly firm-textured, rather than soft and sentimental." Hawthorne, indeed, appears to have been left speechless by the beautiful Miss Lane. "She paid me some compliments," he said, "but I don't remember paying her any."[22]

The Hawthornes spent most of the month of September, 1855, in London, taking a house near Hanover Square. Before Hawthorne could call on Buchanan, the minister came and left his card – "an intimation that I ought sooner to have paid my respects . . .." Hastening to make amends, Hawthorne visited Buchanan at the legation in Harley Street, an establishment, he noted, which "compares shabbily enough with the legations of other great countries, and with the houses of the English aristocracy."[23] Before long the two were again discussing American politics. Buchanan ventured that Pierce – even with great dissension in his cabinet – had a fair chance of being renominated. If Buchanan expected Hawthorne to comment on this speculation, perhaps revealing some clue as to Pierce's intentions which he thought might have reached Hawthorne, he was to be disappointed.

Toward the end of·September, the Hawthornes called on Buchanan again. This time they were shown into the drawing room. They observed that the furniture, while sufficiently splendid, was "rather the worse for wear – being hired furniture, no doubt." Although a bachelor, Buchanan was a charmer among women, and this occasion was no exception. "His deportment towards ladies is highly agreeable and prepossessing, and he paid very kind attention to Sophia . . .," Hawthorne noted. Despite Sophia's views about Buchanan's role in the *San Francisco* arrangements and the episode of Queen Victoria's autograph letter, she liked the minister as a person. On this occasion she found him more aged, infirm and depressed. Perhaps the reason lay in his next announcement: he had decided to return to the United States and Harriet Lane's passage was already booked for October 6th. Hawthorne at first suspected the ministers' motive was to return home and get his political fences mended in time to fight President Pierce for the Democratic nomination, but upon reflection he believed Buchanan's decision to give up his post at the Court of St. James was due to other reasons. "I rather think," he said, "he does really wish to return, and that not for any ambitious views upon the Presidency, but from an old man's natural desire to be at home, and among his own people. I like Mr. Buchanan."[24]

Sophia was anxious to see the Houses of Parliament in action and asked Buchanan if he could arrange for her admission through the Lord Chamberlain's office. "The Ambassador drew from his pocket a colored silk handkerchief (which ought to have gone into this week's wash) and made a knot in it," Hawthorne said, "in order to remind himself to ask the Lord Chamberlain." The visitors were amused at this mannerism, "but," Hawthorne said, "I would rather not have him do it before English people."[25] That evening Buchanan sent around his carriage to convey his guests to dinner at the American Legation. Miss Lane, Hawthorne noted, "looked quite beamingly, more sweet and simple in aspect than when I had seen her in full dress."[26]

Hawthorne called at the American Legation once more during his London stay. Buchanan, learning that Hawthorne was on the premises, burst into the office in his dressing gown. He explained that Harriet Lane's days in Britain were now numbered, and that he shortly would be off to Liverpool to see his niece safely aboard ship. The vivacious Harriet was leaving Britain not a day too soon, for she had come very close to succumbing to the advances of Sir Fitzroy Kelly, a man more than twice her age. Ever an admirer of lovely ladies, Hawthorne was sad to hear that Harriet was leaving Britain. "She has had a good deal of success in society here," he said, "being pretty enough to be remarked among English women, and with cool, self-possessed, frank, and quiet manners, which look very like the highest breeding."[27]

The vexing problem of how to move on incoming dispatch bags to the American Legation in London brought a gentle reprimand from Buchanan toward the end of his ministerial assignment. His letter, and Hawthorne's appended note, reads:

Legation of the United States
London, 3 December 1855

My dear Sir,

It is at all times disagreeable for one to complain and least of all to complain to so valued a friend as yourself.

I am now writing at 3 o'clock and the Despatch Bag has not arrived whilst I received my mail early this morning. It has several times occurred that the mail has arrived early in the morning and the Despatch Bag not till late in the evening, and sometimes not until the next day, etc. At a common time this would make no difference, but it has now twice occurred (it has done so today) that I have had an interview with Lord Clarendon on Monday, *he being in possession of information from Washington* whilst I had not received my despatches. On the former occasion this produced serious inconvenience. It will not do so today because I was "mum" and postponed the interview until Thursday next. Do give your attention to this matter during the pending difficulties.

From your friend
Very respectfully,
James Buchanan

Beneath Buchanan's signature Hawthorne scribbled a note indicating the action taken:

Answered – explained, and the delay thought to be unavoidable under the present arrangements for conveying the despatches.

N.H.

P.S. The system has since been entirely changed, at my suggestion.[28]

Buchanan had every right to be annoyed by the delay in receiving instructions from Washington, for at this time relations between the United States and Britain were strained. His strongly worded letter to Hawthorne was the only instance when the American Minister had something to say about how Hawthorne should perform his duties.

# X
# Mischief at Sea

"A great part of the wear and tear of [my] mind and temper," said Hawthorne of his four-year consular experience, "resulted from bad relations between the seamen and officers of American ships."[1] For one who preferred seclusion and a quiet life, he found himself in a violent new world. From almost the day he became consul, sailors beat a path to his door to display cuts, bruises and other signs of mistreatment aboard ships.

Hawthorne at first tended to side with the seamen, as did the British press who made much of the violence aboard American ships. In time he learned there was another point of view – that of the shipsmaster. His job was to take ships across the sea, but his so-called crew was often no more than a collection of the dregs of humanity – misfits, alcoholics, criminals, returning emigrants and illiterate foreigners with little or no skills. "Looked at judicially," Hawthorne admitted, "there appeared to be no right side to the matter, nor any right side possible in so thoroughly vicious a system as that of the American mercantile marine."[2]

His initiation into the arena of seamen's disputes was mild enough. In January of 1854 he attended a hearing at the Liverpool police court at which a sailor was accused of stealing a comforter from another seaman. When the magistrate ruled he had no jurisdiction in the matter and Hawthorne considered the offence was too trivial to warrant sending the man back to the United States, the case was dismissed.

A month later he was back in the same court, this time concerned with a much more serious affair. The second mate and four seamen from the *John and Albert* were charged with beating up the vessel's chief mate. The victim was brought from the hospital heavily doped with brandy for the trial. Testimony by the five men charged with the assault, plus that of the Captain, revealed that the chief mate had aggravated his attackers and probably got what he deserved. All but one were discharged, and Hawthorne arranged for the fifth to be returned to the United States for trial. The report of the case formed the subject of Hawthorne's first dispatch relating to violence aboard American ships.[3] It opened his eyes to conditions about which he had known little. It also set in motion his resolve to make Washington aware of these bestial conditions in the hope that constructive measures would be taken to eliminate them.

Hawthorne proposed an official inquiry by the United States Government into conditions aboard American ships. ". . . I feel it a duty to express my opinion," Hawthorne wrote, "that, if competent persons were appointed by our government to investigate this matter, great evils would certainly be exposed, and a wholesome and effective remedy might be suggested." This daring proposal – all the more so coming from one so new to the consular service – brought no action from Washington. On the question of providing professional training for American shipmasters and crewmen, Hawthorne had very specific notions which were far in advance of his time. His dispatch to Washington predicted that "some arrangement, on our side of the water, similar to that adopted in this country [Great Britain] under the Mercantile Marine Law, and, in like manner, the establishment of Nautical Schools, day and evening, would be productive of great improvement in our merchant service, both as regards the capacity and character of masters and crews."[4]

Shortly after the first anniversary of taking office, Hawthorne wrote Ticknor that he was

**"LET SLAVERY ALONE!"**
Hawthorne pleaded with his friend, Senator Charles Sumner, to leave the slavery issue alone for a while and join him in the effort to improve conditions aboard American ships where indescribable cruelty was being inflicted upon seamen.

"sick and weary" and would not care if the position were abolished. "What with brutal shipmasters, drunken sailors, vagrant Yankees, mad people, sick people, and dead people," he said, ". . . it is full of damnable annoyances."[5]

In April, 1855, Hawthorne sent the State Department a dispatch detailing the death of a seaman at the hands of the master of the *Charles Sprague*.[6] Depositions from six members of the crew painted a gory picture of intoxication, disobedience, and violence. In May, 1855, a young man – Daniel Smith – came to the consulate and told an amazing story. He had been living in Charleston where he sold produce from his brother's farm located near the South Carolina port. One day he was asked to help take a heavy trunk aboard a ship, the *George A. Ropley* (registered at Charleston). When he got aboard, he was promptly seized by crewmen and impressed into service. On the voyage to Liverpool he was repeatedly assaulted. By the time he arrived at Hawthorne's office he was in a shameful condition with "grievous marks about his face and eyes, and bruises on his head and other parts of his person."[7] After admission to hospital Smith's condition grew worse, and one day Hawthorne was summoned to his bedside at the dying youth's request. When he arrived, Hawthorne found the young man unable to speak. But the house-surgeon thought he could evoke a response by telling the boy he was dying. It worked, and the youth turned first to the surgeon and then to Hawthorne, pleading that he did not want to die, but to get well. Then he lapsed into a dying fit again, and less than an hour later, expired.

Hawthorne was so distressed by the Smith incident that he made it the subject of a vigorously worded dispatch. He described the case as being "one of great cruelty" and asked the State Department if it were "not one in which an example ought to be made of the offender."[8] He followed up the dispatch with a personal letter to Massachusetts Senator Charles Sumner. After outlining the Smith incident, he suggested that Sumner "let slavery alone, for a little while, and attend to this business . . ."[9] This time the State Department acted, although not in the manner Hawthorne had hoped. It sent a copy of his dispatch to U.S. Attorney General Caleb Cushing who readily agreed that the American law should be modified to prevent occurrences like Smith's kidnapping. He added that legislative reform, if desired, was not his concern, but the Department's. There the matter rested and if the master of Smith's ship was ever brought to trial, no one seems to have bothered to inform Hawthorne.

In mid-November Hawthorne had another death on his hands, this time a crew member from the American ship *Assyria*.[10] Accompanied by his junior clerk, Henry Wilding, he went to Liverpool's North Hospital to take a deposition from the dying man. Prompted by the doctor's prognosis that he was about to die and should tell the consul what had happened, the man explained that he had been maltreated from the moment he set foot aboard ship. Several times life almost ebbed away, but – plied with wine – he managed to complete his statement and make his cross at the end. Despite the doctor's discouraging remark, the sailor seemed to think he would recover and said he wanted to get back to his native America. On a pallet next to the dying man was a second crew member from the same ship; if anything, he was even more battered than the man Hawthorne had just interviewed. The next morning a message from the surgeon revealed the first seaman had died, and that his companion was now in a serious condition.[11]

"There is a most dreadful state of things aboard our ships," he wrote in his journal on November 16, 1855. "Hell itself can be no worse than some of them, and I do pray that some New Englander, with the itch of reform in him, may turn his thoughts this way."[12] But his pleas went unheeded, and a month later another death was reported to Washington. This time the victim, a member of the crew of the *Albert Gallatin*, had fallen from the yard after being brutally kicked in the back by the second mate. He died and was buried at sea the next day. Three second class passengers, all Cornishmen, made depositions.[13]

The violence aboard American ships continued unabated and in January, 1857, Hawthorne confessed his despair to Ticknor. "I have had all sorts of trouble in my consulate lately," he said, "– indeed, I always do, but now more than ever." A new source of annoyance were "the Liverpool philanthropists" who, unaware of the consul's strenuous efforts to get better conditions for American seamen, demanded that he "run amuck with them against the American ship-masters . . ." Hawthorne explained to Ticknor that he had made repeated statements to the State Department, and had written Senator Sumner on the subject. "Had he [Sumner] busied himself about this, instead of Abolitionism," he said, "he would have done good service to his country and have escaped Brooks' cudgel. I offered to supply him with any amount of horrible facts, but he never noticed my letter."[14]

With only seven months remaining before the date he planned to resign, Hawthorne – like many a foreign service officer in the last year of an overseas assignment – may well have asked himself: "What have I accomplished?" His letter, quoted above, indicates that he had not yet given up the battle of making his point with Washington. He was to write only fifteen more dispatches dealing with substantive matters, and eleven of these would be concerned with seamen. Taken together, these last eleven dispatches comprise a vigorous, sustained plea for legislation leading to reform aboard American vessels. Hawthorne simplified his approach and hammered away at three essential points: men should not be shipped illegally (i.e., kidnapped, while drunk, or under false pretences); second, punitive measures and other legal provisions were so inadequate or obscure as to leave consuls powerless to act effectively in most cases; and third, the United States badly needed mercantile navy training centres to provide capable crews for the country's growing merchant fleet.

February 13 not only was the day on which Hawthorne would forward one of his most critical dispatches to the State Department; it was also the day he would send his resignation to President Pierce, and write his friend Ticknor. He was well aware that Pierce would relinquish the presidency on March 4 and be succeeded by the former minister to England, James Buchanan. "I have sent my resignation to take effect from August 31st," Hawthorne wrote Ticknor; "Buchanan may choose to turn me out sooner, but I should suppose he would prefer taking the office on my own terms as the old fellow and I are very good friends."[15]

**LIVERPOOL CRUSADER**
William Rathbone was an old man when
Hawthorne arrived in Liverpool, but both he
and his son supported the consul's efforts to
stamp out the cruelty to seamen aboard
American merchant vessels.

In the dispatch of February 13 Hawthorne detailed instances of cruelty and mistreatment. "Something must be done," he pleaded, "as our National character & Commerce
are suffering great damage." He added that he had been told that maritime insurance premiums on American vessels "have materially increased because of the inefficient crews they
are known to have."[16] In the hope that concern by a third party might carry some weight,
Hawthorne attached a copy of a survey made by the Liverpool Society of Friends in
Distress. It confirmed what Hawthorne already knew – that many American sailors had
been lured aboard departing vessels by one stratagem or another. Of the 106 men
interviewed by the Society, 69 had been brought over against their will. Most were totally
unqualified for service aboard ships and it was precisely because of this that their fellow
crew members, especially the mates, turned upon them and inflicted acts of brutality
defying description. The Society reported that aboard the *Ocean Monarch* sailors had been
forced to pull out with their teeth nails which had been driven into the deck floor to a depth
of two inches.

Since Hawthorne had campaigned so long, and with so little result, for reform of the laws
under which American shipping operated, he was understandably piqued when the Society
of Friends in Distress, the British press, and prominent citizens sometimes attached blame
to himself. He was on excellent personal terms with the William Rathbones, senior and
junior, but the latter did not hesitate to condemn the American merchant navy. In reply to
criticisms by Rathbone Brothers and Company, Hawthorne pointed out that he was
"painfully aware of the evils of the present system . . . from the cases almost daily coming
before me." He nevertheless expressed his pleasure that the Rathbones were concerned
about the problem and would use their influence to bring about improvement. Hawthorne
concurred with the firm that American shipowners could do much, for, he said, "the prime
source of the evil lies in the . . . system of shipping seamen, and the want of a nursery for
seamen."[17]

Meanwhile, Washington was preparing for a change in administration. Franklin Pierce,
humiliated over losing his party's renomination, saw the man who had beaten him – James
Buchanan – go on to win the presidency in November, 1856. While there is little doubt that
Buchanan genuinely sought retirement after resigning as U.S. Minister to Great Britain, he
allowed himself to be talked into the candidacy on the grounds that he was the only
Democrat who stood a chance of capturing the presidency.

Following Pierce's departure from the White House many of his supporters, among them

Secretary of State William L. Marcy, resigned. This enabled Buchanan to begin his administration with a Cabinet which owed its allegiance to him. Like Pierce, however, Buchanan was viewed by many as a northerner with southern sympathies – a posture hardly calculated to resolve the issue of slavery which was moving the country nearer to civil war. One appointment of Buchanan's, however, that of Lewis Cass as Secretary of State, was made as much on the grounds of Cass' ability as on his very considerable political power. One of the most gifted American public servants of the nineteenth century, he served as an Army officer, state governor, negotiator, Cabinet member, Minister, and United States Senator. He narrowly missed the presidency in 1848 when he lost to Zachary Taylor.

With Marcy's departure and Cass' assuming the office of Secretary of State, Hawthorne was obliged to make his old points about cruelty aboard American ships. Not that there was any lack of new incidents to report; on March 27 he advised Secretary Cass of a particularly obnoxious case of ill treatment aboard the *Wandering Jew* in which one Daniel McKay died. Depositions taken from two crew members, one English and one Irish, revealed the subterfuges by which they were lured aboard, as well as the subsequent brutality afflicted upon them and the unfortunate McKay.

The Englishman, William Harrison, explained what happened to him in New Orleans at the time he joined the *Wandering Jew*. "I was at the Sailors boarding house kept by Mrs. Smith on the Levee," he said in his deposition. "I was there because I wanted to get a passage home to England. I had been living in New Orleans twelve months and was in bad health made me want to come here I was in the boarding house a week I was supplied with drink Some I paid for and Some I did not."[18]

Edward Moore, the Irishman, had an even more pathetic story to tell. "I am a native of Queens County Ireland," he said in his deposition, "and am a labourer." Moore added that he was not a sailor and had never been at sea except for the original voyage from Ireland. ". . . a Man from the Boarding House (Chocks) accosted me and asked if I wanted to go to Boston that he had a Ship ready that I should only have to work on deck and coil up rope I consented to go and went with him to the Boarding House Two days after he took me to a Shipping office I did sign articles."[19] Moore told a graphic story of how McKay was beaten and kicked by the first and third mates. Later, according to Moore, he managed to get out of the bunk and stagger as far as the door of the forecastle where he said, "I am going to Heaven . . .," collapsed, and never spoke again.[20]

Not the least annoying aspect of Hawthorne's efforts to deal with the perpetrators of violence was the absence of necessary legal provisions. When British and American lawmakers drafted their respective treaties and regulations, they often failed to take into account borderline situations which inevitably were dumped at a consul's door. The case of the death of a crew member from the *Guy Mannering* is typical. The point at issue was the competence of English courts to try a man for a crime committed on the high seas when the victim did not die until he reached hospital in Liverpool. The magistrates held that the existing treaty between Britain and the United States did not permit them to hear such a case. The coroner, on the other hand, said that it did not matter where the injuries were inflicted, and that the essential fact was the victim's death in Liverpool. Eventually two men were tried by the Liverpool Assizes, one being found guilty and the other being discharged. But the case was appealed to London where the judge quashed the conviction. This decision distressed Hawthorne, for once more guilty men had been set free because of the inadequacy of the law. The London Court of Appeals action, he continued, "will do much harm unless met by some such international arrangement as I have before suggested for sending

**DISPATCH CASE**
This is the case used by Hawthorne at the Liverpool consulate. It held copies of his dispatches and the numerous affidavits and other supporting documents.

home persons guilty of Crimes falling below the present Treaty, or giving Jurisdiction to the Courts here to try them."[21]

By the time he neared the end of his consulship Hawthorne thought himself sufficiently qualified to outline some reforms required to improve the quality of the American seamen. His earlier suggestions had included a public inquiry, establishment of training schools for both masters and seamen, and a study of the system of advance payments. Now he ventured into the field of law, and his later dispatches were to contain suggestions about legal measures.

Just as Hawthorne was driving home his arguments for reform, there appeared in the British press an amazing letter – reputed to be from Secretary of State Cass – which shattered any notion the consul may have held that Washington had been reading his dispatches with sympathetic understanding. The letter came to be published in Britain after Lord Napier, the British Minister in Washington, wrote Cass about his unhappiness over treatment of American seamen. Cass duly replied, never dreaming Napier would make public his answer. The Cass letter was printed extensively in Britain, and was given special prominence in commercial journals, including the highly respected *Shipping and Mercantile Gazette*. The *Gazette* was subscribed to by everyone in the Liverpool commercial circles, many of whom were friends and acquaintances of Hawthorne. When these people – the Rathbones and others – had earlier queried the consul about the reasons for the wretched conditions aboard American ships, Hawthorne had largely laid the blame on inadequacies of the law. Cass, in his letter to Lord Napier, had contradicted this view and, worse still, included a reference to consuls that infuriated Hawthorne. "The execution of these [seamen's] laws in foreign countries for the most part devolves upon consuls," Cass wrote. "It is possible that these officers may, in some instances, have been delinquent in the discharge of their duties in Her Majesty's ports."[22]

The enraged Hawthorne sat down and wrote Secretary Cass a two-thousand word dispatch, the longest (disregarding enclosures) of his consular career. If Cass had not bothered to read the consul's previous dispatches, he could not afford to ignore his man in Liverpool now. The dispatch, since widely published, evidences Hawthorne's passion to see a healthy American merchant navy devoid of encumbrances and legal impediments. Hawthorne threw considerations of rank to the wind and disputed the Secretary's assertion that existing American laws were sufficient for the protection of seamen. "I believe," said Hawthorne, "that no man practically connected with our commercial navy, whether as owner, officer, or seaman, would affirm that the present marine laws of the United States are such as the present condition of our nautical affairs imperatively demands."[23]

## "WRONGED" BY THE SECRETARY

A letter from Lewis Cass, the U.S. Secretary of State, appeared in British journals. It accused some consuls of being delinquent; Hawthorne felt the letter was aimed at himself and sent Cass a sharply worded rejoinder.

He pointed out to the Secretary how large numbers of men aboard American ships were totally unqualified to go to sea. "Almost every ship," he said, "on her trip from New York to Liverpool brings a number of returning emigrants, wholly unacquainted with the sea and incapable of performing the duties of seamen, but who have shipped for the purpose merely of accomplishing their homeward voyage." Hawthorne the humanist readily saw the results which ensued – "a state of war between two classes who find themselves, for a period, inextricably opposed on shipboard."[24]

Hawthorne went on to call the seamen's situation "a national emergency," and added: "If there be an interest which required the intervention of the Government, . . . it is this." He concluded by blaming Secretary Cass for the humiliating letter which had been so widely circulated in Britain. ". . . if I have done my utmost, as an executive officer, under a defective law, . . . then, unquestionably the Secretary has wronged me by a suggestion pointing so directly at myself."[25]

When Hawthorne had finished his caustic dispatch, he poured out his heart in a letter to Ticknor. "I send by this mail," he said, "a despatch to General Cass, on receipt of which he will feel much inclined to turn me out of office. . . . If he does not grow wiser, it will not be my fault. I have serious thoughts of writing a pamphlet, or even a book, on the subject of American seamen, and it might be made entertaining by bringing in sketches of people and incidents that have come under my notice, besides being a work imperatively called for by the present state of our merchant marine."[26]

Although Secretary Cass received Hawthorne's long dispatch on July 2, he did not bother to reply until September 24 – nearly two months after the consul's original date of resignation. There was not a word of apology; Cass, in fact, strongly defended his stance. The reply was bound to have disappointed Hawthorne. It was never published in Britain and, if it had been, would have done nothing to assuage the humiliation of Hawthorne caused by the original letter. Whether Hawthorne showed it privately to some of his Liverpool acquaintances is not known. An extract of the Secretary's reply follows:

Department of State, Washington, Sept. 24, 1857

Nathaniel Hawthorne, Esq., Consul, Liverpool.

Sir, – Your despatch, No. 90, of the 17th of June last, upon the maltreatment of seamen on board vessels of the United States, was duly received. The note to

Lord Napier, which accompanied it, was correctly published in the English journals, but without the previous knowledge or consent of this Department. You seem to suppose that some of its expressions may have been intended to charge you with delinquency in your official duties towards seamen. No such intention, however, was entertained, and now that you are about to retire from your position, I am happy to bear testimony to the prudent and efficient manner in which you have discharged your duties. I owe it to myself, however, to add that I perceive nothing in the letter to Lord Napier which justifies the construction you have placed on it. On the contrary, while it admits that some delinquency, on the part of our Consuls, in executing the laws of the United States concerning seamen, is not absolutely impossible, it expressly disclaims all knowledge of such delinquency ... What you say with regard to the evils that afflict our commercial marine, it is not now necessary to consider, but you quite misapprehend my views if you suppose that I am insensible to the magnitude of these evils, or could have ever intended to deny their existence. While, therefore, our statutes may be, and probably are, as well adapted to their objects as those of any other country, it is nonetheless true that our merchant service suffers constantly from the want of American seamen. How this want can be supplied, is a question to which, in my note to Lord Napier, it was not my purpose to reply. I am, sir,

Your obedient servant,

Lewis Cass[27]

Hawthorne's trying four years as judge and arbitrator soon came to an end. He never found time to write the pamphlet he had once considered, but his journal, correspondence and dispatches reveal the lonely fight he conducted to expose, and improve, the conditions under which American seamen worked in his day. His comment in *Our Old Home* sums up his exasperation: "The Consul could do little," he said, "except to take depositions, hold forth the greasy testament to be profaned with perjured kisses, and, in a few instances of murder or manslaughter, carry the case before an English magistrate who generally decided that the evidence was too contradictory to authorise the transmission of the accused for trial in America."[28]

# XI
# The Peregrinations of a Consul

"These sketches of English life and scenery are by a master's hand," wrote Hawthorne's friend, Henry Bright, of passages in *Our Old Home*; "they are fragmentary indeed and there is something of caprice in the choice of subject and treatment. But, with all their wilfulness, they are full of grace and beauty, of tender pathos, and of subtle humour."[1]

Hawthorne, aware that his stay in Britain was limited to a few years, was determined to make the most of the opportunity. If anyone reminded him of the old foreign service adage, "Travel early – and often," such advice would have been wasted on him. Whereas newly arrived diplomats in a strange land may have welcomed this formula as being the quickest and best way to get to know a nation, Hawthorne had his own impelling reasons for travelling. He wished to track down his English ancestry and he was drawn to the sites associated with great names in English literature. There is little doubt but that he also hoped to find ideas for plots of new works as he wandered about the country. But there was an additional reason, one added only after assuming his consular duties: his wish to escape, even for short periods, from Liverpool.

If getting away from Liverpool became an end in itself, one might ask why he did not start his travels earlier. There was a two-fold answer. Except for weekends and when official business was involved, Hawthorne could not leave the consulate until he had accumulated sufficient leave time. Secondly it is true that he could have absconded from his Brunswick Street offices on one pretext or another, but he was conscientious about his official obligations and was determined to be a good consul.

So he toiled away vigorously, determined to master the office routine and meet the civic, commercial and professional leaders of Liverpool who would most help him in his work. After three months he confided to Ticknor that he was "almost worn out with hard work."[2] As the year 1854 began, the pressure of work heightened with his personal involvement in the *San Francisco* affair and his growing awareness of conditions aboard American ships. Another deterrent to travel was Sophia's health; it had not improved with the move into the spacious villa at 26 Rock Park, and Hawthorne was reluctant to leave her and the children for long periods.

Hawthorne's first escape from his Brunswick Street "prison," a brief jaunt into North Wales in mid-July of 1854, was with his Liverpool friend, Henry Bright. From Birkenhead, adjacent to the Hawthorne home in Rock Park, the two men set out by train for Chester, but did not tarry long in the city. They continued on to Bangor where they left the train, took a carriage across the Menai Bridge, and came to Beaumaris. Here Hawthorne saw his first castle, "[it] quite coming up to my idea of what an old castle should be." The next morning Bright and Hawthorne walked from Beaumaris to the point on the Menai Straits where the Bangor ferry departed. "It was really a very pleasant road," Hawthorne said, "overhung by a young growth of wood, exceedingly green and fresh." After putting up for the night at the Penrhyn Arms, the pair set off early the next day by carriage for a circular ride of some forty miles, passing lakes, a slate quarry, numerous mountains (in the distance they saw Snowdon), and Swallow Waterfall. Hawthorne, in his journal, apologized for not remembering the name of the next stop on the itinerary: "neither can I remember a single name of the places (nor could spell them if I hear them pronounced, nor pronounce them, if I saw them spelt) . . ."³

At Betws-y-Coed (an "unutterable village") Hawthorne and Bright visited the old church where they saw a stone image of great antiquity, as well as several monumental brasses. People, of course, mattered as much to Hawthorne's inquiring mind as what he saw, and he did not overlook the Welsh whom he encountered. "Many of the Welshwomen, particularly the elder ones," he said, "wear black beaver hats, high-crowned, and almost precisely like men's." He noted that Welsh was still spoken widely in the region, and was the only language used by some inhabitants. "I have had Welsh people in my office," he recalled, ". . . with whom I could not communicate, except through an interpreter." Late that evening the two friends reached Chester where they remained overnight before going their separate ways the next morning. The North Wales trip had been short, but "very delightful."⁴

Now it was the family's turn to see something of the rest of Britain, and for their first trip they chose the Isle of Man. Hawthorne could only get away for weekend visits, but even these brief sorties from Liverpool cheered him immensely. He was much taken with the little church of Kirk Bradden ("I never saw anything prettier").⁵ ". . . Mr. Hawthorne," Sophia lamented, "after fetching us one day, and staying the two next, went away to the tiresome old Consulate, so conscientious and devoted is he . . ." During one of his visits with the family, Hawthorne took Julian to the Douglas open air market. "My husband," said Sophia, "said that living manners were so interesting and valuable that he would not miss the scene for even Peel Castle."⁶ The stay on the Isle of Man was idyllic for everyone except Una who became homesick for home in Rock Park. Julian was quite content to roam the rocks and beaches. Rose occasionally probed the water (sometimes with her shoes on), but generally stayed near her mother. Hawthorne summed up the adventure in his letter to Ticknor: "The health of my family (and, indeed, my own) required a change of air, and nothing could be purer than the atmosphere of the Isle of Man."⁷

The only other trip in 1854 was with Minister John L. O'Sullivan, then visiting the Hawthornes, to North Wales in September. Their first stop was at Rhyl, a place Hawthorne dismissed with four words – "a most uninteresting place." His opinion of the ancient ruins might have been more elaborate had he been able to gain admittance, but the combination of a deep moat and a fence barred his way, and he was obliged to start back towards Rhyl. When he asked directions of an old man and was told "Dim Sassenach," he was left dumbfounded and no better off. "How odd," he said, "that an hour or two on the railway should have brought me amongst a people who speak no English." What Rhyl lacked was compensated for by Conway's magnificent castle. "Certainly," said Hawthorne, "this must be the most perfect specimen of a ruinous old castle in the whole world."⁸

As they ended their perambulations, an omnibus approached with its horns sounding. It was bound for nearby Llandudno. On the spur of the moment the four travellers decided to visit the town – "knowing no more about it than that it was four miles off . . ." Once aboard, their attention was drawn to a pair of girls, "pleasant looking," who were speaking Welsh – "a guttural, pleasant, childish kind of a babble." Within minutes Hawthorne and his bold companions engaged the girls in conversation, finding them "very agreeable." One, at least, had more than good looks to commend her: she was reading Martin Tupper's popular *Proverbial Philosophy*. In Llandudno the visitors saw an abandoned copper mine around which little boys were hawking ore samples. Hawthorne was amazed at the number of open shafts and holes, some "fearfully deep and black," and which were without the slightest protection. Back in the village for a quick lunch of sandwiches, cakes and ginger

## "A CHARMING LITTLE PARADISE OF GARDENS" – LEAMINGTON

To save on living expenses, Hawthorne hit upon the idea of keeping his family in watering places. They lived briefly on two occasions in Leamington Spa. Sophia termed the town a paradise which only the English "know how to make out of any given flat bit of land."

beer (cost eighteen pence), the party had its meal interrupted by the arrival of "the two prettiest young ladies I have seen in [Britain] . . ."[9]

By four in the afternoon they reached Rhyl; there the family and O'Sullivan had their final meal together before Hawthorne and his guest had to depart. Sophia and the children were to remain on for a few days in the hope that the children would get rid of their whooping cough. The appointments at the hotel were plain and Sophia saw the humour in the family's situation. "Ever since our marriage," she said, "we have always eaten off the finest French china, and had all things pretty and tasteful, because . . . I would never have *second-best* services, considering my husband to be my most illustrious guest. But now! It is really laughable to think of the appointments of the table at which the Ambassador to Lisbon and the American Consul sat down last Saturday . . . And we did laugh, for it was of no consequence . . ."[10]

The winter of 1854–5 at Rock Park was a very happy one and the Hawthornes did not care to travel. The cost of maintaining so large a house and staff, however, was great and thus the family moved to Leamington Spa – renowned for its saline springs, tree-lined avenues and gentle style of living – in mid-June of 1855. They took lodgings in Lansdowne Crescent – "one of the cosiest nooks in England or in the world" – and for the next three weeks led an almost paradisiacal existence.

Hawthorne, ever in search of seclusion, found just that in Leamington Spa. Only the postman, the butcher and the grocer, on their daily rounds, intruded upon his privacy. The house was exactly what he and the rest of his family wanted, a sylvan retreat in a gracious setting. Sophia's letters to the family in America also sang the praises of the town. ". . . we are in a charming little paradise of gardens, with a park in the center," she wrote, "towards

## JOHNSON'S BIRTHPLACE

"A very good, old-fashioned, quiet house," was Hawthorne's description of Dr. Samuel Johnson's birthplace in Lichfield.

which all these gardens converge. It is such a paradise as the English only know how to make out of any given flat bit of land."[11] Pleasant as the town was, Hawthorne's chief enjoyment came from the rural walks leading to the adjacent countryside and nearby places of interest. Within a few minutes of Leamington he could be in villages of thatched cottages, alone on a winding country lane, or even in historic Warwick – a mere two miles distant – with its imposing castle. "... in verdure, in the rich aspect of the country," Hawthorne said, "nothing surely can equal England."[12]

While in Leamington Spa Hawthorne told Ticknor of his latest scheme to reduce the cost of living. "According to my calculation," he said, "we shall be able to live more cheaply at watering places and country towns, or even in London in respectable lodgings, than we have heretofore done in Liverpool . . . Our whole expenditure here with these ample accommodations will not exceed seven guineas a week."[13] Leamington was convenient to Stratford where Hawthorne took the family to see Shakespeare's birthplace. He found the downstairs portion clean and interesting, but was put off by the numerous names which had been scribbled on the walls and window panes. Walter Scott's name was supposed to be among them, but, Hawthorne said, "so many people had sought to immortalize themselves in close vicinity to him that I really could not trace out his signature." His overall impression of the birthplace: "almost a worse house than anyone could dream it to be." He confessed, however, that "it is agreeable enough to reflect that I have seen it."[14] Hawthorne's time with the family was now running out and, after saying yet another temporary farewell, he started back to Liverpool.

En route there he stopped first at Lichfield, and later, at Uttoxeter, to see places associated with Dr. Samuel Johnson. In Lichfield he stayed the night at the Swan Hotel, the city's oldest inn – "a very good, old-fashioned, quiet house." In Lichfield's market square he gazed upon the newly erected statue of Dr. Johnson – "colossal (though perhaps not much bigger than the mountainous Doctor . . .)." A few yards away was Johnson's birthplace where workmen were busy plastering the outer walls. "I set my foot on the worn steps, and laid my hand on the wall of the house," said Hawthorne, "because Johnson's hand and foot might have been in those same places." From the market square Hawthorne made his way up Dam Street to Lichfield Cathedral. He had seen only one other English cathedral – that at Chester – before coming to Lichfield, but had no hesitation in asserting its splendour, "... there may be much more magnificent cathedrals, in England and elsewhere, than this in Lichfield," he said, "but if there were no other, I should be pretty well satisfied with this . . ."[15]

**DINING ROOM OF WORDSWORTH'S HOME AT RYDAL MOUNT**
"Those sacred places," wrote Sophia to her sister Elizabeth when describing the
environs of Rydal Mount. The Hawthorne family visited Wordsworth's grave twice,
saw his cottage and garden, and rambled repeatedly among the paths of Rydal
Mount.

From Lichfield Hawthorne went to Uttoxeter to seek the exact spot in the market place
where Dr. Johnson had performed his act of penance by standing bareheaded and exposed
to the insults of passersby for an hour. Johnson had condemned himself to the punishment
in atonement for refusing, fifty years earlier, to open the family bookstall in the market for
his ailing father. In vain did Hawthorne look for something to mark the historic event.
"How strange and stupid," he observed, "that there should be no local memorial to this
incident – as beautiful and touching an incident as can be cited out of any human life . . ."[16]

Hawthorne arrived back in Liverpool for a week of work at the consulate before setting
out again for Leamington, this time to remove his family to the Lake District. The trip to
the lakes had not been planned as such. ". . . I had an official engagement," he explained,
"which it was convenient to combine with a pleasure excursion." Late one afternoon in July
the family arrived at Milnthorpe Station in southern Westmorland. To their pleasure, they
discovered the first leg of their Lake Country travels would be by a mode of transportation
long since considered obsolete ". . . (at five or six o'clock) we took seats in an old-fashioned
English stage-coach, and came to Newby Bridge," Hawthorne said. "I suppose there are
not many of these machines now running on any road in Great Britain, but this appears to

**THE LAKE COUNTRY**
"Man," wrote Hawthorne of the Lake Country, "[is] in entire possession of Nature here." The family stayed near Ambleside on Lake Windermere, pictured at the right.

be the genuine article in all respects, and especially in the round, ruddy coachman, well-moistened with ale, good-natured, courteous, with a proper sense of his dignity and important position." The party "bowled off merrily towards the heart of the hills," arriving at Newby Bridge a little after nine-thirty. The family relaxed for several days, using the Swan Hotel as a base for short excursions to nearby points of interest (Furness Abbey, Ulverston and Dalton), and for walks into the countryside. Hawthorne pondered deeply over the Lake Country's magnetic appeal, and especially how it struck an American. "On the rudest surfaces of English earth," he said, "there is seen the effect of centuries of civilization, so that you do not quite get at naked Nature anywhere. . . . Man has, in short, got in entire possession of Nature here, and I should think young men might sometimes yearn for a fresher draught. But an American likes it."[17]

From Newby Bridge the family voyaged up Lake Windermere aboard a lake steamer, stopping at Lowwood Hotel a few miles south of Ambleside. Here Hawthorne found time to write Ticknor an assessment of the effect of the travels on Sophia's constitution – probably his real reason for making the trip in the first place. "Mrs. Hawthorne's health and strength seem to improve," he reported, "and I feel more encouraged about her than when I wrote last. She shall never reside in Liverpool again, for any length of time, whether I keep the office or resign it."[18] Hawthorne was intrigued with the pattern of hotel life in which other families, like his own, kept entirely to themselves. He found neither the service nor the food so good as that at Newby Bridge. He attempted to keep the damp, chill air from penetrating through a broken window of their parlour by pinning his copy of *The Times* over the opening. ". . . I shall remember Lowwood not very agreeably," he said, "– as far as we are concerned, it is a scrambling, ill ordered hotel, with insufficient attendance, wretched sleeping accommodations, a pretty fair victualling-department, but German silver forks and spoons." Immediately behind the hotel, however, Hawthorne discovered a footpath which led directly to the summit of a hill from which he could see almost the whole of Lake Windermere. ". . . I think there can hardly be anything more beautiful in the world," he extolled. "The water was like a strip and gleam of sky, fitly set among lovely slopes of earth."[19]

The days in the Lake Country passed happily in spite of the dullness of resort hotels. The family saw most of the region's main attractions – Grasmere, Ullswater, the Vale of St. John, Keswick, Derwentwater, Skiddaw, Thirlmere – and, of course, Wordsworth's cottage. They visited Wordsworth's grave twice, and attempted to walk the same paths, sit on the same benches, and enjoy the same views known to the poet. To her sister Elizabeth in America Sophia wrote ecstatically:

[July, 1855]

MY DEAR ELIZABETH, – . . . I had set my heart upon writing you a long letter about those sacred places, especially sacred to you, the true lover of Wordsworth. . . . We presently came to a fine old crag by the shore [of Rydal Water], up which were some friendly steps, and we were entirely sure that Wordsworth had often gone up there and looked off upon his beloved Rydal from the summit. We went up and sat down where we knew he must have sat, and there I could have dreamed for many hours. . . . The gardener opened a wicket, after passing the deep, shady nook, and said, "This is Mr. Words-worth's garden." I looked about and saw troops of flowers, and sought for the white fox-glove, which was a favorite of his, and found it . . . Presently, after so much mounting of steps, and threading of embowered paths and lanes of flowers, we were ushered into the grounds immediately around the actual house. And the man first took us upon that memorable terraced lawn, in great part made by Wordsworth's own hands.[20]

Hawthorne found no fault with Wordsworth's grave, situated as it was, near the hills and streams he loved. But he wondered why the poet was "packed so closely with his kindred" and why he could not have had some "fresh earth to himself." He contented himself that Wordsworth had picked the spot himself and, therefore, must have liked it; certainly, Hawthorne added, "he did not care for a stately monument."[21]

In his rambles through the Lake District, Hawthorne was sometimes amused that exceedingly small bodies of water were called lakes – and even had names assigned to them. Rydal Water, he said, could be carried away in a porringer and was nothing more than a grassy-covered pool which looked more like a recent accumulation of rainwater than a lake. "Now," he said, "the best thing these little ponds can do is to keep perfectly calm and smooth and not attempt to show off any airs of their own, but to content themselves with serving as a mirror for whatever of beautiful or picturesque there may be in the scenery around them."[22]

The beauty of the Wordsworth country did not prevent Hawthorne from noticing the people about him. One day a band of itinerant musicians appeared, consisting of a young woman with a child, and four men. They sat down at the roadside house, played several tunes, and departed after being served a large pitcher of ale by the waiter. "One would like to follow these people through their vagrant-life," mused Hawthorne, "and see them at meal-time and bed-time, and overhear their intercourse among themselves.[23]

Tourist sites are seldom the best yardsticks by which to judge a nation's hotels, but since Hawthorne was being exposed to a succession of them among the lakes, he took the liberty of passing judgment on their standards. When one particular stay ended and the account

## HAMPTON COURT PALACE
Despite his admitted republican sympathies, Hawthorne was in awe of Hampton Court Palace, and said the English were well-advised to retain it.

was paid, he was confronted by the members of the hotel staff obviously awaiting gratuities. "You can always know," he said, ". . . when you have less than satisfied them by the aspect of the waiter, which I wish I could describe, – not disrespectful in the slightest degree, but a look of profound surprise, a gaze at the offered coin (which he nevertheless pockets) as if he either did not see it or did not know it, or could not believe his eyesight – all this, however, with the most quiet forbearance, a Christian-like non-recognition of an unmerited wrong and insult . . ."[24]

Yet, with all its drawbacks, the Lake District had its charms. "I question," said Hawthorne, "whether any part of the world looks so beautiful as England – this part of England, at least – on a fine summer morning." He turned his thoughts to English homes which he felt were built, and cared for, with more attention and love than were homes in America – perhaps, he thought, "by people who mean to live there a great while, and feel as if their children might live there after them." Pondering on the future, he ventured that the blissful, well-ordered English scene, might not always remain as he saw it. "All this is passing away," he said, "and society must assume new relations."[25]

In the first week of September, 1855, the Hawthornes left Merseyside for the south. En route to London the family stopped briefly in Shrewsbury where Hawthorne enjoyed pleasant walks among the old streets. "There was a delightful want of plan in the laying out of these ancient towns," he said, "in fact, they were never laid out at all, nor were [they] restrained by any plan whatever, but grew naturally, with streets as eccentric as the pathway of a young child toddling about the floor."[26] At Shrewsbury station an incident occurred which was amusing to the consul but which must have been embarrassing to Sophia. To guard against travelling without food and drink, the Hawthornes carried with them a small store of provisions. Somehow a bottle of port fell from the family luggage and broke upon the pavement of the station. "This mishap," Hawthorne noted, "and the fragrance of the port-wine, caused the railway officials to gather round us like flies round a drop of molasses, and drew on us the smiling notice of a whole train of passengers, waiting to set off."[27]

In London – "the dream-city of my youth" – Hawthorne sated a lifetime of curiosity with his perambulations among the city's "thronged thoroughfares, the broad, lonely squares, the lanes, alleys, and strange labyrinthine courts, the parks, the gardens and inclosures of ancient studious societies, so retired and silent amid the city uproar, the markets, the foggy

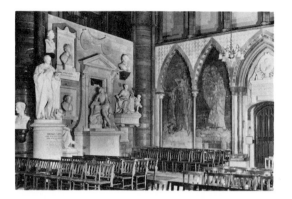

## "POETS' CORNER"

"The spot which I had dreamed about more reverentially than any other in the world," was Hawthorne's tribute. Americans, he added, have a right to be proud of Westminster Abbey because "most of the men who sleep in it are our great men, as well as theirs."

streets along the riverside, the bridges . . ."[28] Sometimes alone, sometimes with Julian, and sometimes with Sophia and the two older children, Hawthorne saw the wonders of the capital. From the moment he first set foot in the city, he felt an exhilaration akin to that of boyish enthusiasm. "It is a long time," he said, "since I have had such a childish feeling, but all that I had heard, and felt, about the vastness of London, made it like swimming in a boundless ocean . . ." During this visit and one he was to make to the city the following year, Hawthorne saw many of the city's outstanding attractions. But it was sometimes the places associated with the ordinary folk of London that made the city come alive to Hawthorne. Once, when hungry, he decided to try his luck at the "Albert Dining Rooms," a name which gave little hint of what the diner would find inside. "I got a mutton chop in [this] the very meanest and dirtiest eating-place I ever chanced upon," Hawthorne said, "a filthy table-cloth, covered with other people's crumbs; iron forks, a leaden salt cellar, the commonest earthen plates; a little dark stall, to sit and eat in."[29]

Hawthorne's interest in the world's less fortunate creatures was manifested one evening when the family returned to their Hanover Square quarters after a day of intense sightseeing. A woman busker, who had performed alone in the street outside the house on other occasions, now reappeared. She hesitated between the windows and began singing "Kathleen O'Moore" in a voice so rich and sweet that it "made our heart throb in unison with it, here in the comfortable drawing room." When neighbours protested at the disturbance, the woman stopped "like a nightingale suddenly shot." It was more than Hawthorne could bear – "I never heard a voice that touched me more," he said. Sophia, too, was moved, and Fanny, the nurse and a maid were sent after the singer. They found her, invited her in, and listened to her life story. She claimed to have been trained for the opera and had once been married to an Italian opera singer – now dead. She said she stayed at a lodging house every evening, provided she could raise the necessary three pence. She did plain sewing to keep alive, but frequently had to raise the odd penny by singing in the streets. "It seems very strange," lamented Hawthorne, "that, with such a gift of heaven, so cultivated, too, as her voice is, and making even an unsusceptible heart vibrate like a harpstring, she should not have some sort of an engagement among the hundred theaters and singing rooms of London, – that she should throw away her melody in the streets, for the mere chance of a penny, when sounds not a hundredth part so sweet are worth purses of gold from other lips."[30]

What impressed Hawthorne most in London? Undoubtedly, it was Westminster Abbey. He repeatedly visited Poets' Corner, a place where he did not feel a stranger. "It was

**SCOTT'S STUDY**
Hawthorne was told by the attendant that he might "catch some inspiration" for writing if he sat in Scott's chair.

delightful to be among them," he said, and pleasing to see them, in companionship, "mutually recognized and duly honored." But it was not only the poets who made Westminster Abbey so memorable to Hawthorne; it was also the "crowd of [other] personages" interred in the Abbey. All these by-gone notables, he said, were imbued "with the venerable and awful character of the spot." He considered England fortunate to have a church where so many of the nation's worthies were "incrusted" within its walls. "An American," he added, "has a right to be proud of Westminster Abbey, for most of the men, who sleep in it, are our great men, as well as theirs."[31]

After Sophia, Una and Rose embarked for Portugal on October 8 to spend the winter with Minister O'Sullivan and his family, Hawthorne and Julian left Southampton by train for Liverpool. They halted at Worcester to pass the night, and next morning had a hasty look at the cathedral. Hawthorne was only "moderately impressed" but Julian was much attracted to the nature collection in one of the city's museums. After lunch, the pair again set off for the north, arriving at "the abominable Mersey" after dark.[32]

Hawthorne had seen more of Britain in 1855 than in the previous two years combined, but the sight of the River Mersey, which symbolized his unhappy relationship with Liverpool, was depressing. The lonely winter lay ahead, and once more the call of London sounded. He was determined to visit the capital again in the New Year, this time on his own.

With Julian entrusted to the care of the Brights and the Channings, he made plans to revisit London in March of 1856. He explained the arrangements to Sophia, still in Lisbon. ". . . [Mr. Bright] has often besought me that Julian might come and spend a few days at Sandheys," he said, "and I think I shall let him go and take the opportunity to run up to London."[33] Although Hawthorne's second sojourn in London was more taken up with dinners and social engagements than his earlier visit, he nonetheless managed to see some

**THE CASTLE INN**
The Hawthornes stayed at this modest Southampton hotel. Though small, it had the attraction of being built into the town's ancient wall, overlooked the harbour, and was inexpensive.

attractions he had missed previously – mainly places connected with literary personalities. These included Bolt-court (Dr. Samuel Johnson), St. James Place (Addison), Upper Thames Street (Dickens), and the church of St. Giles (Milton).

Hampton Court, Hawthorne was convinced, was a national monument entirely worthy of retention. ". . . what a noble palace, nobly enriched, this Hampton Court is!" he exclaimed. "The English government does well to keep it up and to admit people freely into it . . ." He admitted that even a republican like himself could not escape the feeling of awe and respect which Hampton Court conveyed to the visitor. "By no possibility," he said, "can we ever have such a place in America."[34] Although not a connoisseur of art, Hawthorne visited the National Art Gallery. There he admitted to liking some pictures better than others, adding: ". . . I have an idea I might get up a taste, with some little attention to the subject." His tour of the British Museum, on the other hand, was "an exceedingly tiresome affair," for, he said, "it quite crushes a person to see so much at once."[35]

Two months after his London visit, Hawthorne toured Scotland with a friend, James Bowman. The weather was cold and he missed Sophia's companionship. Nonetheless, he managed to see both Edinburgh and Glasgow, scenic points in the Highlands, and Scott's home at Abbotsford. He took his time to examine meticulously the various articles at Abbotsford that had once belonged to Scott. When he came to the chair which Scott had used while writing his romances, he was asked by the attendant if he might like to sit in it. ". . . perhaps," the attendant said, "you may catch some inspiration." The man did not know Hawthorne, but the irony was not lost on the visitor. "No," he said, "I shall never be inspired to write romances."[36]

In June Hawthorne and Julian went to Southampton to meet Sophia and the girls on their return to England. While in the south they decided to see something of the area. Southampton earned special praise – "a very pretty town . . . [that] has not the dinginess to which I have been accustomed in English towns."[37] In Salisbury Hawthorne was captivated by the cathedral spire. "I do not remember any cathedral," he said, "with so fine a site as this, rising up out of the centre of a beautiful green, extensive enough to show its full proportions, relieved and insulated from all other patch-work and impertinences of rusty edifices." He considered Salisbury Cathedral far more beautiful than York Minster, but despaired of describing it in detail. "I am weary of trying to describe cathedrals," he said; "it is utterly useless; there is no possibility of giving the general effect, or any shadow of it."

He confessed his envy for the dean and other officials who inhabited the charming quarters set round Salisbury Cathedral. "I never beheld anything," he said, "— so cozy, so indicative of domestic comfort for whole centuries together – houses so fit to live in, or to die in, and where it would be so pleasant to lead a young maiden beneath the antique portal, and dwell with her till husband and wife were patriarchal – as those delectable houses."[38]

## THE KING'S HOUSE, SALISBURY CATHEDRAL CLOSE

Hawthorne was captivated by both Salisbury Cathedral and its Close. Of the living quarters in the Close, he said: "I never beheld anything so cozy, so indicative of domestic comfort."

From Salisbury's Lamb Hotel Hawthorne engaged a one-horse fly to take his party to Stonehenge. At length he spied in the distance a cluster of large grey stones which he knew had to be Stonehenge, and whose reality he feared would not measure up to his ideal. "There never was a ruder thing than Stonehenge made by mortal hands;" he said, "it is so very rude, that it seems as if Nature and man had worked upon it with one consent, and so it is all the stranger and more impressive from its rudeness." An hour's examination of the stones, undertaken with the help of a self-imposed artist-guide, left Hawthorne unmoved. "Apart from the moral considerations suggested by it," he said, "Stonehenge is not very well worth seeing."[39]

In July the family took up residence in Francis Bennoch's home in Blackheath outside London, while the Bennochs toured the Continent. The arrangement was ideal for the Hawthornes: he could return quickly to Liverpool when required; and Sophia could postpone the moment when she would have to return to Merseyside. Blackheath's proximity to London allowed Hawthorne to continue his tour of sights there, some for the second or third time (St. Paul's and Westminster) and some for the first time (the Royal Academy and the vaults of London Docks).

Hawthorne's last expedition in 1856 was with Sophia to Oxford during the last days of August and the first week in September. The previous June, when travelling with Julian to meet Sophia's incoming ship at Southampton, he had stopped between trains to see the city. The day was hot and oppressive, the impending departure of the train weighed on his mind, and in the end his introduction to Oxford was most unpleasant. He must have communicated this negative picture of Oxford to his friend, Francis Bennoch, for on arriving with Sophia, he clearly was unaware of the plans. "I do not quite understand the matter,"

**AN OXFORD LANDMARK**
Richard Spiers, who went to great trouble to show the Hawthornes the principal attractions of Oxford and the surrounding area, was nationally renowned for his shop which specialized in *papier-machè* articles.

he said, "but it appears that we were expected guests of Mr. Spiers, a very hospitable gentleman, an ex-Mayor of Oxford, and a friend of Bennoch's and of the Halls [Mr. and Mrs. S. C. Hall]."[40] Richard Spiers, indeed, was one of the city's best known citizens. He was proprietor of the stationers, Spiers and Son, an emporium much favoured by Oxford University students during Queen Victoria's reign. The shop specialized in fancy stationery items, particularly *papier-machè* goods which had been made to order for the firm. In Alden's guide of the period, the firm's advertisement told of its wide range of merchandise:

> [SPIERS] Invite TOURISTS to VISIT their extensive establishments for useful and ornamental manufactures, suitable for presents and for Remembrances of Oxford. Copies of every published Guide Book and Map of Oxford and its neighbourhood are kept in stock, as well as a most extensive variety of goods useful and interesting to the Tourist.[41]

Spiers and Son featured prominently in Cuthbert Bede's classic, *The Adventures of Mr. Verdant Green*, which was published only three years before Hawthorne's visit to Oxford. It was enormously popular and Richard Spiers could not have wished for a better advertisement. The relevant passage describes how the mischievous Charles Larkyns lured the naive Verdant Green into Spiers' shop on Oxford's ancient High Street:

> "... Do you ever read Wordsworth, Verdant?" continued Mr. Larkyns, as they stopped at the corner of Oriel Street, to look in at a spacious range of shop windows, that were crowded with a costly and glittering profusion of *papier maché* articles, statuettes, bronzes, glass, and every kind of 'fancy goods' that could be classed as 'art-workmanship.'
> "Why, I've not read much of Wordsworth myself," replied our hero; "but I've heard my sister Mary read a great deal of his poetry."
> "Shows her taste," said Charles Larkyns. "Well, this shop – you see the name – is Spiers'; and Wordsworth, in his sonnet to Oxford, has immortalised him. Don't you remember the lines? –
> O ye Spiers of Oxford! your presence overpowers
> The soberness of reason!"[42]

Larkyns was referring to one of Wordsworth's miscellaneous sonnets which actually begins: "O ye *spires* of Oxford . . ." Before leaving Spiers, the dazzled Verdant Green was persuaded by Larkyns to buy two firescreens (one for each parent), a writing case, a netting-box, a card-case, a model of the famous Martyrs' Memorial, and a paper-knife.

Richard Spiers, the proprietor, was first elected to the Oxford City Council in 1832. Nineteen years later he was made an Alderman, and on November 9, 1853, became the city's Mayor. He lived at 14 St. Giles Street, and when the Hawthornes came to Oxford as his guests, they were housed directly across the street. There was an excellent reason why Spiers could not receive the Hawthornes at 14 St. Giles; they had thirteen children, and Mrs. Spiers was expecting another.

Francis Bennoch had brought together the authors, Mr. and Mrs. S. C. Hall (already well known to Hawthorne), and the former Mayor in an effort to alter, through carefully planned visits to Oxford's colleges and the city's nearby attractions, the negative impression previously gained by Hawthorne.

As soon as the party was settled into lodgings, Bennoch and Mr. Hall took Hawthorne and Sophia for their first walk in the ancient seat of learning. It did not take the consul long to realize that his earlier judgment was faulty. ". . . I spoke very slightingly of the exterior aspect of Oxford, as I saw it with Julian during an hour or two's stop here on my way to Southampton," he said. "I am bound to say that my impressions are now very different and that I find Oxford exceedingly picturesque, and rich in beauty and grandeur and its antique stateliness."[43] During the ensuing week he visited several colleges (Magdalen, New College, Christ Church, St. John's, and Merton), as well as such well known University centres as the Bodleian and the Taylorian. He reserved his highest praise for the gardens of New College. ". . . [they] are indescribably beautiful," he said. "Such a sweet, quiet, sacred, stately seclusion – so age-long as this has been, and, I hope, will continue to be – cannot exist anywhere else."[44]

Spiers, Bennoch and the Halls were determined that the Hawthornes should see more of Oxford and Oxfordshire than the city's renowned university. Early one morning they set out in a four-horse carriage to see Blenheim Palace, some seven miles north. Hawthorne and a companion sat on the box up front, Bennoch and a friend in the dicky behind, and the rest inside. The weather was fine, the journey passed quickly and they reached the Black Bear ("an ancient inn, large and respectable") to water their horses. As the hour was early, they decided to carry on to Blenheim, but not before first ordering lunch ("the most delightful of English institutions, next to dinner"). In the park they mounted a tower to see the spires of Oxford, descended and then saw majestic oaks and cedars, the various works of Capability Brown, and, at last, entered the house itself. The party went from room to room, being impressed variously with rich tapestries, handsome paintings, beautiful furniture and a library whose atmosphere was "brighter and more cheerful than that of most libraries." Hawthorne reflected on the great men who claimed Blenheim as home – past and present. ". . . I should still love to think," he said, "that noblemen lead noble lives, and that all this stately and beautiful environment may serve to elevate them a little way above the rest of us." The Woodstock outing ended when the party returned to the Black Bear, somewhat late, where they sat down to "a cold collation, of which we ate abundantly, and drank (in the good old English fashion) a due proportion of various delightful liquors."[45]

A few days later they were taken to Cumnor where they saw the ancient village church, and to Stanton Harcourt, where they were graciously welcomed by the vicar, Mr. Welsh. Hawthorne was momentarily puzzled when the vicar asked him if he was the author of *The Red Letter A*. ". . . after some consideration (for I really did not recognize my own book, at first, under this queer title)," said Hawthorne, "I answered that I was." Hawthorne was amazed at the fine state of preservation of the tombs and statues. "I have seen [no tombs

**GLIDING ALONG**
One highlight of the Hawthornes'
Oxford visit was a trip by barge to
Nuneham Courtenay. The route
took the guests past Christ
Church meadows and, the consul
said, "through the loveliest park
and woodland scenery I ever
saw."

and statues] so well preserved," he said. He put this miracle down to the loyalty of Oxfordshire to the royal cause during the English civil war, and to the Harcourt family, whose
peasantry, "among whom they had lived for ages, did not desecrate their tombs, when it
might have been done with impunity."[46]

Another highlight was the visit to one of the barges which once comprised such a happy
part of Oxford college life. S. C. Hall was something of an authority on these craft and no
doubt provided ready replies to the Americans' questions. Hawthorne described their vessel
as "a spacious barge, with a house in it, and a comfortable dining-room or drawing-room
within the house, and a level roof, on which we could sit at ease, or dance if so inclined." A
horse was attached to their barge and soon it was gliding through the water "like no motion
at all." In this ideal state, the party passed through Christ Church meadows and saw many
of the sights which every Oxford graduate retains through life – the receding spires and
towers of the various colleges, students punting, small boys swimming, simple cottages, and
familiar waterside inns. After a while a feast was spread in the dining room – ham, fowl,
pigeon-pie, beef "and other substantial cheer, such as the English love, and Yankees, too
. . ." Eventually the barge tied up at the landing for Nuneham Courtenay, the estate
inhabited by the Harcourt family. "Thence we proceeded onward," he said, 'through the
loveliest park and woodland scenery I ever saw, and under as beautiful a declining sunshine
as heaven ever shed on earth . . ." With the visit to Blenheim still fresh in his memory, he
did not hesitate to draw a comparison. "The grounds . . .," he said, "seemed to me even
more beautiful than those of Blenheim."[47]

Toward the end of their Oxford stay the Hawthornes were asked by Spiers to pose for a
group photograph which also would include Mr. and Mrs. Hall, Spiers' son, Mrs. Spiers,
and other guests. Richard Spiers had engaged one of the nation's foremost craftsman,
Philip H. Delamotte of London, to make the group picture in the Spiers' garden.
Delamotte, professor of drawing at King's College, may have come to Oxford in the first
instance to photograph some of the city's best known landmarks for his forthcoming book,
*Views of Oxford*, which Spiers seems to have jointly commissioned with a London publisher.

He assembled the group under a tree beside the garden wall. Photographic subjects were
not then accustomed either to remaining stationary or looking toward the camera; thus,
both Sophia and Mrs. Hall managed to turn their backs just as Delamotte snapped his
picture. Hawthorne, placed on the extreme right of the group, came out very well, as did
most of the others. The former Mayor's son, who had cut his finger badly while trying to
capture a snake on one of the outings arranged by his father for the Hawthornes, appears
with his arm in a sling. This group photograph was the only one made of the Hawthornes
during their English sojourn.

The visit to Oxford and its environs was now over and Hawthorne realized that his first,

**THE "OXFORD PHOTOGRAPH" COMMISSIONED BY SPIERS**
The former Oxford mayor arranged for the noted photographer, Philip Delamotte, to take this group picture in the garden of his St. Giles Street home. Left to right are Sophia Hawthorne, Mrs. Spiers, Richard Spiers, Jr., Fanny Hall, Mr. Addison, S. C. Hall, Mrs. S. C. Hall (seated), and Hawthorne.

hasty impression of the city had been unfair. But he was at a loss as how best to portray the ancient seat of learning – and gave up without trying. ". . . I take leave of Oxford," he said, "without even an attempt to describe it, – there being no literary faculty, attainable or conceivable by me, which can avail to put it adequately, or even tolerably, upon paper." Hawthorne acknowledged that without the hospitality afforded by Richard Spiers, it would have been impossible for Sophia and himself to have obtained such a "happy coloring" of Oxford.[48] Spiers had to have a suitable gift in return, and Sophia's next letter to William Ticknor revealed what she had in mind.

[Sept. 7th, 1856]

My Dear Mr. Ticknor,
    We have been the objects of perfectly magnificent hospitality to a gentleman of Oxford – former mayor of Oxford, now alderman – a gentleman of the kindest heart – most liberal hand – sagacious, sensible – & of indefatigable activity. We wish to make a delicate return in the way of a memorial, & I have suggested to Mr. Hawthorne a set of his own works – *very splendidly* bound – Wonder book & all – Will you order this to be done as soon as possible – to send by the next steamer, if that is not too soon? In greatest haste with very kindest regards, dear Mr. Ticknor – I am

truly yours

S. Hawthorne[49]

## YORK MINSTER AND PETERBOROUGH CATHEDRAL

Hawthorne much admired the beauty of York Minster but found himself "almost congealed with cold" after listening to a sermon lasting an hour and a half. He was appalled at the damage caused to Peterborough Cathedral by Cromwell's soldiers, an incident that led him to ponder "how suddenly the English people lost their sense of sanctity."

In his own handwriting at the bottom of Sophia's letter, Hawthorne instructed Ticknor to have the recipient's name embossed in gilt Old English lettering thus:

R. J. SPIERS. ESQ.

Hawthorne paid another tribute to Spiers at the end of the chapter in *Our Old Home* devoted to the Oxford visit. Instead of identifying the former mayor by name, he borrowed Cuthbert Bede's epithet from *Verdant Green* to show his and Sophia's appreciation for all Spiers had done to make the Oxford experience such a memorable affair: "He has inseparably mingled his image with our remembrance of the Spires of Oxford."[50]

By February of 1857 Hawthorne had notified Washington he would leave the consulate on August 31. But in the months remaining he hoped to see as much of Britain as his duties would permit. At Easter he planned to visit York briefly with Sophia and Julian. Up to then he had seen nothing of East Anglia; that deficiency, too, he hoped to remedy before the summer was over. Finally, he hoped to pay another visit to Scotland – this time with Sophia – for his venture there the previous year, like his first visit to Oxford, had not been entirely satisfactory.

The York expedition was accomplished as planned, with side trips to the castle at Skipton and Bolton Priory. As the family visited York Minster on Easter Sunday,

**LINCOLN CATHEDRAL**
"Certainly," Hawthorne said, "the Bishop and Clergy of Lincoln ought not to be fat men, but of very spiritual, saint-like, almost angelic, habit." To climb the hill to the cathedral, he added, "is a real penance."

Hawthorne, Sophia and Julian duly attended the morning service. Sophia and Julian were ushered into distant seats, but Hawthorne was led to the choir stalls where he had an excellent view of the interior architecture and magnificent stained glass windows. Despite his choice seat, Hawthorne soon tired of the long service. ". . . nearly an hour and a half were . . . employed, with some intermixture of prayers and reading of scriptures," he said, "and being almost congealed with cold, I thought it would never come to an end. The spirit of my Puritan ancestors was mighty in me, and I did not wonder at their being out of patience with all this mummery . . ."[51]

Bad weather persisted in May when the Hawthornes planned to make their pilgrimage to "old Boston" and other places in East Anglia. Arriving in Lincoln late one afternoon, they had a meal of cold beef, cold trout, and cold boiled crab, and then set out on foot to see Lincoln Cathedral. The lane leading to the cathedral became steeper and steeper – "At last, it got to be the steepest street I ever saw . . ."[52]

Then Hawthorne reflected on how the steepness must affect those associated with the cathedral who had to climb the hill regularly. "Certainly," he said, "the Bishop and Clergy of Lincoln ought not to be fat men, but of very spiritual, saint-like, almost angelic, habit, if it be a frequent part of their ecclesiastical duty to climb this hill, for it is a real penance, and was probably performed as such, and groaned over accordingly, in monkish times." He considered those fortunate enough to live in the cathedral close the luckiest of mortals. "How delightful," he said, "to combine all this with the service of the temple!"[53]

Finding that a small steamer operated on the River Witham between Lincoln and Boston, Hawthorne decided to try this mode of transportation for a change. The venture proved a mistake, for the little craft was not intended for sightseers, but as a cheap means for conveying passengers and cargo. It provided few comforts and, by stopping at any place along the river bank where there was business, its progress was painfully slow. After a "cruise" of some five to six hours, the craft reached Boston and Nathaniel, Sophia and Julian were pleased to escape. Hawthorne's primary interest in Boston derived from its association with his own Boston, whose Custom House and docks had been so much a part of his early life. He was somewhat disappointed in what he saw. "The whole scene made an odd impression of bustle, and sluggishness, and decay, and a remnant of wholesome life," he said, "and I could but contrast it with the mighty and populous activity of our own Boston, which was once the feeble infant of this old English town . . ."[54]

In an unpretentious bookshop the Hawthornes encountered a Mr. Porter, the proprietor, who knew of Hawthorne and his works and promptly left his business to make his guests welcome. He led the trio into his upstairs apartment which turned out to house hundreds of antiquities – some, he said, that were not held even by the British Museum. There was a quilt said to have been embroidered by Mary Queen of Scots; a waistcoat attributed to Lord Burleigh; fine drawings by Raphael, Rembrandt, and Cellini; a "Secret-Book" which had belonged to Queen Elizabeth; and a rare collection of old coins and medals. Nor did Mr. Porter's hospitality end here; he brought forth wine "as old and genuine as the curiosities of his cabinet," and afterwards introduced his guests to the vicar of St. Botolph's Church.[55]

The concept of "twinning" cities of the old world and the new, such as the two Bostons, had not then evolved, but Hawthorne, in a letter to Ticknor describing his visit, foresaw the value of such links. "There is a strong feeling of pride among the inhabitants in the greatness and prosperity of our American Boston, which they consider as the daughter of their old town," he said. "There is going to be a celebration, this summer, in honor of John Cotton, the first minister of our Boston, and Americans will be in great demand on the occasion. Our Boston ought to send a special representative."[56]

With their pilgrimage to Boston over, the trio started back to Liverpool, halting briefly in Peterborough to see the cathedral. Hawthorne was horrified at the damage done by Cromwell's soldiers to the carved woodwork and other interior features of the cathedral. "It is wonderful," he said, "how suddenly the English people lost their sense of the sanctity of all manner of externals in religion, without losing their religion, too."[57] By slow stages they continued their way towards Liverpool, stopping at Nottingham to have a look at Newstead Abbey (associated with Lord Byron) and at Matlock, the Derbyshire beauty spot. On June 2 Hawthorne returned to Liverpool, having left Sophia in Manchester for sight-seeing on her own.

Three weeks later the trio went to Scotland for their last vacation before Hawthorne gave up his consular position. It was a trip he had promised Sophia, because she had never been, and himself, because his first visit there had been marred by bad weather. Not long after leaving Carlisle, the Hawthornes crossed the Scottish border and came to Gretna Green, a place where thousands of young English couples were wed under the more lenient marriage laws of Scotland. Hawthorne promptly dubbed it "a spot which many people have visited to their woe."[58]

During much of Hawthorne's travels his object was to visit places associated with British literary figures; such was now the primary objective in choosing Dumfries as the centre for their exploration to sites connected with Robert Burns. On arriving they immediately set out to find Burns' home, and eventually were directed to a modest building being used as an industrial school. Hawthorne was much disappointed with what he saw. "Altogether," he said, "it is an exceedingly unsuitable place for a pastoral and rural poet to live or die in, – even more unsatisfactory than Shakespeare's house, which has a certain homely picturesqueness that contrasts favorably with the suburban sordidness of the abode before us."[59] In St. Michael's churchyard the family saw the grave of Burns under the watchful eye of a lady attendant. She was more interested in the seamy side of the Burns family than in the poet's works, an emphasis Hawthorne found somewhat irreverent. Inside the church, she led the family to Burns' pew, located squarely behind a massive column. ". . . Robin," she said, "was no great friends with the ministers."[60]

From Dumfries the party continued to Mauchline, whose village church was the scene of the poet's "The Holy Fair," and to nearby Moss Giel, the dreary farmhouse where Burns made his mark in the literary world. After stopping briefly at spots mentioned in works of Burns, Hawthorne and his family arrived at the hamlet of Alloway, just outside Ayr, where

## "A WELL-PADDED MAN"

Sophia also said the cricket players were dressed in "buff leather, very much like a child's sun-bonnet." Hawthorne could not understand the game: "It is necessary to be born an Englishman to enjoy [it]," he said. The scene above is at Stanway, Gloucestershire.

Burns was born. The birthplace had been converted into a public house, complete with tables on which hundreds of visitors had inscribed their names. Covered, too, were the wooden walls, the wooden cupboard – in fact, anything made of wood seemed to have been "much oversubscribed with names of visitors."[61]

Before turning southward for Liverpool, the family saw other well known features of the Burns country – stark Kirk Alloway, the graceful Bridge of Doon, and the Bonny Doon itself "with its wooded banks and the boughs dipping into the water."[62] On their way to Liverpool they stopped at Glasgow, where they saw its cathedral and university, Dumbarton Castle, Loch Lomond, the Trossachs, Stirling, Edinburgh, and Abbotsford. Now south of the border, they attended a Sunday service in Durham Cathedral before continuing to York. Here Hawthorne led the family to the Black Swan, an ancient and friendly inn where he had stayed previously.

After nearly four years in Britain, Hawthorne had seen many of the country's cathedrals and was constantly revising his opinion as to which deserved the most praise. With the advantage of hindsight, he now accorded York Minster the top honour. "York Cathedral," he said, "(I say it now, for it is my present feeling) is the most wonderful work that ever came from the hands of man. Indeed, it seems like a 'house not made with hands,' but rather to have come down from above, bringing an awful majesty and sweetness with it . . ."[63]

It was the memory of Robert Burns and the places connected with his life and works that Hawthorne was to cherish most from his last trip. ". . . we had been holding intercourse," he said, "if not with the reality, at least with the stalwart ghost of one of Earth's memorable sons, amid the scenes where he lived and sung. . . . Henceforth, there will be a personal warmth for us in everything he wrote, and like his countrymen, we shall know him in a kind of personal way, as if we had shaken hands with him and felt the thrill of his actual voice."[64]

The Hawthornes could not travel the length and breadth of Britain without being exposed to the national game of cricket, and both Sophia and Nathaniel had something to say about the sport. Neither's description of cricket was likely to recommend it to Americans, and doubtless some Englishmen would have difficulty recognizing it. In a letter to her father Sophia explained that the game was played on "a perfectly level plain of eight or nine acres – a smooth, sunny, velvet lawn." The players, who appeared to her as being in a fashion parade, were "dressed in pale buff washleather or felt doublet in strips over the

## MANCHESTER EXHIBITION

While attending the Exhibition of Art Treasures at Manchester in 1857, Hawthorne spotted Tennyson among the viewers but held back from introducing himself to the poet.

instep, and those who stood before each wicket with a bat in hand were guarded from the severe blows of the ball by a peculiar coat-of-mail reaching from the ankles above the knee. This shin-guard was made of buff leather, very much like a child's sun-bonnet, but instead of pasteboard sewed in, it is thickly padded with wool, and I do not know but a thin wooden board or whalebone besides – making the limb look very clumsy."[65]

She then turned to the players and their mysterious antics. "At each wicket," she said, "stood . . . a well-padded man with a bat. Behind him and each wicket stood another man who threw the ball and tried to knock down the wicket, which the man with the bat was studious to prevent. In a vast circle from these four stood, I believe, eight men, at exact distances from one another, who were to catch the ball when a bat sent it off from either wicket." Scoring, at least, said Sophia, was a simple matter. "If the man with the bat was so fortunate as to drive it to a great distance," she explained, "he and the other batsman ran from one wicket to another, and just as many times as they could exchange places, so much the better for them, for each time counts one in the game."[66]

Hawthorne had less patience and gave up trying to understand the game. "It is necessary," he concluded, "to be born an Englishman . . . to enjoy this great national game."[67]

After the consular duties ended, the Hawthornes lived in Manchester. The most pleasant aspect of this stay undoubtedly was the family's visit to the Exhibition of Art Treasures which had been opened by Prince Albert in March of 1857. One day, while viewing the exhibition, Hawthorne spotted Tennyson and rushed off to find Sophia, Rose and Fanny. By the time he had found them and brought them to the spot where he had seen the poet, Tennyson had moved on. Eventually they found him, but Hawthorne held back from introducing himself. ". . . it seemed mean to be dogging him through the saloons, or even to have looked at him," he said, "since it was to be done stealthily, if at all." Yet, Hawthorne admitted, he would have enjoyed smoking a cigar with him.[68] When Tennyson learned afterwards that Hawthorne had seen him at the exhibition but had been reluctant to make his presence known, he expressed regret that the meeting had not taken place.

In his four years as consul, Hawthorne had made good the traditional diplomat's vow to know well the nation to which he has been assigned. The only areas of England he missed were the southwest and the easternmost tip of East Anglia. His time and observations were necessarily limited by the constraints of his official duties, but his voluminous *English Notebooks* nonetheless offers a graphic, and often lively description of Victorian Britain as seen by American eyes.

As Hawthorne himself realized, he had not seen the entire country; yet, what he had seen had given him immense pleasure. Towards the end of one of his expeditions he recorded his affection for the land he had come to love. "If England were all the world," he said, "it still would have been worthwhile for the Creator to have made it . . ."[69]

# XII
# Mrs. Blodget and the Lonely Consul

"I am persuaded," said Julian Hawthorne in later life, "that no other establishment like Mrs. Blodget's exists now, nor did even then."[1] This tribute was directed at the remarkable boarding house located at 133–135 Duke Street in Liverpool and its equally remarkable proprietress, Mrs. Mary Blodget. Julian was not content to praise the establishment as being merely unique; he considered it pre-eminent in this world, and the next. "It has vanished from earth long since," he added, "but if there were boarding houses in paradise, I should certainly expect it to be found again there."[2]

Neither Hawthorne nor his son recorded Mary Blodget's early life or the reason why American sea captains were attracted to her house. That she had once been a lady of means in Gibraltar was beyond doubt, but the precise circumstances of her early life were obscure. The Gibraltar census return of 1834 confirms that she lived on "The Rock" at that time with her American husband, Samuel Chase Blodget, his (or their) son, Samuel Chase Blodget, Junior, and Mary's sister, Anne Williams.[3] While in Gibraltar Mrs Blodget earned a considerable reputation as a hostess.[4]

Working with Anne, Mary established a glowing reputation for her Duke Street establishment. In a short time its fame spread among the colony of Americans in Liverpool and, through them and successive consuls, across the Atlantic. This word-of-mouth advertising was sufficient to bring any sensible master of an American ship to Duke Street, and he often counted himself lucky to find a room free. Either through her fame or cleverness, Mary Blodget had succeeded in attracting two of Hawthorne's predecessors to the boarding house. They were General Robert Armstrong, who was named consul to Liverpool in 1845 by President Polk, and Thomas Crittenden, Hawthorne's immediate predecessor.

Mary Blodget was like a character out of Dickens – short and plump, bespectacled, with brown curls splashing down each side of her face and blessed with a pleasant disposition. She was always immaculately dressed, her standard attire being a black dress with white apron and matching white cap.[5] When she first opened the boarding house, it was limited to 133 Duke Street. As the demand for rooms grew, she took over the adjacent house. The houses could not be termed elegant, but Mary Blodget did not stake her reputation on the appearance of the place, but rather on her generous hospitality.

The Hawthornes stayed at Mrs. Blodget's several times during the family's English residence. The first occasion, the nine days following their departure from the Waterloo Hotel, found the entire family there. This stay, however, came to an abrupt end with the move across the River Mersey to search for a house. Two years later, after Sophia and the two girls had gone to Portugal, Hawthorne and Julian began a prolonged, lonely stay through the winter of 1855–6 and into the spring.

Julian, more than any other member of the family, came to look upon Mrs. Blodget's as his new home. This was largely due to his mother's absence, a period which often found the boy living a boarding-house existence with only Mrs. Blodget's motherly attentions to cheer him. During this time father and son became great friends. Julian also had lessons to attend, but there were, nonetheless, many hours when the patient Mary Blodget was the only adult in the boy's daily life.

**MRS. BLODGET'S BOARDING HOUSE**
Julian Hawthorne, who looked upon the boarding house as a second home, said no other place could match it. Two of Hawthorne's predecessors had rooms there, and Mrs. Blodget's hospitality was known to ships' masters on both sides of the Atlantic.

Never at a loss for amusement, Julian was especially fond of sliding down the banisters which led to the ground floor from the public rooms on the next storey. Kept highly polished, they insured maximum speed. Happily for Julian, there were no obstructions on the way or offending knobs at the end; instead they broadened into a magnificent flat section which insured a smooth flight. This thoughtful arrangement, Julian recalled, allowed him "at the end of his thrilling sweep from top to bottom, to fly off unscathed and land heroically on his feet in the hall."[6]

If a guest escaped Julian's flight and mounted the staircase to the next floor, he found the various public rooms where Mrs. Blodget's boarders gathered for meals and other pleasures. The parlour was a fair-sized room, furnished with a piano. It was here that a delegation from the American Chamber of Commerce welcomed Hawthorne to the city within a few days of his arrival. There was also the smoking room, usually inhabited only by captains and the American Consul, but which on occasion was invaded by the ladies. It was in the dining room, however, that Mrs. Blodget gained the reputation that made her name a by-word among American mariners. This room boasted a single long table capable of accommodating up to twenty people. From her vantage point Mary Blodget kept a watchful eye on her guests, making sure that all had as many helpings as they wished, and that each of her specialities was sampled. Julian's impression was that Mrs. Blodget drove hard bargains when reaching agreement on terms, but once these were settled her object "was not to make money, but happiness."[7]

Hawthorne and Julian accompanied Sophia, Una and Rose to Southampton early in

October when the *Madrid* was due to sail for Lisbon. Neither husband nor wife wanted to be parted, but Sophia's health was at risk and the milder climate of Portugal offered the prospect of recovery. The parting was tearful, but Julian did not allow the consul a chance to ponder his grief. "[He] took occasion to remind me," Hawthorne said, "that he now had no one but myself to depend upon, and therefore suggested that I should be very kind to him."[8]

It was natural that the servants tended to spoil Julian, and in the process become his close friends. His vantage point at meal times was the broad end of the banisters at the top of the stairs, just outside the dining room. From this spot he caught occasional views of meal-time activity. Better still, he was able to get the first glimpse of every new dish as it passed between the kitchen and its intended consumers. The serving maid was an indispensable ally. ". . . as rosy Mary passed me at intervals with the heaped platters she would pause a moment," Julian recalled, "and I would lift a tid-bit with the eleemosynary kitchen fork supplied for that purpose." Once Mrs. Blodget caught Julian in his sampling act and feigned great astonishment, but the lad sensed she was fully aware of his "immoralities."[9]

Breakfasts at the boarding house were substantial affairs. Besides the usual muffins, crumpets and marmalade, there was smoked haddock or fresh-boiled mackerel. Where the latter came from was no riddle for Julian, for he had only to peer out of his window for the answer. "In the dawn," he remembered, "I would be awakened by the fisher-girls passing along the street: 'Mackere-eel fresh, fresh, fresh!' in long-drawn, strong notes with the tang of the sea in them, and sometimes I would tumble out of bed and [dash] to the open window to catch a glimpse of the big baskets on their heads." He retained a lifelong impression of Mrs. Blodget's bountiful breakfasts. "There have never been any such in America," he said, "and I doubt whether in England either, and only a boy would know. The marmalade was the only marmalade then or since, the Dundee marmalade . . ."[10] Even Liverpool's prestigious Adelphi would have been hard pressed to equal Mrs. Blodget's daily fare which, Julian recalled, could consist of roast beef and Yorkshire pudding, fried sole, chicken pie, roast duck, tripe fried in butter, boiled salmon, green peas, puddings, tarts, custards, musk melons, and plums.

Hawthorne now resumed his routine of dealing with an unending stream of marine folk and their problems and documents, but without Sophia's usual support. Happily, letters flowed freely between the separated members of the family and these boosted morale. Extracts from Sophia's correspondence reveal not only the fond love of a mother for an only son, but contain expected parental admonitions. She told Julian that his previous note to her "delighted me extremely," adding: "It was very well expressed and spelt pretty well." She also related how, as the guest of the American Minister to Portugal, she was privileged to mix in the same circles as the O'Sullivans. On one occasion she attended a ballet during which she decided to sneak a peek at the King. ". . . just as I got his face well into my glass," she wrote Julian, "he raised his glass to look at me and discover what new person was in the American Minister's box, and so in this way we could neither see the other."[11]

Sophia's thrust into Lisbon's high society prompted Hawthorne to write Ticknor that she "sees kings, princes, dukes, and ambassadors as familiarly as I do Liverpool merchants."[12] One result of this social activity was Sophia's obligation to present a gift to Fernando II, the king-regent. The gift, she suggested, should be a specially bound set of her husband's works.

While Sophia was enjoying life in Lisbon, Hawthorne was miserable in Liverpool. "Julian and I live here at a boarding house," he wrote Longfellow in November of 1855; "I

**SOPHIA AND ROYALTY**
Hawthorne's lonely stay at
Mrs. Blodget's was enlivened
by Sophia's letters detailing
her social life in Lisbon.
Among the dignitaries she
saw were young King Pedro
V (left) and the king regent,
Fernando II.

feel quite homeless and stray, and as if I belonged to nowhere."[13] The loneliness was temporarily cast aside during Christmas, for Mrs. Blodget saw to it that her establishment provided not only the expected feasts of the season, but traditional holiday fun and frolic as well. The custom of kissing beneath the mistletoe was new to Hawthorne, and one of which he did not entirely approve. "The maids of the house," he said, "did their utmost to entrap the gentleman-boarders, old and young, under these privileged places, and there to kiss them, after which they were expected to pay a shilling. It is very queer, being customarily so respectful, that they should assume this license now, absolutely trying to pull the gentlemen into the kitchen by main force, and kissing the harder and more abundantly the more they resisted. I doubt whether any gentleman but myself escaped."[14]

Despite Sophia's regular letters and Mrs. Blodget's well-stocked table, Hawthorne's morale and health were adversely affected by the long separation. Not until the end of February, 1856, was he able to tell Ticknor that the worst was over. "My health and spirits," he said, "are considerably better than in the earlier part of the winter. I begin to eat and drink again."[15] Not that Mrs. Blodget had failed to do her part. She was constantly urging Hawthorne and his fellow boarders to take more of the food placed before them. To one of her ship masters she would say, "Captain Green, you must let me give you a bit of tenderloin," and to another she would ask, "What's wrong with your appetite, Captain Purdy?"[16]

Mrs. Blodget's "old men," Julian said, "were her brothers, her young men were her sons, all children were her children."[17] She did, indeed, do her best to take Sophia's place during the eight months when Julian lived at the boarding house. "She would beseech me . . .," he said, "to part my hair straight, to forbear to soil my jacket, and even to get my shoes blacked." Mrs. Blodget's attentions did not stop with the boy's appearance. "Sometimes at table," Julian added, "I would glance up to find her eyes dwelling with mild reproach upon me . . ."[18] There was little, in fact, that Mrs. Blodget could do about the lad's manners and overall discipline, for Hawthorne himself abetted Julian in his boyish whims. He was allowed in the smoking room – not to smoke – but to join in games of "yucca" (euchre) with his father and the old sea captains. He much relished this privilege and listened with rapt attention to the yarns and jokes that accompanied the games.

For Hawthorne, Mrs. Blodget's boarding house – and the smoking room in particular – was Little America. "There," he said, "we criticize and ridicule John Bull, and assert American superiority, in a way that it would probably chafe him a little to hear . . ." Some captains brought their wives along on their voyages, and a few even took their children. So much did these sea-faring folk talk of their crews, cargoes, tempests, business prospects, and all the rest that at least one captain could not stomach it. "Captain Johnson," Hawthorne said, "assigned as a reason for not boarding at this house, that the conversation made him sea-sick."[19] Many and varied were the boarders who entered the portals of Mrs. Blodget's esteemed establishment, but none attracted Hawthorne's attention so much as the Amazonian wife of a certain Captain Devereux from Marblehead. She was nicknamed "Oakum," and was described by Hawthorne as being six-feet tall, possessing "a vast amount of connubial bliss,"[20] and probably as capable of commanding a ship as her husband.

Separated from Sophia and the girls and removed from the homelike atmosphere of the Rock Park villa, Hawthorne would have found it difficult to carry on his consular duties while living in a hotel, or in more pretentious English accommodations. But Mrs. Blodget's establishment was a place where, at the end of each day, he could relax in the company of his fellow countrymen. The ships' captains may have bored him at times with their yarns, but at least he understood their language and their humour. Julian Hawthorne recalled "there were no quarrels or heartburnings among the jolly occupants of Mrs. Blodget's table; first, because they were all Americans in the country of their hereditary enemies, and secondly, because they were all men of the same calling, and that calling the sea."[21]

Undoubtedly the highlight of Julian's eight-month stay at Mrs. Blodget's was a sensational robbery to which he was almost a party. The only male member of the boarding house staff was Charley, commonly known as "Boots" because his principal job was blacking the boots of Mrs. Blodget's boarders. He and Julian became close friends. One day the boy came upon Charley unexpectedly in the kitchen, working at something in the floor beneath the table. After hesitating briefly and exacting a pledge of secrecy, Charley showed Julian his handiwork – a plank neatly sawn through, and which could be lifted out with the blade of a knife. Then he produced a small box which fitted into the cavity perfectly. When Julian asked the purpose of the operation, Charley replied he merely was "passing the time" and added, "Might be I'd want a place to hide away my watch and jewelry if I was taking the day off. I'd slip it in there, and they'd not find it in a day's hunting." Julian promptly forgot about the incident, but several days later he remembered it when he awoke to find the household in turmoil. A thief had taken Mrs. Blodget's silver, Captain Howe's seals and watch, and Mrs. Perkins' rings. His empty box was found beneath the kitchen table. The police came and confirmed the culprit to be Charley. Julian then related his encounter, but it was too late. Nothing was heard of him, and Julian surmised he may have gone to the United States, "as he once had told me he meant to do, when he had made his pile."[22]

In mid-March Hawthorne reported to Sophia that he and Julian were "plodding on here . . . in the same dull way." He told her of the boy's romance with Minnie Warren, and his almost adult-like analysis of her. An American girl slightly older than Julian, Minnie attended Monsieur Victor Regnier's dancing class. It was here that Julian met her and in a short time the pair became the star pupils of the dancing master. Later they were to play the feature roles of "Beauty and the Beast" given in the home of a Liverpool hostess. "He sees . . . [Minnie's] character," said Hawthorne, "and criticizes her with a shrewdness that quite astonishes me."[23] Meanwhile Sophia reported the weather in Madeira, where she had gone with the O'Sullivans, was worse than England's and said she was suffering greatly. This depressing revelation caused Nathaniel to write another letter, partly by way of commiseration and partly to distract Sophia by calling attention to Julian's latest antics:

> It was a most foolish project of O'Sullivan's (as all his projects are) to lead thee from his comfortable fireside, to that comfortless Madeira. And thou

sayest, or Una says, that the rainy season is just commencing there, and that this month and the next are the two worst months of the year! . . . Thou wilt find . . . [Julian] a good and honest boy, healthy in mind, and healthier in heart than when he left thee; ready to begin his effectual education as soon as circumstances permit. . . . I find it an arduous business nowadays to take him across my knees and spank him, and unless I give up the attempt betimes, he will soon be the spanker and his poor father the spankee.[24]

Both parents, during the enforced separation, took great pains to send individually written notes to the children. Among them was one to Rose from her father:

MY DEAR LITTLE ROSEBUD, – I have put a kiss for you in this nice, clean piece of paper. I shall fold it up carefully and I hope it will not drop out before it gets to Lisbon. If you cannot find it, you must ask Mamma to look for it. Perhaps you will find it on her lips. . . .

Your affection father,

N.H.[25]

By now it was clear that any expected improvement in Sophia's health was not taking place. Hawthorne was almost frantic with anxiety and, at least twice, considered joining his wife and daughters. Then he had a new thought: why not resign the consulship and take the family to Italy now, instead of waiting for his assignment to run its course. But the notion of quitting Liverpool shocked Sophia, and she hurriedly made another suggestion. "Dearest," she said, "I have an idea! Next winter, if you wish to remain in England and my coughing continues, I will tell you how I might do and be most happy and comfortable. I might remain in my chamber all winter and keep it at an even temperature, and exercise by means of the portable gymnasium. . . . I hate to be the means of your resigning from the Consulate."[26]

Hawthorne's letters to Sophia constantly refer to her illness, offering advice of one remedy or another – some supplied by himself, some by others. In one he begged her not to rely solely on Lisbon's climate to restore her health, but to seek the counsel of a competent physician as well. Then he offered his own cure: "*Do* take cod-liver oil. It is the only thing I ever really had any faith in, and thou wilt not take it. Thou dost confess to growing thin. Take cod-liver oil, and, at all events, grow fat."[27]

Sophia, for her part, was as concerned about the welfare of Julian as her husband had been for her and the girls. Hawthorne assured her the boy's health was fine, that he never ate between meals – "unless it be apples" – and that his only real grievance was not being allowed to have his dinner with everyone else. "The intercourse which he holds with the people of Mrs. Blodget's seems to me of a healthy kind," he added. "They make a playmate of him, to a certain extent, but do him no mischief . . ."[28] In another letter he passed on to Sophia Julian's latest gem: "I don't remember," the boy said, "how I came down from Heaven, but I'm very glad I happened to tumble into so good a family."[29]

The days of spring came and went as Hawthorne's longing for the family grew. He particularly missed the girls who, he feared, may have altered greatly. "I think a great deal about poor little Rosebud," he wrote Sophia, "and find that I loved her about ten million times as much as I had any idea of. . . . Una, too! I long unutterably to see her and cannot

**CAPTAIN HUDSON AND THE U.S. FRIGATE *NIAGARA***
Mrs. Blodget had known Captain Hudson when she lived in Gibraltar; when Hudson brought the *Niagara* to Liverpool he invited the boarding house proprietress aboard for an official visit. The *Niagara* took part in the initial attempt to link Britain and America by cable.

bear to think that she has been growing out of her childhood, all the time, without my witnessing each day's change. But the first moment when we meet again, will set everything right. Oh, blessed moment!"[30]

The "blessed moment" came not on June 14, as Sophia had written, but on June 12. News of the earlier arrival came on the evening of June 9 just as Hawthorne was going to bed. The next day he hastily put his consular business in order and by five in the afternoon set off south with Julian. They reached Birmingham by nightfall, where they remained the evening, and the next day continued to Southampton. There, on the quayside, the family at last was reunited.

Both at Sophia's departure and now on her return, the family stayed at the modest Castle Inn – a mere fifty yards from the water's edge. The inn was small and lacked the amenities of the town's larger hotels, but it had the advantage of being near to arriving and departing vessels. After a few days in the inn, the family removed to the suburb of Shirley where they took rooms with the proprietress of a girls' school. The surroundings were pleasant enough, but the family did not take kindly to the lady's meagre servings of food. "If she fed us better," Hawthorne remarked wryly, "I suppose I might be more lenient in my judgments, but eight months at Mrs. Blodget's table have not been a very good preparation for the schoolgirls' bread and butter, morning and night, and the simple joint of mutton."[31]

On return to Liverpool Hawthorne could at last put behind him the loneliest winter of his life. There is no record of what gift, if any, he may have presented Mrs. Blodget for her kindness to Julian and himself, but through his consular position he was able to demonstrate his gratitude and respect. One such opportunity arose in June of 1857 when Hawthorne was influential in arranging for Mrs. Blodget to be an honoured guest aboard an American naval vessel.

When the United States and Great Britain were making arrangements to link the two countries by transatlantic cable, special ships were designated for the project. The U.S. frigate *Niagara*, commanded by Captain William L. Hudson, was to lay that half of the

**THE LAST RESTING PLACE OF MRS. BLODGET**
Located at the upper end of Duke Street, St. James' Cemetery was perhaps the most
striking of Britain's great 19th century burial grounds. Mrs. Blodget lived for only
two years after the Hawthornes left England; she was 68 at her death.

cable terminating in the United States. Hudson brought the *Niagara* into Liverpool in June,
1857, and shortly after disembarking called on the American Consul. Hawthorne found
him "a somewhat meager, elderly gentleman of simple and hearty manners and address."[32]
He was pleasantly surprised when Captain Hudson revealed that he had come ashore, in
part, to pay his respects to Mrs. Blodget. He was also to be guest of honour at an elaborate
dinner given by the American Chamber of Commerce.

"The Captain," said Hawthorne, "is an old acquaintance of Mrs. Blodget . . . so, after
we left our cards on the Mayor, I showed these gentlemen [the Captain and his purser] the
way to her house. Mrs. Blodget and [her sister] Miss Williams were prodigiously glad to
see him, and all three began to talk of old times and old acquaintances, for when Mrs.
Blodget was a rich lady at Gibraltar, she used to have our whole navy-list at her table –
young midshipmen and lieutenants then, perhaps, but old gouty, paralytic Commodores
now, if still partly alive."[33]

But the gallant Captain Hudson was not content merely to see Mrs. Blodget and her
sister again; he would count it a privilege to have the ladies come aboard the *Niagara* while
she was in port. "It was arranged," said Hawthorne, "that Mrs. Blodget, with as many of
the ladies of her family as she chose to bring, should accompany me on my official visit to
the Ship . . ."[34] When Hawthorne's party went aboard the following day, Mrs. Blodget and
Miss Williams were numbered among them. The vessel was anchored near Rock Ferry
and, when the tour was over, the various guests – including Mrs. Blodget, her sister,
Hawthorne and Julian – went ashore on the Cheshire side of the Mersey and retired to the
gardens of the Royal Rock Hotel to savour the day's adventure.

When Hawthorne finished the last volume of his Liverpool diary, he remembered the
gentle lady whose boarding house had been his second home. "My friend Mrs. Blodget, for
whom I feel respect and affection," he said, "is as good, kind, and hospitable as ever, and I
take pleasure in putting her name last in this last volume of my English journal."[35]

# XIII
## War Fears and Calming Words

Toward the middle of Hawthorne's consular assignment there occurred a series of events which were to bring the United States and Great Britain as close to conflict as anything since the war of 1812.

The circumstances unfortunately coincided with a period in which Anglo-American relations had already become strained. The initial cause of the bad feelings arose from the American contention that the Monroe Doctrine made Latin America a zone of United States influence and that outsiders, including Britain, were unwelcome there. The United States was seeking a canal route across Central America to give the eastern and western halves of the country a sea link. Britain, as the world's leading maritime nation, was uneasy about what it saw as American expansionism in an area where it already had established footholds — Jamaica and Belize (the latter was to become British Honduras). These conflicting interests in the same part of the world seemed bound to put Britain and the United States on a collision course unless some joint initiative was taken to ease the tension. Such a joint effort, indeed, was made and the resulting Clayton-Bulwer Treaty of 1850, although deliberately ambiguous in its wording, at first seemed the desired palliative. By the treaty the Americans promised not to construct an isthmus canal unilaterally, and the British seemed to commit themselves to no new territories. But when the British seized the Bay Islands off the coast of independent Honduras and declared them to be a Crown Colony in 1852, the United States at once doubted Britain's intention to keep to the treaty. The Bay Islands incident was widely debated in America, and Franklin Pierce referred to it in his inaugural address of 1853, but Britain took no notice and continued its Caribbean adventures. American anger thus was already great when Britain's recruiting programme in the Crimean War flung the two nations into a bitter quarrel — one in which Hawthorne, aided by his friend, Francis Bennoch, would attempt to calm.

Late in 1854 the British public was shocked to learn of heavy losses sustained by Her Majesty's forces in the Crimea, but the shock turned to fury when it heard that many of the deaths were due to poor organization and, in particular, inadequate medical support. It was this war which Florence Nightingale and others would point to as evidence that casualties from wounds and sickness, if not treated properly, could outstrip battlefield deaths. With British fortunes faring badly, the government in London belatedly set about to replenish the wasted manpower and to improve its lines of supply, both to the Crimea and in the actual fighting area.

It was the British effort to bolster its depleted forces by inaugurating an intense recruiting programme in North America that almost brought the two English-speaking nations to war. The central figure in the bizarre episode was the British Minister to the United States, John F. Crampton. This was the same Minister whom the Hawthornes had met when they sailed on the *Niagara* from Boston in 1853. At that time Sophia was charmed by Crampton's manners and speech, but during the recruitment dispute his name became synonymous with British imperialism in the eyes of many Americans. To Crampton's credit, it should be said that he was so concerned about Britain's precarious military situation in the Crimea that he was determined to raise recruits at all possible speed.

To meet the demand for more able-bodied men, the British Parliament in December, 1854, enacted a foreign recruitment law which was mainly intended to facilitate recruitment of British forces in North America. While Crampton knew that Anglophiles residing in the United States might be eager to join the British forces, he was also aware that he had to tread carefully because of American neutrality laws. He studied the recruitment act and took legal advice from an American lawyer, but did not rush to implement the new provision. Lord Clarendon, the British Foreign Minister, became impatient and pressed Crampton for action, but it was not until February of 1855 that the Minister developed a plan which he considered workable and which would not infringe on American law. The plan was a simple one: potential American recruits (to be known as "voluntary emigrants") would be supplied with transportation to eastern Canada and there formally enlisted. Neither Crampton nor any British Consul serving in the United States was to approach the recruits; this task was to be left to selected agents who would be paid from a special secret account.[1]

Canadian authorities were lukewarm to Crampton's plan, but he found a more sympathetic response in Nova Scotia whose governor, Sir Gaspard le Marchant, not only liked the scheme, but urged Crampton quickly to put it into effect. Thus encouraged, Crampton authorized the implementation of his plan and soon a small network of British agents fanned out over northeastern United States. Most, adhering to the minister's advice, acted with caution, but others – no doubt imbued with feeling for a cause to which they had committed themselves – made little or no effort to keep a low profile. One New York agent went so far as to advertise for men, while another openly distributed handbills and passed out fare money or tickets. Not unexpectedly, these blatant recruiting techniques soon came to the attention of the public and the incidents were not long being picked up by the press.

As news of the agents' activities became common knowledge, each country reacted as might be expected. To many in Britain, the men were merely doing their duty; to Americans, the recruiting was regarded as an insult to national pride. Hawthorne expressed his own dilemma in a letter to Ticknor. "It is very difficult," he said, "for an American to speak in public in a manner to suit both countries . . . when there is a great deal of hostile feeling towards England on your side of the water, and not a little on the part of England towards us." In philosophical vein, he dared to look into the future. "I shall be true to my country," he said, "and get along with John Bull as well as I can."[2]

In March of 1855, after further reports of British recruiting reached Washington, Secretary of State Marcy called in Minister Crampton and demanded an explanation. The minister assured the secretary that neither he nor any British Consul had done anything in violation of American neutrality. But a few days later, after additional evidence was uncovered in New York, the U.S. District Attorney began an investigation with the approval of the U.S. Attorney General, Caleb Cushing. The findings revealed British complicity.

By May, Crampton was becoming concerned that the recruiting campaign was not going as well as he had hoped. His principal agent, Joseph Howe, was both zealous and secretive in his operations. This air of mystery, which Howe seemed deliberately to foster, was unnecessary in Crampton's view. Although at all times he urged compliance with American law, Crampton thought too much secrecy could only prove counter-productive to the British recruiting drive.[3] Determined to see for himself how the enlistment was proceeding in Canada and Nova Scotia and how the recruiting was faring in Boston and New York, he spent the three last weeks of May on a fact-finding mission. During his wanderings he saw only a handful of recruits, mainly Germans, and now had doubts as to whether the effort was worth the expense and the political risk it entailed.

**PUNCH CARTOON**
When Anglo-American relations deteriorated after British recruitment drives in the United States, *Punch* side-stepped the sovereignty issue and instead had John Bull asking "Come Jonathan, why should we fight – am I not a man, a brother?"

In June Secretary Marcy notified the American Minister in London, James Buchanan, that British agents undoubtedly were at work recruiting American citizens, and most likely with the knowledge of Her Majesty's Government. Two weeks later Buchanan was instructed by Washington to inform the British Foreign Secretary of the known facts, and to ask for an explanation. Meanwhile, several agents had been arrested and brought to trial, but hard evidence was often lacking. The publicity surrounding the trials and the realization by the American public of what was going on in their midst, soon led to bitter feelings against Britain. In London doubts were raised as to whether the alleged agents had, in fact, done anything wrong, and – in any case – why all the sensitivity by the American "cousins?" A full-page cartoon in *Punch* showed John Bull proffering the hand of friendship to Jonathan (Uncle Sam) over the caption, "Come, Jonathan why should we fight – 'Am I not a man, and a brother?'." To make sure its readers got the point, *Punch* supplied its own explanation: "An alleged infraction of International Law by Great Britain, in permitting, in Canada, the enlistment of American citizens under the recently passed Foreign Enlistment Act, caused relations between England and America to become very strained."[4]

Nonetheless, Lord Clarendon was aware that the British public was becoming increasingly sceptical about the enlistment tactics in the United States and on June 22 he wrote Crampton to stop the recruiting programme. It was at this point that the minister in Washington committed the unforgivable error of not complying with instructions from a superior. In replying to Lord Clarendon, Crampton said he was taking no *fresh* initiatives, but that he was allowing two agents – to whom firm promises had been given – to continue until they could deliver the recruits already contacted. Lord Clarendon, however, told Minister Buchanan on July 16 that the recruiting had been stopped; in fact, it continued to the end of the month when Crampton at last ordered all his agents to cease their activities.

James Buchanan, as U.S. Minister in London, was increasingly caught up in the role of "postman," relaying messages between Washington and the British Foreign Office. His preoccupation with the Crampton affair did not prevent him from passing on words of advice to his niece, Harriet Lane, who had returned to the United States in the autumn. "Take good care," he advised, "not to display any foreign airs and graces in society at home nor decant upon your intercourse with titled people. . . . I shall be happy on my return to learn that it has been truly said of you, – 'she has not been a bit spoiled by her visit to England'."[5]

By late 1855 relations had become so cool that some people on both sides of the Atlantic spoke openly of the possibility of war. Hawthorne wisely refrained from putting any war-like thoughts in his diary at this point, but he did write Sophia, then in Lisbon, and Ticknor, in New England, of his feelings. He recounted to Sophia how Julian was preparing for the forthcoming conflict. "Since the war-cloud has begun to darken over us," he said, "he insists on buckling on his sword the moment he is dressed, and never lays it aside till he is ready to go to bed – after drawing it, and making blows and thrusts at Miss Williams' tom-cat for lack of a better antagonist." Hawthorne considered the likelihood of war so great that he pondered the immediate consequences to himself and his family. "One great effect of a war," he said, "would be that I should speedily be warned out of England. . . . But how are we to get home?"[6]

Sophia, removed from the scene of the war scare, did not share Julian's enthusiasm about fighting John Bull. "I am much obliged to you," she wrote back hastily from Lisbon, "for your important conclusions about the war. But not even the prospect of seeing *The Wayside* could make me welcome a war between mother and daughter, as I consider England and America. A daughter, to be sure, quite independent of her mother – married to the eagle, that free citizen of the air – but still inalienably her daughter." Then, in a gentle reproof which was equally intended for her husband, she added: ". . . I trust that neither your sword nor that of any other young or old American will ever find its way to an English heart."[7]

Hawthorne's letters to Ticknor document his distaste for war on one hand, and his intense patriotism on the other. "We have all been in commotion here, for a fortnight past [November, 1855], in expectation of a war," he said, "but the peaceful tenor of the last accounts from America have gone far towards quieting us. No man would be justified in wishing for war, but I trust America will not bate an inch of honor for the sake of avoiding it. . . . I HATE England, though I love some Englishmen, and like them generally, in fact."[8] Here Hawthorne was making a fine distinction. He despised the government of England, which he felt was dominated by the country's aristocracy and was not representative of the popular will. Yet, he was prepared to like individual Englishmen – even aristocratic ones. Thus the Crampton affair did not diminish Hawthorne's respect for his English friends and acquaintances, or his sincere desire to see war thwarted.

Through his letters to Sophia in Portugal, Nathaniel kept his family posted on the war rumours. After Sophia's New England friend, the Rev. William Channing, called at the consulate one day and spoke in surprisingly belligerent terms, Hawthorne hastened to inform Sophia. ". . . thou wouldst be (as I am)," he said, "at once confounded and delighted to hear the warlike tone in which he talks. He thinks that the Government of England is trying to force us into a war and he says, in so many words, LET IT COME ! ! !" Then he told Sophia about the latest report circulating in England. "There was a rumor yesterday," he said, "that our minister had demanded his passports, and I am mistaken in Frank Pierce if Mr. Crampton has not already been ejected from Washington."[9]

**BARBARITY IN AMERICA**
At the height of the Crampton affair *Punch* printed this cartoon depicting life in an American hotel. At gunpoint, a guest shouts "Pass the mustard!"

Indeed, as more facts about Crampton's involvement in the recruiting emerged, the British public came to doubt the propriety of its government. People were far from satisfied with the few, rather reluctant statements it issued. Now Hawthorne had a new thought: the British people might be led into a war by their government which they neither wanted, nor believed they could win. His next letter to Ticknor reflected this thinking. "The English people will not let their Government go to war with us," he said, "not from any liking of America, but from a wholesome apprehension of the consequences. This feeling is very manifest, all over the country."[10]

On December 28, 1855, the Crampton question reached a critical stage when Secretary of State Marcy prepared a letter for Minister Buchanan to read out before Lord Clarendon in London. After outlining Crampton's involvement in the recruiting programme, the letter categorically stated that "his connection with that affair has rendered him as an unacceptable representative of Her Majesty near this Government."[11] The letter ended by asking Buchanan to request the recall of Crampton and the British Consuls in New York City, Philadelphia, and Cincinnati. Marcy followed up the official letter with a personal one to Buchanan. "I really believe," he told Buchanan, ". . . [Lord Clarendon] does not know how offensively British officers have behaved in this recruiting business . . . We are willing – more – anxious to be on friendly terms with our 'transatlantic cousins,' but they must recollect that we do not believe in the doctrine of primogeniture. The younger branch of the family has equal rights with the elder."[12]

After hearing the contents of the American letter demanding the recall of Crampton and three British Consuls, Lord Clarendon expressed astonishment and bluntly refused to act as requested. He said he would wait to hear Crampton's side of the story before deciding on his next course of action. While Clarendon's inaction was a rebuff to the United States, it had the effect of calming tempers in Britain. "There has been a marked and favorable change of feeling here within the last month toward the United States," reported Minister Buchanan on February 29, 1856. "I am now made something of a lion wherever I go, and I go much into society as a matter of duty."[13] But Buchanan was to relinquish his ministerial position and be succeeded by George M. Dallas, an experienced politician who also had been U.S. Minister to Russia and Vice President under President James K. Polk. Dallas arrived in London with high hopes of resolving the issues growing out of the disputed

**LORD CLARENDON**
The British Foreign Secretary was the central figure in the war scare that erupted out of the Crampton affair. Although Crampton had been declared *personna non grata* by the United States, Clarendon stopped short of direct retaliation, thereby easing tensions in both countries.

Clayton-Bulwer Treaty, but the Crampton question was entirely to dominate his first days in London.

Meanwhile, news of the Crampton recall demand eventually became public knowledge, and some wondered if the United States had over-played its hand and would now have to back down. At this stage the correspondence passing between Washington and London was anything but cordial, but the general public was unaware of this and many people assumed the controversy was being disposed of amicably behind the scenes. Hawthorne himself now became optimistic of a peaceful outcome, and so told Ticknor. "The war-talk has entirely died away," he wrote on March 1, "and I hope, on the American side of the water, we shall say nothing more about fighting unless we really mean to come to the scratch."[14] A few weeks later, after having seen the new American Minister, George M. Dallas, his old fears returned. In pessimistic terms he told Sophia, now in Madeira, of his latest feelings. "Dost thou know that we are going to have a war?" he asked. "It is now quite certain and I hope I shall be ordered out of the country in season to meet thee in Madeira. Dost thou not believe me?"[15] His assumption that he was on the verge of being dismissed was well founded, for if the United States expelled Minister Crampton and three British Consuls, it would have followed that the British government would ask the American Minister and three American Consuls to depart. In that event the consul at Liverpool – the busiest in the United Kingdom – would certainly have been among those sent packing.

Due largely to chance, Hawthorne was about to be thrust into the unexpected role of peace-maker. In the first half of April he at last realized his dream of visiting London unencumbered by family. But after a week of sightseeing he appealed to his friend, Francis Bennoch, for suggestions as to how best to spend his time. Bennoch recalled that an old friend, Captain Shaw, was then serving with the North Cork Rifles at Aldershot Camp. He hurriedly arranged with Shaw for Hawthorne and himself to visit the camp. The timing was shrewd for two reasons: Hawthorne, as author, was known and appreciated in British literary circles and, secondly, Hawthorne, the friend of Britain, could not have chosen a better time to allow himself to be exposed before influential Englishmen. There is nothing to suggest that Bennoch, either alone or with Hawthorne's consent, concocted a deliberate campaign to foster Anglo-American amity at this moment of bitter relations between the two English-speaking countries. On the other hand, Bennoch's deep friendship with Hawthorne and his own liking for the United States, very likely led him to arrange functions at which the consul's positive views would receive sympathetic hearings.

Certainly the choice of Aldershot Camp as a place to visit in late March, had to be made

## ALDERSHOT CAMP

"Of all discomfortable places," the consul said, "I am inclined to reckon Aldershot camp the worst." Nonetheless, Hawthorne found the officers there "really gentlemen, . . . courteous, kind, most hospitable."

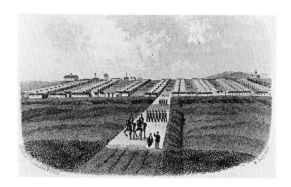

on grounds other than its scenic value. Hawthorne's first impression of the camp was dismal enough – "a large city composed of numberless wooden barracks, arranged in regular streets, on a wide bleak heath, with an extensive and dreary aspect on all sides." Captain Shaw did his best for Hawthorne by assigning him a room in his own hut. Small and by no means airtight, the room let the sharp wind enter freely. ". . . of all discomfortable places," the consul said, "I am inclined to reckon Aldershot camp the worst."[16]

That evening Hawthorne and Bennoch were guests of honour at a superb dinner given by the Colonel of the Regiment. Hawthorne liked the officers – all of them Irish – and reasoned, because of their chosen profession, that they deserved the finest of food and drink. But living among them, he imagined, would be a bore. ". . . they have no thought, no intellectual movement, no ideas, that I was aware of, beyond horses, dogs, drill, garrison, field days, whist, women, wine, cigars, and all that kind of miscellany; yet they were really gentlemen, living on the best terms with one another, courteous, kind, most hospitable, with a rich Irish humor, softened down by social refinement . . ."[17]

Only the warmest sympathies were expressed by the officers toward the United States, but when it came to France "there was no real friendliness."[18] When the time came to play the traditional national anthem in honour of a visiting dignitary, the Colonel apologized that "Hail Columbia" was not within the capability of the band. Instead, he said, they would play a few melodies which, he hoped, would suffice. "It was really funny," Hawthorne said, "that the 'wood notes wild' of . . . poor black slaves should have been played, in a foreign land, as an honorable compliment to one of their white countrymen." Hawthorne and Bennoch spent two nights at the camp, and during neither were they able to get much sleep. ". . . I don't wonder," Hawthorne said, "[that] these gentlemen sit up as long as they can keep their eyes open, for never was anything so utterly comfortless as their camp-beds."[19]

He also learned, comfortable beds or otherwise, that the Army does not intend to sleep long. ". . . almost as soon as I did close my eyes," he said, "the bugles sounded, the drums beat reveille, and from that moment the camp was all astir . . ." The Aldershot visit ended with Hawthorne and Bennoch viewing an exercise staged by upwards of 12,000 troops and in which the Duke of Cambridge was the central figure. Throughout the visit the officers with whom Hawthorne spoke had expressed the warmest sympathies towards the United States. "For my part," he said, "I fraternized with these military gentlemen in a way that augurs the very best things for the future peace of the two countries."[20]

Meanwhile, the Crampton affair remained unresolved as it seemed Lord Clarendon had no intention of recalling his minister. By now the British public was aware that the nature of the Foreign Secretary's next act might very well spell the difference between war and peace. Whether or not Francis Bennoch shared the same anxiety is not known, but he did set in motion an intensive social programme for Hawthorne during the remainder of the consul's London stay. Within the space of a few days Hawthorne was to be seen and heard by a large number of the most influential residents of the capital, including editors and writers with access to some of England's important newspapers and journals.

With the auspicious premises of the Milton Club as the locale, Hawthorne's first function was a dinner attended by about sixteen prominent Londoners – most of them editors, publishers, and literary figures. Those present included Herbert Ingram whose voice was heard in two forums – Parliament, and the pages of the *Illustrated London News*, which he owned. Dr. Charles Mackay, the editor of the *Illustrated London News*, also was present, as was William Howitt, editor of *Howitt's Journal*, and S. C. Hall, well known author and editor of the *Art Union Journal*. Martin Tupper, who had written the immensely popular *Proverbial Philosophy*, also was there. So, too, was Captain Shaw from the camp at Aldershot.

"It was a good dinner," said Hawthorne of the meal at the Milton Club, "[with an] abundance of wine which Bennoch sent round faster than was for the next day's comfort of his guests." When the cloth was taken away Bennoch made a warm speech in praise of Hawthorne, after which other members of the group joined in. ". . . I was done entirely brown," Hawthorne said, "Certainly, if I never get any more soft soap in my life, I have had enough of it for once." But praise for the consul brought on the inevitable obligation for a response. "I made another little bit of speech . . .," he said, "in response to something that was said in reference to the present difficulties between England and America, and ended with (as proof that I deemed war impossible) drinking success to the British Army and calling on my friend Lieutenant [sic] Shaw of the Aldershot Camp to reply. I am afraid I must have said something very wrong, for the applause was vociferous and I could hear them whispering about the table, 'Good! Good!' 'Yes! He is a fine fellow!' – and other such ill-earned praises . . ."[21]

The Hawthorne–Bennoch "team" had effectively placed on record, before persons bound to put their views in print or in public assemblies, the peaceful sentiments of one of the most prominent Americans resident in Britain. Dr. Mackay was the first of the group to comment on the Crampton issue after the Milton Club dinner. In the very next issue of the *Illustrated London News* he pled for broader understanding. "We trust," he said, "that . . . the good sense and good feeling existent on both sides of the Atlantic will preserve the world from so fratricidal a catastrophe as war."[22]

That same evening Hawthorne had another chance to demonstrate his spirit of good-will. An editorial writer of *The Times*, Eneas Dallas, and another staff member, invited Hawthorne to a late supper at the home of Dallas. Much of the evening was spent in discussing the unique characteristics of the London paper and some of the great men connected with it. Hawthorne had his own view of *The Times'* success secret. "Every sensible man in England," he said, "finds his own commonsense there . . ." Dallas' wife, the actress Isabella Glyn, amused the consul when she said she had read *The House of the Seven Gables* thirteen years before. ". . . I thought [this] remarkable," he said, "because I did not write it till eight or nine years afterwards."[23]

Herbert Ingram, the publisher-parliamentarian, invited Hawthorne to dine in the refectory of the House of Commons. He accepted and much enjoyed being in the company of British lawmakers. He did not speak with, but saw Benjamin Disraeli at a nearby table.[24]

Now came the highlight of the consul's London adventures and the one at which he would make the greatest impact for a peaceful resolution of the dispute which had brought

**THE LORD MAYOR**
Sir David Salomons was the first Jewish Lord Mayor; he later represented Greenwich in the House of Commons for 14 years. Hawthorne considered Salomons "a rather hearty man."

Britain and America to the brink of war. The occasion, one which any visiting foreigner would relish, was the Easter Banquet of London's Lord Mayor. The event was historic in itself for the host, David Salomons, was the city's first Jewish Lord Mayor. Salomons, who later was knighted, was elected to the House of Commons in 1851 but was refused a seat because Jews were then barred. His dramatic defiance of the Speaker on that occasion drew public attention to the anti-Semitic provision which eventually was thrown out; Salomons went on to represent Greenwich in the House for fourteen years (1859–1873).[25]

Bennoch very probably told Hawthorne of Salomons' civil rights crusade, thus adding to the interest of the evening. But it was neither Salomons' renown nor the banquet itself that most excited the consul. "Tonight," he wrote Sophia hastily, "I am to dine with the Lord Mayor and shall have to make a speech!!" As an after-thought, he added: "Good Heavens! I wish I might have been spared this."[26] City of London archives do not show that Minister Dallas was present at the banquet.

Hawthorne, apprehensive about speaking at all, no doubt was now concerned about the appropriateness of his remarks which he instinctively knew would reflect his Anglo-American sympathies. Although truly in a difficult position, he momentarily put aside his worry and determined to enjoy the dinner – easily the most elaborate social function of his stay in Britain.

He arrived at the Mansion House with Bennoch at six-thirty and for the better part of five hours was treated to a glorious spectacle of pomp and culinary delight. The guests were received, Hawthorne noted, "by some of the most gorgeously dressed footmen I ever saw. Their livery is blue and buff and they look something like American revolutionary generals, only far more splendid." Two others, attired in scarlet coats, helped the guests to find seats. "... there is a great deal of state and ceremony in this place of the city-king," Hawthorne said, "and the Mansion House is worthy of its inhabitants ..."[27]

In the receiving line he was introduced to David Salomons and the Lady Mayoress. Hawthorne found Salomons "a rather hearty man," but was momentarily taken aback when the Lord Mayor reminded him that he should be prepared to respond to the toast. "... though I hinted that I would much rather be spared," Hawthorne said, "he showed no signs of mercy."[28]

Soon he encountered the famous husband-and-wife writing team, Mr. and Mrs. S. C. Hall, who introduced him to various of their friends who were present. It was agreed that Mrs. Hall would sit next to Hawthorne during the dinner. After the blessing was said, the meal began with turtle soup. "The rest of the meal," he said, ". . . was very good, and of variety enough, though not better than those given by the Mayors of Liverpool . . ." Hawthorne's attention was soon drawn to a remarkable young lady, the sister-in-law of the Lord Mayor, who sat nearly opposite him across the table. She seemed, he said, "to be of pure white marble, yet not white, but the purest and finest complexion . . that I ever beheld. Her hair was a wonderful deep, raven black . . . hair never to be painted, nor described . . ." The girl's beauty left Hawthorne incapable of description. ". . . all her features," he said, "were so fine that sculpture seemed a despicable art beside her, and certainly my pen is good for nothing."[29] When Hawthorne came to write *The Marble Faun*, the picture of the beautiful Jewess flooded back into his memory; in the book she becomes the strikingly lovely Miriam.

When the guests had finished dinner the Lord Mayor introduced the notables present – among them Hawthorne. Then, according to ancient custom, two loving cups were passed among the guests. Each person had to remove the cover and take a sip before passing it on to his neighbour. Most guests, Hawthorne noted, only pretended to drink, but when the cup reached him, he sampled the contents. "[I] found it to be claret, spiced and sweetened, and hardly preferable to sweetened water," he said. Then came a series of toasts, that phase of the proceedings Hawthorne most feared since his name was among those obliged to respond. He tried desperately to think of something appropriate. His near-neighbour, S. C. Hall, suggested "a whole rivulet of lukewarm stuff, which I saw would be sufficiently to the purpose."[30] Hall, writing later in his memoirs, relates how he offered a solution to Hawthorne's nervousness. "I said to him," Hall recalled, "Now, if you attend to me, you may be safe from all apprehension, and be sure to make a good speech. When you hear your name and I take the glass in my hand and drink the toast, *look only at me:* do not turn your eyes towards the lord mayor or on any one of the magnates. Consider you are thanking *only me* for the honour done you'."[31]

The Lord Mayor then began some remarks which, Hawthorne noted, were aimed at him. ". . . after paying me some high compliments in reference to my works (I don't believe he ever read a word of them)," he said, "he drank prosperity to my country, and my own health, which was received with great applause." With that the band played "Hail Columbia" and Hawthorne's moment had come. ". . . I arose amid much cheering, so screwed up to the point that I did not care what happened next. The Lord Mayor might have fired a pistol, instead of a speech at me, and I should not have flinched." He started off by using some of Hall's "flummery," and added a few points of his own. As usual on such occasions, he was interrupted frequently by interjections and applause. He admitted it was "a very tolerable little speech" which had been helped along by the kind cheers. "It is wonderful," he said, "how conscious the speaker is of sympathy, and how it warms and animates him."[32] On resuming his seat Hawthorne was roundly congratulated by the Halls and Bennoch – and by other people later in the evening.

If Hawthorne's response was both short and spontaneous, it contained several sentences which pleased those of his listeners who still feared a war. "There was never yet a moment," he said, "when America was not ready to extend her hand to meet the hand of England outstretched in earnestness and good faith. It would be strange, indeed, if it were not so, for Providence had connected the two countries by indissoluble ties." The next sentence may well have struck some present as being an official American declaration of

The Right Hon. David Salomons, Lord Mayor,

MANSION HOUSE.

**MONDAY, APRIL 7th, 1856.**

TURTLE SOUP.

TURBOT.            SALMON.            RED MULLET À LA GÉNÉVOISE.
SLICES OF CODFISH AU GRATIN.            FRIED SMELTS.
DORY À L'ITALIENNE.

COTELETTES DE MOUTON AUX CONCOMBRES.
RIS DE VEAU AUX ÉPINARDS.            FRICASSÉ DE POULET AUX TRUFFES.
VOL-AU-VENT AUX HUÎTRES.
COMPOTE DE PIGEONS À LA MARÉCHALE.
BOUDIN DE PTARMIGAN À L'ESSENCE.

CHICKENS À LA TOULOUSE.            QUARTERS OF HOUSE LAMB.
CHINES OF MUTTON.            BOILED PULLETS.            TONGUES.
ROAST CHICKENS.            ALOYAUX DE BŒUF À LA JARDINIÈRE.
ROAST CAPONS.

PEA FOWL.            GOSLINGS.            GUINEA FOWLS.            WILD DUCKS.

MUSHROOMS À LA BORDELAISE.
HARICOTS VERTS À LA MAÎTRE D'HÔTEL.

GELÉE À LA DAUPHINE.            BLANCMANGER.
SUÉDOISE D'ORANGES.            CRÈME À L'ITALIENNE.            NOYEAU JELLY.
RHUBARBE À LA RÉGENCE.            MADEIRA JELLY.
PASTRY.            CHEESECAKES.

ICE PUDDING.            SIR WATKIN PUDDING.            GINGER PUDDING.
COMPOTES DE FRUITS.

ICES.

RASPBERRY.            GINGER.            RATAFIA CREAM.
LEMON WATER.            ORANGE WATER.

J. & C. STAPLES.            THE ALBION.

**MENU OF THE LORD MAYOR'S EASTER BANQUET**
"There is a great deal of state and ceremony in this place of the city-king," said Hawthorne.

intent regarding the Crampton issue. "There never was yet," Hawthorne went on, "a kind word spoken, or a kind action performed by an Englishman towards an American that the American was not ready to respond by an action, or a word at least as kind, if not more so." The consul ended his brief response with a vow that "friendly relations between the two nations could never be broken." Loud cheers and cries of "Hear! Hear!" erupted, to Hawthorne's embarrassment.[33]

Mackay printed the consul's words in the next issue of the *Illustrated London News* and so did some of London's dailies and the country's provincial weeklies. If any literate Englishmen previously had feared America's intentions, Hawthorne's words seemed the assurance that moderation would prevail. On reflection, Hawthorne wondered if he had overdone the peace-making emphasis of his remarks. "I should not care for England," he said, "but America will read it, too."[34] For the time being the consul's and Bennoch's efforts to calm British public opinion was over. In the space of a fortnight Hawthorne had made his points eloquently, first at a military garrison, then at a respected club, next to a gathering of prominent journalists, and finally, at the Lord Mayor's banquet.

But had the extending of the olive branch been noticed by British officialdom? It appeared not, for there was only silence from the Foreign Office. Then, suddenly on April 30, Minister Dallas was summoned by Lord Clarendon. The Foreign Secretary's attitude was conciliatory, but his position was an unyielding as ever. He told Dallas he had now received, and studied, reports from Crampton and the accused British Consuls in the United States, and had concluded there was nothing to justify their recall. Minister Dallas returned to the American Legation, deeply disappointed. He realized he had no choice but to report the Foreign Secretary's statement and attitude exactly as he had understood them, whatever the consequences.

American ire was now at boiling point and within thirty days Secretary of State Marcy, invoking the name of President Pierce, dismissed Crampton as minister and at the same time revoked the exequaturs of three British Consuls. The American response, however, was mildly worded; it accepted Clarendon's statement that Britain had never *intended* to violate American neutrality, but made clear that four of Her Majesty's diplomats had, in fact, violated the law.

First news of the dismissal reached Britain through a passenger arriving aboard the *America* early in June. His comment, carried in the *London Globe*, was treated as a rumour by *The Times* in its June 6 issue. ". . . we have every reason," it said, "to disbelieve the announcement that so grave a circumstance [as Crampton's dismissal] has actually occurred."[35] Other newspapers wrote in much the same vein, causing Dallas to communicate immediately his concern to Secretary Marcy. "The dread of a war with the United States," he said, "is very general; and the two great interests, manufacturing and mercantile, are beginning to bestir themselves to prevent it if they can."[36] To a friend, to whom he wrote the same day, he was more candid about his own prospects. "If *The Times* and *Post* are reliable organs," he said, "I shall probably quit England soon, *never* to return . . . It will not surprise me if I should turn out to be the last minister from the United States to the British Court, and that will certainly be fame if not honour."[37] When the British government confirmed that Crampton's dismissal was indeed fact, to many war seemed inevitable.

Whatever Clarendon thought of Crampton's innocence, not all British politicians agreed. A letter, signed by "A Statesman," and published in the June 9 issue of *The Times*, put in print what many others no doubt thought. "Some persons believe, and many fear," it began, "that war between Great Britain and the United States will be the upshot of the wily expedients, flat contradictions, and sharp practice which, growing out of . . . the recruiting scheme, have lately kept the reflecting, moral, industrious, and really responsible portions of two great communities in a state of wonderment bordering upon terror . . . The truth, in my opinion, is that Mr. Crampton was not up to his work."[38]

Did the British people now believe that America was ready to do battle? *The Times* assumed so, for on June 11 it reprinted a terse comment from the New York *Tribune* which stated flatly: "We have a foreign war close upon us."[39] But the following day the same newspaper expressed the hope that the American government would not "push the point to such an extremity as would force upon us an appeal to the sword."[40]

The new question on everyone's mind was, would Britain retaliate by dismissing Minister Dallas? He had no doubts about this possibility himself and asked Secretary Marcy "precisely the wishes of yourself and the President in regard to my course of action, should . . . I be dismissed in turn."[41] Hawthorne, in a letter to Ticknor shortly after Crampton left Washington, that "most people think Dallas will be sent home and I believe he is himself very uneasy."[42]

*Punch* came to the defence of Lord Clarendon and Minister Crampton with a satirical article entitled, "A Challenge to America." Ostensibly a dare to the United States, in reality it sought to frighten Americans from going to war by emphasizing the gory side of the expected conflict. "Let us quarrel, American kinsmen," it said. "Let us plunge into war. We have been friends too long." Then, after pointing out the immense damage which a war would bring to each country's shipping, banks, towns and property, it catalogued the horrors of war. "Let us maim and mutilate one another!" it said, "let us make of each other miserable objects, cripples, halt, and blind adapted . . . to beg during life. Come, let us render the wives of each other widows, and the mothers childless, and cause them to weep rivers of tears. . . . Oh, how good it is – oh, how pleasant it is for brethren to engage in internecine strife!"[43]

The *Punch* diatribe ended, not with a defence of Crampton, but with a bitter denunciation of President Pierce and Caleb Cushing, the Attorney General who had conducted the investigation of Crampton's activities. ". . . Let us murder and ruin each other," it exhorted, "to suit the purposes of MR. PRESIDENT PIERCE. Let PIERCE, with CUSHING by his side, come hot from their conclave of evil spirits, cry havoc, and let slip the dogs of war, and do you be mad enough to be those mad dogs and permit yourselves to be hounded upon us by MR. PIERCE."[44]

The respected *Quarterly Review*, while denouncing the Foreign Enlistment Act, deplored the deterioration of relations between the two countries. "We will not disguise from the Americans," it said, "that these late events have tended greatly to alienate the affection which it is in the nature of Englishmen to feel towards those of a common origin and speaking the English language in a commonwealth governed by free laws."[45] *Blackwood's*, in a long essay about the dispute, concluded: "the best preventive of war is to be prepared for it. The better prepared we are, the more peaceful-minded will be our American brethren. Therefore we would say to our Government, do not be in such a haste to reduce your armaments; you may need them sooner than you imagine."[46]

The British Parliament, meanwhile, continued to debate the Crampton affair and, under increasing pressure from its own members, forced the Foreign Office to release more and more of the unsavoury details about the crude recruitment efforts. As new facts emerged, it became clear that Crampton's actions were indefensible. Disraeli seemed to speak for many when he asserted publicly: "I think . . . it would be wise if England would at last recognize that the United States, like all the great countries of Europe, have a policy, and that they

**SECRETARY OF STATE MARCY**
After Lord Clarendon refused to recall Minister Crampton it fell to Marcy to dismiss the minister and three British consuls in the United States.

have a right to have a policy."[47] This pronouncement, and others like it, led the British government to hestitate about dismissing Dallas. By June 10 no declaration of war had been made, and Dallas wrote optimistically to Secretary Marcy: "I do not think the [foreign] ministry will make a further stand and hazard a war, in defense of a person now proved so unworthy. If they do, Parliament will drive them from their places."[48] When Clarendon continued to keep silent about his next move, Hawthorne, too, assumed Dallas would be allowed to remain in London. Gleefully he wrote Ticknor his view on June 20.

"You see," he said, "I was right in my opinion that Dallas would not be sent home. We have gained a great triumph over England and I begin to like her better now. . . . We have gone through a crisis and come out right side up. Give Frank Pierce credit for this, at least, for it was his spirit that did it."[49] On the same day he wrote in similar vein to Horatio Bridge. ". . . the course of our Government," he said, "deserves all praise, and the result is a triumph that will be felt and recognized long hereafter. Frank has brought us safely and honorably through a great crisis, and England begins now to understand her own position and ours, and will never again assume the tone which hitherto she has always held towards us."[50]

For the first time since the crisis had erupted, Minister Dallas had reason to believe he would not be sent home. On June 20 he wrote Secretary Marcy that the press was lining up solidly behind the American viewpoint. "Even the newspapers, The *Times* and the *Post*," he said, "are slowly but obviously retreating from the positions they have heretofore so audaciously maintained."[51] Clarendon's own retreat came on June 26 when he wrote Minister Dallas in reply to the formal notification about the dismissed British diplomats. His note, again conciliatory, implied that Dallas' continued presence in London would be sanctioned.

Dallas established something of a record by remaining as his country's principal representative in the United Kingdom during the rest of Franklin Pierce's term, throughout the administration of James Buchanan, and for two months of Abraham Lincoln's presidency. Crampton, meanwhile, saw his name go into a standard work of reference, *The Dictionary of English History*, when that volume accorded him a paragraph under the heading, "The Crampton Question."[52] His career, however, was unaffected by the episode; he was given a knighthood the same year and went on to become his country's Minister to Hanover the following year.

# XIV
# The Lion of Liverpool

Whether Hawthorne liked it or not, he was the foremost social lion of Liverpool during his years as consul. The commercial community sought him out because he was the official representative of the nation with whom most of Liverpool's trade was conducted. The wives of the town's prominent families were eager to make him the main attraction of their elaborate dinners. Four successive Liverpool mayors were pleased when he attended their civic functions either as consul or as popular author. Added to these demands was the traditional custom of ship owners and ships' masters of inviting the American Consul aboard their vessels for meals.

Thus the man who arrived in Liverpool with a reputation for extreme shyness and a pronounced dislike for public speaking found himself in a situation which demanded constant public exposure. By moving to Rock Ferry across the River Mersey he hoped to reduce the obligations on his private life, but – except for fewer functions in the evening – invitations continued unabated throughout his consulship. He struggled hard to overcome his fear of speaking in public and, much to his surprise, was to acquit himself well, as his journal, correspondence, and press accounts attest.

On August 5, 1853, less than a week after taking over the consulate, Hawthorne received an invitation to dine with the mayor of Liverpool at the Town Hall. His instant reaction was of apprehension. "I had rather dine at the humblest eating-cellar in the city," he said in his journal, "inasmuch as a speech will doubtless be expected from me. However, things must be as they may."[1]

Promptly at seven on the evening of the dinner, Hawthorne turned up to find a large number of judges already assembled, for the repast was being given mainly in their honour. He was fascinated by the ceremonial side of this, his first, mayoral affair. "Nothing struck me more than the footmen in the city-livery," he noted, "they really looked more magnificent, in their gold-lace and breeches, and white silk stockings, than any officers of state whom I have ever seen." The speaking began with the mayor offering several toasts, the first to Queen Victoria. "And by-and-by," Hawthorne continued, "came a toast to the United States and me as their representative." Then the band played some American national tune – what, he could not quite make out – after which everyone turned to him for a response. "They received me and listened to my nonsense with a great deal of rapping," he said, "and my speech seemed to give great satisfaction. . . . I hardly thought it was in me, but once being on my legs, I felt no embarrassment, and went through it as coolly as if I were going to be hanged."[2]

Hawthorne was understandably more at ease at private dinner parties which were less formal. He accepted many such invitations during his four years, some intended for him alone while others included Sophia. The first affair occurred during Hawthorne's hectic first week in office, his host being William Barber, president of the American Chamber of Commerce. He invited the Hawthornes to dinner at his home, Poulton Hall, not far from Rock Ferry, where the family was to take hotel rooms until a house could be found. He also mentioned that he could provide a pleasant ride in his carriage. Hawthorne misunderstood and thought the invitation was only for the ride. When the appointed day (a Sunday) came, the Hawthornes were in the midst of dinner when Mr. Barber arrived in his carriage. When the embarrassing error was explained, Hawthorne agreed that the family should immediately leave with Mr. Barber in his carriage. Sophia, in a letter to a relative afterwards, described the carriage as "a chariot . . . with a coachman as straight as a lightning-rod."[3] Poulton Hall and its grounds made a great impression upon the Hawthornes, no doubt abetted by Mr. Barber's accounts of ancient legends and ghost-stories associated with the house.

Barber was typical of the group of Liverpool merchants belonging to the American Chamber of Commerce. Unmarried but with two sisters to keep house for him, he had lived for several years in New Orleans. Now a successful merchant, he had the undoubted advantage of knowing a great deal about cotton production in the southern states, and in particular about the shipment of bales from the port of New Orleans.

The Hawthornes, once arrived at Poulton Hall, were left to roam the grounds while Barber and his other guests had their meal. "By-and-by a footman, looking very quaint and queer in his livery-coat, drab breeches, and white stockings, came to invite me to the table," Hawthorne said. There he found Barber, his two sisters, and the guests sitting before an array of fruit and wine. "There was port, sherry, madeira, and one bottle of claret, all very good," said Hawthorne, "but they addict themselves, here, to much heavier wines than we now drink in America." The delightful interlude at Poulton Hall, coming as it did after the family's initial unsettled period in Liverpool, cheered up the Hawthornes. "Mr. Barber and his sisters," he said, "have shown us genuine kindness, and they give us a hearty invitation to come and ramble over the house, whenever we please, during their absence in Scotland."[4]

A few weeks later Hawthorne was invited to dinner at the home of another Liverpool merchant to meet two sons of Robert Burns. About a dozen people were present, but all eyes were turned on the sons, both seasoned Indian Army officers. One was persuaded to sing a song of his father's, a feat he performed well and with good humour. "I liked them both," Hawthorne said, "and they liked me."[5] Among the guests that evening were Mr. and Mrs. Charles Holland of Liscard Vale, near Liverpool. They promptly invited the Hawthornes to dinner two weeks later.

The visit to the Hollands was the first elaborate social affair for Sophia, and she described it at length in her correspondence home. "The table was very handsome;" she noted "two enormous silver dishcovers, with the gleam of Damascus blades, putting out all the rest of the light." After a fish course the table was cleared. Sophia was then amazed at the variety of meats offered during the main course: "A boiled turkey . . . before Mrs. Holland, . . . a roasted goose before Mr. Holland, and in the intermediate spaces, cutlets, fricassées, ragouts, tongue, chicken-pies, and many things whose names I did not know, and on a side-table a boiled round of beef as large as the dome of St. Peter's." She was equally ecstatic about the pastry, and other features of the meal. "The wines," she said, "were port, sherry, madeira, claret, hock, and champagne. I refused the five first, but the champagne was poured into my glass without any question." After a session of lively conversation, the evening ended with coffee, served separately for the ladies in the drawing room. Here Sophia much admired the "exquisite little china cups all flowers and gold."[6]

Twice during the first half of 1854 Hawthorne attended dinners at the home of a former Liverpool Mayor, John Bramley-Moore. On the first occasion Bramley-Moore took trouble to serve an American speciality, delectable prairie-hen. "It was a most delicate bird," Hawthorne said, "and a gentleman carved it most skilfully to a dozen guests and still had a second slice to offer."[7] At the second dinner Hawthorne gave the former mayor high marks

**LIVERPOOL'S TOWN HALL**

As befitted the town's maritime importance, Liverpool mayors were given generous allowances for entertaining the merchants and commercial leaders who had brought prosperity to Merseyside. Few provincial towns could match Liverpool's excellence on these ceremonial occasions.

again for his "eatables and drinkables," but was sometimes annoyed by his host's habit of stating the price of everything he possessed.[8]

As the months went by, there were other invitations – sometimes to the homes of Liverpool's merchant princes, sometimes to the Brights and other friends. As these social occasions became commonplace, Hawthorne and Sophia referred to them less frequently in their letters. One result of partaking so frequently of fine English fare was the consul's robust appearance. ". . . from the compliments which I receive about my healthy aspect . . .," he said, "I am getting a little too John Bullish and must diminish my allowance of roast beef, brown-stout, port and sherry. I never felt better in my life. England is certainly the country to eat in, and to drink in."[9]

Hawthorne's first recorded repast aboard a ship, the *James Baines*, was in October of 1854. Six months earlier this ship, and others made by the American shipbuilder, Donald Mackay, were the subject of an inquiry initiated by Hawthorne. Mackay's firm built six clipper ships for James Baines and Company of Liverpool, among them the *James Baines*. The transaction appeared to Hawthorne to be illegal, but after investigation by the State Department and officials of U.S. courts, no irregularities were uncovered, and the sale was allowed to proceed.[10]

The *déjeuner* marked the passing of the ship from the American to the British flag, and was a major social event for Liverpool's maritime community. Hawthorne observed that the *James Baines* was both a splendid vessel and magnificently fitted, "though not with consummate taste." He estimated that between four and five hundred people had been invited, for whom tables were set up between decks in the space where berths were later to be installed. Unfortunately the day was overcast and the lighting poor, but – Hawthorne noted – "the cheer was very good." There were cold fowl and cold pies, wines of several varieties, and champagne. He had been told he would be called on to respond to a toast, and this intelligence left him somewhat unsettled. He confided his nervousness to a Mrs. Schomberg, who sat next to him, but she treated his concern lightly. She persuaded him to laugh over his predicament which, Hawthorne admitted, "was good for me, inasmuch as . . . I came to regard it in a light and ludicrous way, and so, when the time actually came, I stood up with a careless, dare-devil feeling, being indeed, rather pot-valiant with champagne."[11]

After the customary loyal toast, the health of the American President was drunk. Turning to Hawthorne for the response, the chairman referred to him as "great by his position under the Republic – greater still, I am bold to say, in the Republic of letters!!" Hawthorne ignored "this dole of soft-sodder" and went on to thank the assembled company, on behalf of the president, and added a few more remarks "with no very decided point to them." To his astonishment and pleasure, everyone cheered and applauded during which he seized the chance to sit down. Then, in a rare admission, he confessed to a certain satisfaction in giving the remarks. ". . . after sitting down," he said, "I was conscious of an enjoyment in speaking to a public assembly, and felt as if I should like to rise again; it is something like being under fire – a sort of excitement, not exactly pleasure, but more piquant than most pleasures . . ." The following day Hawthorne noted that the Liverpool papers had reported the luncheon. One sentence from his remarks was bound to warm the hearts of any devotee of Anglo-American relations: "No good thing could happen on one side of the Atlantic without having an equally good effect upon the other, no advancement in the arts of life could take place in one country without being equally made by the other . . ."[12]

In February of 1855 Hawthorne was again an honoured guest at the Liverpool Town Hall. In his journal he gave an interesting sidelight on the cost of the mayoral banquets. "[A Mayor] is supposed to spend much more than his salary on these entertainments," he said. "The Town provides the wines, I am told . . . Each Mayor might lay in a supply of the best vintage he could find and trust his good name with posterity to the credit of that wine, and so he would be kindly and warmly remembered, long after his own nose had lost its rubicundity. In point of fact, the wines seem to be good, but not remarkable."[13]

Hawthorne bemoaned the fact, on this occasion as on many others, that the prospect of an agreeable dinner was somewhat offset by his obligation to reply to a toast. "The Mayor toasted me by name," Hawthorne said, ". . . whereupon, I got upon my legs and responded for my country rather more decidedly than I might have found in my conscience to do, anywhere save at an English Mayor's table." On this occasion Hawthorne experienced the same mixture of elation and uneasiness which marked some of his previous speeches. "After sitting down," he said, "as usual, I felt that there might be great enjoyment in public speaking, but while up my great object is to get down again as soon as possible."[14]

Two months later (April, 1855), the John Baines Company received another American-made ship, this time christened the *Donald Mackay* after its builder. As in the case of the *John Baines*, an elaborate *déjeuner* was served to the guests. Hawthorne sat at the table of honour, which meant he would again be called upon during the after-dinner toasts. "It would have been a very pleasant entertainment," he said, "only that my pleasure in it was much marred by having to acknowledge a toast in honor of the President," But he noted that "such things don't trouble me nearly so much as they did, and I came through it tolerably enough."[15]

Smithill's Hall, one of the finest and oldest manor houses in the north of England, was visited by Hawthorne in August of 1855. It was at that time occupied by the family of Peter Ainsworth, a former Member of Parliament. Even in Hawthorne's time the hall was renowned for its "Bloody Footstep," and he was to give the legend a firm footing in literature by incorporating it into four posthumously published manuscripts: *Septimus Felton*, "The Ancestral Footstep," *Dr. Grimshawe's Secret*, and "The Ghost of Doctor Harris." Parts of Smithill's Hall date back to the 14th century, but it was during the reign of Mary Tudor that the bloody imprint is supposed to have been made. A Protestant clergyman, having just had his fate decreed by the master of Smithill's, stamped his foot mightily upon a flagstone in protest. From this act came the legend of the bloody impression, although Hawthorne was quick to term it nonsense. His hosts selected for his bedroom one of the finest in the hall – the "Beam Chamber." In the night Hawthorne was roused by a clap of thunder, but did not see the ghost which Mr. Ainsworth assured him still lurked about the place.

**A TYPICAL DINNER AT LIVERPOOL'S TOWN HALL**
Hawthorne may have found Liverpool's climate unfriendly, but he had only praise for the numerous dinners enjoyed in the banquet room pictured above. After dining at the Lord Mayor's Easter Banquet in London, he remarked that the fare there was not better than that "given by the mayor of Liverpool."

Next morning the Victorian custom of family prayers, led by Mr. Ainsworth, was held before breakfast with the servants joining in. There was some apprehension by Mr. and Mrs. Ainsworth lest the family parrot misbehave during prayers. The bird was usually kept in the kitchen and had acquired a vocabulary unsuited for a religious service. ". . . when prayers were over," Hawthorne said, "Mrs. Ainsworth praised it very highly for having been so silent . . ." Polly, however, could not restrain herself for long, for by the time breakfast was served, she "began to whistle and talk very vociferously, and in a tone and with expressions" – Hawthorne said – "that surprised me."[16]

Early in 1856 the merchant, Benjamin F. Babcock, invited Hawthorne to an all-American dinner. He had gone to great trouble and expense to provide American specialities ranging from New York oysters and terrapin soup to Yankee pork-and-beans, a thirty-one pound American turkey, and canvas-back ducks. Then in March Hawthorne went aboard another ship, the *Princeton*, for lunch. He was as much fascinated by the hearty manner in which three elderly English guests pitched into their meals as by the variety of dishes placed before the guests. "In America," he said, "what squeamishness, what delicacy, what stomachic apprehensions, would there not be among three stomachs of sixty or seventy years' experience!"[17]

In October of 1856, Hawthorne – aware of his obligation to repay some of his friends for their hospitality and kindness – decided to give a dinner at Radley's Adelphi Hotel. By this time he had seen a great deal of the elderly, dignified James Radley, whose turtle soup was acclaimed throughout the land, and whose hotel was renowned as among the finest in Europe. Radley, the enterprising *hotelier*, had amassed a fortune estimated at over £100,000 (half a million dollars). Hawthorne was sure that Radley, had he been an American, surely would have become a Member of Congress[18] On the appointed evening James Radley himself served the guests. Counting Hawthorne, there were ten people in the party – among them the consul's two staunch friends, Francis Bennoch and Henry Bright. The meal began, of course, with the exquisite turtle soup, followed by haunch of venison with all the trimmings, and for dessert there was fruit, pastry and ice cream. The tea and coffee afterwards were somewhat overshadowed by an astounding variety of liquid refreshment – sherry, punch, hock, ale, champagne, "Moselle Cup," brandy, liqueurs, port, claret, and Madeira. And there were the inevitable cigars. Hawthorne saved the bill, which revealed that the drinks cost almost as much as the dinner. He sent it on to Ticknor for his "edification." "It was an excellent dinner," he added, "and cost me over £20."[19]

By December Liverpool had a new mayor, Francis Shand, and it was now his turn to offer an official dinner – one to which Hawthorne was invited. It was the last recorded visit of the consul to a Town Hall dinner. Hawthorne believed that these affairs were important for community spirit. "The Mayor's dinner-parties occur as often as once a fortnight, and, inviting his guests by fifty or sixty at a time," he said, "his Worship probably assembles at his board most of the eminent citizens and distinguished personages of the town and neighborhood more than once during his year's incumbency, and very much, no doubt, to the promotion of good feeling among individuals of opposite parties and diverse pursuits in life."[20]

Perhaps conscious that he was enjoying one of the last of the mayoral feasts, he recorded in his journal a good reason for remembering the civic functions. "I want to preserve all the characteristic traits of such banquets," he said, "because, being peculiar to England, these municipal feasts may do well to picture in a novel." On his previous visits to the Liverpool Town Hall he had failed to note one distinctive accoutrement – an ancient silver tobacco-box from which guests formerly filled their pipes after eating. "The date of 1690 was on the lid," he said, "It is now used as a snuff-box, and wends its way from guest to guest, around the table." Although Hawthorne was accorded the position of honour at the mayor's right hand, France, Turkey, and Austria were toasted before the United States. His Worship explained why. ". . . the Mayor whispered me," Hawthorne said, "he must first get his allies out of the way."[21]

To the consul's joy, Mayor Shand – in his toast to Hawthorne – alluded to the recent return of the bark *Resolute* by the United States. This unfortunate ship, abandoned by its crew in the Arctic in 1854, was found and towed to the United States the following year, and in a subsequent ceremony at Cowes, Isle of Wight, was handed over to Queen Victoria. Thanks to the astute and well-informed mayor, Hawthorne's speaking chore on this occasion probably was the least onerous of his consular career. More toasts followed, this time to the various professions – merchants, bankers, solicitors, and so on – with one person from each responding. Then there was a humorous touch towards the end of the evening when a toast was proposed to "the Ladies" – to which an old bachelor responded.[22]

In April of 1857, when Hawthorne had less than five months remaining as consul, there was an event which was to be the highlight of his Liverpool official life – a foundation-stone ceremony to mark the start of construction on the Liverpool Free Public Library. The creation of the library was mainly due to the generosity of a wealthy citizen, William Brown. Born in Ireland in 1784, Brown went with his parents to Baltimore, where the firm of Alexander Brown and Sons, dealing mainly in the linen trade, was established. When the firm prospered, an English branch was opened in Liverpool, and two more domestic outlets in New York and Philadelphia. At the age of twenty-five, young William was entrusted with

## LORD STREET, LIVERPOOL

"The windows were alive with heads," said Hawthorne as he walked with other guests down Lord Street and other Liverpool thoroughfares en route to the site of the foundation-stone ceremony for Liverpool's free public library.

launching the Liverpool branch. Old Alexander Brown could only have been proud of William, both as businessman and as benefactor. William became an Anglo-American banker, an alderman (1831), and for fourteen years represented South Lancashire in the House of Commons. In keeping with the liberal views of many merchants, Brown early advocated free trade.

Brown cherished knowledge and the means of acquiring it. Thus, a free public library in the town that had bestowed so many honours upon him seemed entirely suited to his philanthropic inclinations. His gift of £40,000 thus assured Liverpool of one of Britain's finest libraries. April 15, 1857 was selected as the date for laying the foundation-stone of the new library, although it was another four years before the structure was completed.

Guests were asked to assemble before noon in the ball-room of the Town Hall before beginning their procession through the streets. Hawthorne arrived at eleven and was greeted by Richard Monckton Milnes (later Lord Houghton) who was to introduce him at the banquet. Milnes, whom Hawthorne had come to know well, was a poet and man of letters who derived great pleasure from encouraging and assisting fellow writers. In some ways, Hawthorne said, Milnes reminded him of Longfellow. Presently the order was given for the assembled dignitaries to form themselves into a procession – four abreast – for the two-mile walk through James Street, Lord Street, Church Street, Lime Street and thence to the site of the ceremony in what is now William Brown Street.

The participants plodded their way "through a line of policemen and a throng of people, and the windows were alive with heads." Hawthorne mused how lucky the walkers were not to be caught in rain, although most carried precautionary umbrellas. "... we should have been in a strange pickle for the banquet," he said, "had we been compelled to wade through the ordinary mud of Liverpool." At least two members of the procession wore costumes – the Bishop of Chester "in his flat cap and black silk gown," and the British Army general for the area, who was in full uniform and bedecked with medals. "Mr. Brown himself, the hero of the day," Hawthorne noted, "was the plainest, and simplest man of all, an exceedingly unpretending old gentleman in black, small, withered, white-haired, pale, quiet, and respectable."[23]

At length the procession reached its objective, the short street on which the library was to be erected. "... when we came within the enclosure," recalled Hawthorne, "the corner stone (a large square of red free-stone) was already suspended over its destined place." Then followed photographs of the ceremony, a prayer by the Bishop, and speeches by several dignitaries.

The formal part of the occasion was yet to come. To commemorate the event, a huge banquet was arranged across the street in Liverpool's elegant St. George's Hall, Here,

**RICHARD MONCKTON MILNES**
Milnes, later Lord Houghton, introduced
Hawthorne at the banquet following the
foundation-stone ceremony for the Liverpool
library and museum. Hawthorne, however,
could not hear Milnes distinctly and did not
know how to respond. In the end he praised
Milnes, the spirit of English literature and the
library donor, William Brown, and received
several rounds of applause.

before the nine hundred assembled guests, more speeches were scheduled. Hawthorne was
already aware of the hall's architectural excellence, but William Brown insisted on taking
him into the gallery for a panoramic view. ". . . by this time [it] was full of ladies,"
Hawthorne said, "and thence we had a fine view of the noble hall, with the tables laid, in
readiness for the banquet. I cannot conceive of anything finer than this hall; it needs
nothing but painted windows to make it perfect, and those I hope it may have, one day or
another."[24]

When he took his seat for the banquet, Hawthorne found that he no longer experienced
the nervousness which formerly marked such occasions. "These things," he said, "do not
trouble me quite so much as they did, though it still sufficed to prevent much of the enjoyment which I might have had, if I could have felt myself merely a spectator." There were so
many toasts proposed that he was weary before his turn came "sitting, all that time, as it
were, on the scaffold with the rope round my neck." When at last, Milnes was called upon
to toast the United States, Hawthorne had the greatest difficulty in hearing him, for the
speaker turned his head first one way and then another, so that only portions of his remarks
were audible. Milnes, in fact, paid a glowing tribute to Hawthorne as author, and another
to the ties binding Britain and the United States.

Because Milnes was too far away to be heard distinctly, Hawthorne did not know
whether he had been toasted as one representing American literature, or as consul. This
was awkward, for his own response – at least in part – ought to refer to his introducer's
words. But there was no time to find out what Milnes had said. ". . . there was a vast deal of
clamor," Hawthorne said, "and uprose peers and bishop, general, mayor, knights, and
gentlemen, everybody in the hall, greeting me with all the honors. I had uprisen, too, to
commence my speech, but had to sit down again till matters grew more quiet . . ."
Eventually he stood up again and proceeded to deliver his address with complete com-
posure. "It is very strange," he observed, "this self-possession and clear-sightedness . . .
showed my way through all the difficulties resulting from my not having heard Monckton
Milnes' speech, and, since reading the latter, I do not see how I could have answered it
better."[25]

When he sat down, Hawthorne was immensely relieved – and pleased. "Upon my word,"
he admitted, "I think my speech was about the best of the occasion, and certainly it was
better cheered than any other, expecially one passage, where I made a colossus of poor little
Mr. Brown."[26]

## LIVERPOOL FOUNDATION-STONE CEREMONY
One of Britain's leading journals, the *Illustrated London News*, devoted much space to the ceremony. Afterwards the dignitaries assembled in nearby St. George's Hall for more speeches; it was here that Hawthorne paid a glowing tribute to the library donor, William Brown.

### WILLIAM BROWN
Irish born, Brown first worked with his father in Baltimore and then set up the Liverpool branch of the family business. He prospered, became a banker and Member of Parliament. Three years after donating the library and museum to Liverpool he was knighted.

### LIVERPOOL LIBRARY
This medal was issued in 1860 to mark the completion of the free public library made possible by William Brown's generosity.

The library dedication was probably the last official occasion when Hawthorne was obliged to speak. Having given August 31 as the date when he expected to relinquish office, he had every intention of keeping to his word. As it turned out, however, his successor, Beverley Tucker, did not arrive until two months later. With the precise date of his departure unknown, there was little the consul's friends could do to organize a farewell party, and it seems that none was given.

When Tucker eventually arrived Hawthorne conceded to Ticknor that his replacement was a different type of man and probably possessed all the qualities designed to make a popular consul. "[He is] a bluff, jolly, good-natured gentleman, fond of society and an excellent companion," he said, "– wholly unlike me in every possible respect."[27]

"I do not know what Sophia may have said about my conduct in the Consulate," Hawthorne wrote his sister-in-law before quitting Liverpool; "I only know that I have done no good, none whatever. . . . The good of others, like our own happiness, is not to be attained by direct effort, but incidentally. All history and observation confirm this. . . . God's ways are in nothing more mysterious than in the matter of trying to do good."[28]

# XV
## Provide, Provide, Provide

One of Hawthorne's most amazing acts of philanthropy was to underwrite a ponderous work on Shakespeare by an obscure American writer, Delia Bacon. Many scholars have suggested that one or another person – among them Sir Francis Bacon, the Earl of Oxford, Sir Edward Dyer, the Earl of Rutland, and the Countess of Pembroke – was the real author of works attributed to Shakespeare. But Delia Bacon was the first to develop the theory that the works were written by a *group*. Delia considered Sir Francis Bacon to be *one* of the group, but not the only one. Nonetheless, she was misunderstood and erroneously called a "Baconist" by her contemporaries. She unfortunately ended her days in an insane asylum and some critics in recent times have assumed she was mad when she outlined her group theory. Nothing could be farther from the truth, as the Shakespearean scholar, R. C. Churchill, has pointed out.[1]

Hawthorne defended his countrywoman's philosophy in the company of eminent Britons, some of whom were aghast at the suggestion that Shakespeare's reputation was being questioned. He did not himself subscribe to Miss Bacon's views, but believed her to be sincere and worthy of hearing. He agreed to do the foreword for her work and, unbeknown to her, to underwrite the printing costs. The book appeared near the end of Hawthorne's consulship, in 1000 copies, with 500 copies being assigned each to Britain and the United States. Ticknor was to handle the volumes for the American market. "The 500 copies of Miss Bacon's book have been sent to me," Hawthorne wrote in April of 1857, "[and they are] ready for exportation. . . . The London retail-price is 18/-. You will know what to charge in America. The 1000 copies, as they come from the printer's hands (exclusive of binding) have cost £238.7.9. 'A fool and his money are soon parted.' However, I do not repent what I have done, nor will I, even if I lose by it."[2]

The consul, indeed, did lose badly. "Matters look dark," he wrote Ticknor a month later, "as regards Miss Bacon's book. I shall certainly not 'save my bacon' there. It was absurd in me to let her publish such a heavy volume . . . which is enough to swamp a ship of the line. However, this will be the last of my benevolent follies, and I never will be kind to anybody again as long as I live."[3] Delia Bacon lived only two years after her work was published, and Hawthorne was to deal kindly with her when his recollections of the authoress were recounted later in *Our Old Home*.[4]

Hawthorne's backing of Delia Bacon cost him almost $1,200 before binding and shipping costs were added. Apart from loans made to friends, the venture was the costliest of his consular period. Ironically, this large outlay occurred when his income was diminishing.

When Hawthorne was named consul he was entitled to keep virtually all fees received for conducting American consular business in Liverpool. Had this arrangement continued to the end of his four-year appointment, he could have expected to save about $40,000.[1] His actual receipts would have been much higher, but he was obliged to meet all expenses, personal and office (including wages of his staff), from the income. He received no allowance for entertaining his Liverpool contacts, men upon whom he relied constantly for assistance and information. But consuls were not alone in this oversight by the American Congress. James Buchanan, the American Minister in London, was also worried about

### DELIA BACON

One of Hawthorne's most extravagant ventures was to underwrite a ponderous work by Delia Bacon, the first to advance the "group" theory of the authorship of works attributed to Shakespeare. From the outset the book was a failure, leading the consul to remark wryly, "I shall certainly not save my bacon."

making ends meet. "I pay for my house £700, which is exactly equal to $3,388," he wrote his niece, Harriet Lane, in 1853, "but I am allowed £80 for office rent, which reduces the amount to $3,000.80. According to my estimate, the outfit and salary will not hold out longer than the first year, and I shall have to supply the deficiency in the second year from my private means."[5]

Midway through his term of office Hawthorne received a shock over his prospects of receiving the expected consular fees. Advocates of reform in the U.S. diplomatic and consular service proposed that the fee basis of remuneration for consuls be abolished, and that these officers be put on salaries. Nothing was said about expenses in maintaining contact with members of the commercial community on whom a consul had to call for help following disasters at sea, injuries and deaths of Americans, financial crises, or whatever. Nor was there a penny proposed to cover the cost of renting and maintaining the consul's home or apartment. Hawthorne greeted the news of the reform bill with dread, and its eventual implementation with horror. Only when it became apparent that the Liverpool consul would receive a relatively favourable salary ($7,500) and would be permitted to retain the purely clerical (i.e., copying) fees, was he convinced he should remain in his job.

A chronological scrutiny of references to financial matters in his letters to Ticknor affords a fascinating picture of Hawthorne's alternating moods of joy and despair as his prospects for acquiring a modest fortune rose and fell. This scrutiny also reveals Hawthorne's expenditures for official purposes, his family, and the various causes he supported. Even in his first month as consul, when Ticknor was still visiting in England, Hawthorne wrote twice to let his friend know how he was faring. "If you want money before sailing," he wrote on August 22, "I can let you have £50 or thereabouts – perhaps more. I have had to pay for the furniture of the office and other preliminary expenses, so that there is less on hand than would otherwise have been the case . . ."[6] Two days later, he was more encouraged. "I shall probably have £100 for you," he said, "perhaps more. The gold begins to clink."[7]

In October he reminded Ticknor to pay the taxes due on The Wayside in Concord. A month later he indicated £300 had been deposited to the credit of the publishing house of Ticknor, Reed and Fields – the arrangement through which he was to remit regularly his savings to Ticknor over the next four years. "I wish to Heaven I had made up my whole pile," he added, "and were off to Italy."[8]

Hawthorne's gullibility during the early part of his consulship cost him sizeable sums. Various characters presented themselves at the consulate with stories of need or hardship, and he, unsuspectingly, advanced them money. "I enclose a small draft," he wrote on December 8, "drawn by an old gentleman whose funds failed him here, and whom I have had to assist and send home – as I am compelled to do in many other cases, at my own risk. He is now on his passage to Philadelphia by a screw-steamer. I think the draft will prove a good one, although my clerks (who have seen a thousand such cases) tell me that it will never be paid. In that event, I shall lose not only this, but a much larger sum for his passage-money."[9]

In the same letter Hawthorne informed Ticknor that the newly appointed American Consul to Pernambuco, William Lilley, had passed through Liverpool. While there, he asked Hawthorne to endorse a bill for £50 drawn on an American who neither held funds for Lilley nor had authorized him to draw any. "If I lose the money," Hawthorne vowed, "he shall lose the consulship." Then he lamented over the constant procession of "swindlers" who turned up at his office. "They almost always get short of money here," he told Ticknor, "and never can raise a shilling without my endorsement, for the Liverpool merchants seem to know their character of old."[10]

After forwarding Ticknor another £300, Hawthorne added: "If it had been £3,000. I would kick the office to the devil and come home again. I am sick of it and long for my hillside, and – what I thought I would never long for – my pen! When a man is thoroughly imbued with ink, he never can wash out the stain."[11]

As the year 1854 began, Hawthorne found he was able to remit sums of £200 or £300, regularly. In early February he related the latest in the affair of the consul from Pernambuco. "I have paid Lilley's protested bill some time ago and have drawn upon him for the amount and damages, at three days' sight," he said. "In my letter of advice, I gave him to understand what my course will be in case he does not honor the draft."[12]

By mid-February his income from fees was so promising that Hawthorne fancied himself becoming one of the wealthier citizens of his home state. "Redding," he informed Ticknor, "has published a list of the monied men of Massachusetts. I consider myself one of them since you tell me I have $3,000 safely invested. Send me the pamphlet, for I ought to be acquainted with the names of my brethren."[13]

"Invest – invest – invest!" he urged Ticknor, "I am in a hurry to be rich enough to get away from this dismal and forlorn hole. If I can once see $20,000 in a pile, I shan't care much for being turned out of office, and yet I ought to be a little richer than that. It won't be quite so easy for us to live on a thousand dollars or less, as it used to be. I am getting spoilt, you see."[14]

In April Hawthorne told Ticknor that his old Bowdoin classmate, Horatio Bridge, wished to borrow $3,000. This was a large sum, but he had no hesitation in approving it. Bridge, after all, was the one who had guaranteed the publication costs of Hawthorne's first book. "In my last," he said, ". . . I mentioned that Bridge wished to borrow $3,000. . . . consult his convenience on this point and do not let him hear of any difficulty."[15]

Hawthorne had been in office only nine months when he received news that the reformers of the American foreign service were completing their proposal which, among other things, would abolish the fee system of paying consuls. Although the bill was not yet enacted, Hawthorne realized the prospects of his receiving what he had hoped from the Liverpool position were now slim. The Secretary of the Treasury forwarded a copy of the circular outlining the principal provisions of the proposed act, and he was not long in telling Ticknor about it.". . . [The new act] will seriously affect the emoluments of the office," he said, "but, if nothing worse happens, I shall still get more than my $20,000 out of it. The truth is, it is a devilish good office – if those jackasses at Washington (of course, I do not include the President under this polite phrase) will but let it alone. They are now tinkering at a bill

## BRIDGE THE FAITHFUL

Horatio Bridge had backed Hawthorne's early attempt to become an author. Now, as consul, Hawthorne had no hesitation in lending his friend $3,000. "Do not let him hear of any difficulty," he instructed his financial advisor.

involving the whole subject of diplomatic and consular emoluments, and if they touch the Liverpool consulate at all, it will be to limit my salary. Now, with the inevitable expenses of a residence here, a salary of ten thousand dollars would hardly make it worth my while to keep the office – and they would never think of giving me more than six. But, I trust in God, Pierce will not let them meddle with me . . ."[16]

By the following month (June, 1854) the $3,000 loan to Bridge had been completed. Hawthorne was pleased to hear the transaction had been made, and commented to Ticknor that there was no one else, except Pierce, to whom he would feel obliged to lend any considerable sum.[17] But, as will be seen, he was no more able to refuse requests for loans and gifts than before. He told Ticknor that he was constantly remitting sums of from one to five pounds to beggars and borrowers. There is no record of these small payments, but taken together they must represent a sizeable sum.

The consul in Pernambuco, under threat of being reported to the State Department, eventually repaid the £50 loan to Hawthorne. But this small item of good news did not prevent Hawthorne from expressing to Ticknor his concern over the foreign service reform bill. "I shall fairly bag $10,000 within the year," he said, "and my expenses have been very heavy, too. I am terribly afraid Congress will cut down the office with a salary – in which case it will not be worth holding. If I can have the full swing of the emolument for one more year, I shall not grumble much . . ."[18]

As the anniversary of his assumption of office (August 1st) approached, Hawthorne told Ticknor confidently of his savings goal for the first year. "I think," he wrote, "I am quite up to the $10,000 mark now."[19] He admitted, however, that he would "not find the second year so profitable."[20] The pending legislation which inevitably would curtail his earnings was ever present in his mind, and his letters to Ticknor at this period reflect his growing anxiety. "I observe," he wrote in mid-August, "that a bill for the remodelling of the

Diplomatic and Consular Service was reported in Congress . . . [but] I should suppose they can hardly have acted on it in the brief remnant of the session . . . . . . I am so sick and weary of this office that I should hardly regret it if they were to abolish it altogether. What with brutal shipmasters, drunken sailors, vagrant Yankees, mad people, sick people, and dead people (for just now I have to attend to the removal of the bones of a man who has been dead these twenty years) it is full of damnable annoyances."[21]

Shipping activity in the port of Liverpool slumped badly in the autumn of 1854 and Hawthorne's fees dropped dramatically. "Business is terribly dull," he told Ticknor in September, "and I hardly make enough to live on."[22] Two weeks later he wrote in similar vein, adding: "I shall thank my stars if I do not have to draw on you."[23] Then, in October came notice from the Cunard line that Hawthorne was likely to be held accountable for paying the cost of passage for one Mr. Rogers, whose security now seemed worthless. The incident reveals both Hawthorne's naivety, and devices used by confidence men to obtain money and free passage from a consul. ". . . [Rogers] came to me on his return from St. Petersburg (where he had been to volunteer in the Russian service) destitute of funds and without the means of getting to America," he said. "I supplied him with money and became security for his passage. He said [a] Captain Bell was in possession of funds belonging to him. If these facts are represented to Captain Bell, there can be no question that he will pay the draft which is still in the hands of the agent of the Cunard line in New York. At all events, he will give you the address of Mr. Rogers, in Kentucky or Tennessee – I forget which." But the Cunard agent had not found a Captain Bell at the address given by Rogers, and Hawthorne had enlisted Ticknor's aid in ascertaining the true position. "If . . . [Rogers] turns out to be a rogue," he lamented, "I will give up all pretence to being a judge of human nature."[24]

Ticknor, meanwhile, asked Hawthorne if he could produce another book while carrying out his consular duties. "There is no prospect of that," he replied, "so long as I continue in office, but if the consular bill should pass at the next session I shall soon be an author again." He told Ticknor that the salary proposed for the Liverpool job was reported to be $7,500, plus a supplement for expenses. "No consul," he said, "can live as a gentleman in English society and carry on the official business on those terms."[25]

Hawthorne's inability to say "no" to would-be borrowers worried Ticknor, and in January of 1855 he begged the consul to be more careful. Hawthorne defended his actions strongly. ". . . as to your advice not to lend any more money," he told Ticknor, "I acknowledge it to be good and shall follow it so far as I can and ought. But when a friend of half my lifetime asks me to assist him and when I have perfect confidence in his honor, what is to be done?" The friend in this instance was probably John L. O'Sullivan, the American Minister to Portugal. Nonetheless, Hawthorne calculated his total worth was not far off the $20,000 figure he had earlier set for himself. "Reckoning O'Sullivan's three thousand dollars, I shall have bagged about $15,000," he said, "and I shall estimate the Concord place and my copyrights together at $5,000 more – so that you see I have the twenty thousand after all!"[26]

By March the American House of Representatives had passed the foreign service reform bill, and it went to the Senate for consideration. Hawthorne took it for granted that Senate ratification would be swift. "If I find I can hold the office without a positive expense to myself," he told Ticknor, "I think I shall remain here for one year longer for the sake of seeing more of England – then go to Italy for perhaps another year – and then home."[27] The bill was passed by the Senate, but because some parts of it were deemed likely to be unconstitutional, the act was not to come into force until the summer of 1855. The delay was gratifying to Hawthorne. "The affair turns out so much better than I at first expected," he said, "that I feel as if a piece of good luck had happened to me."[28]

In the spring and summer of 1855 Hawthorne continued to forward remittances to Ticknor, painfully aware that he had only a few months left before the consular fees no longer would be his own. "I don't think I am quite so well contented here," he told his friend, "as before this disturbance about the Consular bill."[29] By June he felt that he *must* have reached his original goal. "The amount of these [enclosed remittances], together with whatever may accrue during the month," he said, "will not fall much short of my *minimum* which I have always set at $20,000 . . ."[30]

With the exception of his threat to expose the U.S. Consul (Lilley) at Pernambuco to the State Department unless he repaid his loan, Hawthorne did not rely on his friendship with President Pierce to gain favour. Indeed, he was to write the president only twice during his tenure of office, and on both occasions for official reasons. The first letter, sent on June 7, 1855, was not so much a protest over the recently enacted consular reform bill as it was a plea for a better understanding of the expenses borne by American consuls abroad.

Hawthorne's letter to Pierce is remarkable for its insight into the thorny question of whether American or foreign clerks should be employed in consulates, what their pay should be, and how they should be appointed. In his view, only foreign clerks would accept the low pay offered. "I employ three . . .," he said, "a smaller number could not manage the business. . . . It will be found impracticable to obtain an American capable of filling the office of head-clerk at a less salary than $1,500, or, better, $2,000. The truth is, no such man is in existence at this moment; he must be caught young and brought over here and educated in the business before he is fit for it." He went on to tell the president the advantages of having a clerk who is a citizen of the country where the consulate is located. "One must have lived abroad," he said, "in order to understand the innumerable ways in which foreign customs and modes of business require an interpreter and how necessary it is that a stranger should . . . have the help of a native."[31]

On the question of how appointments should be made, Hawthorne was equally emphatic. "In my opinion," he said, "the whole staff of clerks should be appointed, not by the Consul, but by the State Department of which they should be the servants, and not removable by the Consul except on grounds approved by the Secretary of State." He added that it was possible, with clerks appointed by himself, to falsify official records to the extent that up to half the fees received would be lost to the government – "without the possibility of proof against me." No man, he said, ought to be exposed to so great a temptation.[32]

Hawthorne then turned to the question of a just salary for the American Consul in Liverpool. A consul, he said, "cannot possibly live here with a family (unless he secludes himself from society and forgoes all the social advantages of a residence in England) at a less expense than $5,000 per annum." Clerk-hire took $3,500 of this figure, he estimated, and office rent and other expenses the remaining $1,500. From the salary of $7,500 paid the consul at Liverpool under the new Act of Congress, there remained only $2,500 for the officer's living expenses. "A man might be comfortable with this sum in a New England village," Hawthorne told the president, "but not, I assure you, as the representative of America in the greatest commercial city of England. For Heaven's sake, do not let the next session [of Congress] pass without having this matter amended."[33]

Hawthorne ended his letter by giving news of each member of his family, and by explaining why he had not written regularly since becoming consul. ". . . it is not quite so easy," he said, "to write to the President of the United States as it used to be to write to Frank Pierce."[34]

Time was fast running out under the old fee-retention system when Hawthorne remitted $2,200 to Ticknor in August. "Don't you think I have property enough now to resign upon?" he asked. "I want to do so most damnably, but will try to hold on another year unless Congress makes the office worse than it looks now."[35] In October Hawthorne calculated he owed the U.S. Government $4,000 for fees taken in during the first quarter of the new act's life. "This is sheer robbery," he wrote Ticknor. "I am disgusted with the business and hardly bear to think of continuing at the present miserably reduced rate of compensation."[36]

From now on Hawthorne's remittances were smaller, for he was only allowed to retain fees for notarial and copying services. Previously he had not kept large sums in the consulate, having sent remittances weekly or fortnightly. Now, under the new act, he was saddled with a worrying responsibility. "I have many thousand dollars of public money (which should have been my own) now in my keeping," he said, "and I must remain at my post, either to take care of it or to pay it over. I cannot express, nor can you conceive, the irksomeness of my position and how I long to get free from it."[37]

Meanwhile, the 1855 reform act had been amended to eliminate provisions likely to be ruled unconstitutional, but the amended version did nothing to restore a consul's fees. It did, however, provide a small allowance for renting the consulate premises. Hawthorne added relatively little to his savings in 1856. Early in 1857 he asked Ticknor for a statement of his finances. He was pleased by his friend's reply and told him, were he now living in Concord, that it would hardly be worth his while to be any richer. But, with further travel and residence abroad envisaged, he considered his savings "a bare competence."[38] Still, he added, he would be content to wait "because I live at Uncle Sam's expense and do him very little service – the old scoundrel!"[39] But these final months were not without considerable drama. Hawthorne's clerk, Henry Wilding, became seriously ill and almost died, leaving the consul to complete the complicated fiscal returns for Washington. In November there was a further worry when the Liverpool Borough Bank, in which both his and government fees were deposited, was the subject of closure rumours. He managed to withdraw the funds in the nick of time, thereby escaping "serious embarrassment."[40]

Just how much Hawthorne had managed to save when he left Liverpool is not clear. If the consular reform act had not been enacted, there seems little doubt that he would have maintained the $10,000 annual saving rate compiled in his first year of service. He seems certain to have reached his minimum goal of $20,000, but probably not much more. Had the family immediately returned to the United States, it very likely would have provided the cushion against hard times that he envisaged. But fate was to decree a devious and difficult route before the family would again take up residence in New England.

# XVI
# Near-Tragedy and Tribulation

"You will be sorry to hear," wrote Hawthorne to William Ticknor on January 7, 1858 from Paris, "that I was detained in England until the day before yesterday by the impossibility of getting my complicated accounts ready at an earlier date. . . . We reached Paris last night by way of Boulogne. The weather is terribly cold and we find it difficult to keep ourselves from freezing by these wretched little wood-fires. Indeed, I find how English I have grown in five years past by my antipathy to French fires and everything else that is French."[1]

The Hawthornes did not intend to remain long in Paris; to them, it was merely a stop on the route to Italy – the exotic Mediterranean land about which they had dreamed during their long stay in England. Sophia regarded a sojourn in Italy as being necessary for anyone with an appreciation of the fine arts, while Hawthorne looked forward to the Italian sojourn as a time when his earlier talent for writing might return.

While in the French capital, Hawthorne offered a classic comment on the usefulness of ambassadors. Judge John Y. Mason of Virginia had been named the American Minister to France by President Pierce in the same year that Hawthorne went to Liverpool. When James Buchanan became president he allowed Mason to retain his post in Paris, much to the chagrin of those politicians who had entertained hopes of succeeding him. Hawthorne's remark was made in defence of Buchanan's action, but its satirical flavour embraced both Mason and ambassadors of all time. "There is no good reason," he said, "why Uncle Sam should not pay Judge Mason seventeen thousand dollars a year for sleeping at the dignified post of Ambassador to France. The true ground of complaint is that whether he slept or waked, the result would be the same."[2]

Rome in mid-winter was hardly the pleasant place the Hawthornes had imagined. In a letter to Ticknor, Hawthorne said he had a cold almost from the day he arrived, and that he found the climate most unsuitable. "I doubt," he added, ". . . whether I shall be able to settle down to serious literary labor as long as I remain abroad; at all events, not in Italy. In England, if not interrupted by other avocations, I could have worked to good purpose." His thoughts then turned naturally to his financial position, for he was now without an income and encumbered by maintaining his family indefinitely in Rome. "We find," he told Ticknor, "living in Rome quite as expensive, in most particulars, as it was in England. Rent is a good deal dearer and nothing is cheaper except macaroni, figs, bad cigars, and sour wine." He then made an observation about the quality of life in the United States. ". . . I had rather be a sojourner in any country than return to my own," he said. "The United States are fit for many excellent purposes, but they certainly are not fit to live in . . ."[3]

The Hawthornes experienced difficulty in adjusting to life in Italy. "The utmost caution is requisite in regard to diet and exposure to air," he wrote Ticknor, "and after all the care that can be taken there is a lurking poison in the atmosphere that will be likely enough to do your business. I never knew that I had either bowels or lungs till I came to Rome, but I have found it now, to my cost."[4]

With the coming of spring the family's morale was restored, although at least one member of the family sometimes pined for England. "We are having perfectly splendid weather now," wrote Una. "But the sky is too blue, the sun is too blazing, everything is too vivid. Often I long for the more cloudy skies and peace of that dear, beautiful England. . . . We have to pay a fearful price for the supreme enjoyment there is in standing on the very spots made interesting by poetry or by prose, imagination, or (which is still more absorbing) truth. Sometimes I wish there had never been anything done or written in the world! My father and I seem to feel this way more than the rest."[5]

Hawthorne's presence in Rome had not gone unnoticed by the New York *Times'* correspondent. Writing under the pseudonym "Pericles," he said: "Hawthorne I frequently see in the street, swinging along in a sort of land-measuring pace, smoking, and occasionally looking out from under his shaggy brow and otherwise tenacious face. He avoids all society and is said to be engaged on some new work, the subject of which is not even known by his wife."[6] The *Times'* correspondent erred in thinking the author was a recluse; Rome's large Anglo-American community obliged him to enter into society probably more than he wished. Nonetheless, he did find time and the will to complete a draft of the work that later became *The Marble Faun* (*Transformation* in England). He also selected a tentative date on which to sail for the United States (early July), and even had thoughts about how he would enlarge The Wayside. "I feel in somewhat better spirits to come home," he told Ticknor, "because I see how an addition may be made to the house, which need not be enormously expensive and yet will afford us the necessary space. I want a drawing room, two bed-chambers, and two chambers for servants in addition to what we now have; . . . these, if I mistake not, I can get by adding on a wing to the southern end of the house."[7]

Hawthorne was apprehensive about the new romance, for his last work of fiction, *The Blithedale Romance*, had appeared seven years earlier. ". . . I feel," he confessed to Ticknor, "that I shall come before the public, after so long an interval, with all the uncertainties of a new author. If I were only rich enough, I do not believe I should ever publish another book. . . . But, with a wing of a house to build, and my girls to educate, and Julian to send to Cambridge [i.e., Harvard], I see little prospect of the '*dolce far niente*,' as long as there shall be any faculty in me."[8]

Two months later (May, 1859) Hawthorne explained to Ticknor why he had not written recently. ". . . we have suffered a great deal of trouble and anxiety from Una's illness," he said, "and, at one period, we had scarcely no hope of ever taking her out of Rome. Indeed, the physician did not encourage us to think that she would live even from one day to another."[9] Una had contracted malaria from the Campagna marshes near Rome and her frequent fits of fevers and deliriums left Hawthorne distraught. Her illness also came as a shock to the family's English-speaking friends in Rome, among whom Una – at fifteen with an engaging manner – had been extremely popular. "Carriages were constantly driving to the door with enquiries," Sophia recalled. "People were always coming. . . . Magnificent flowers were always coming, baskets and bouquets, which were presented with tearful eyes. The American Minister [John M. Daniel] constantly called. Everyone who had seen Una in society or anywhere came to ask."[10]

Robert and Elizabeth Barrett Browning; the artist, C. G. Thompson; the sculptor, William W. Story (whose *Cleopatra* Hawthorne was to describe in *The Marble Faun*); the historian-diplomat, John L. Motley and his wife, Mary (who had been taught by Hawthorne's sister, Elizabeth, in Salem) – all these, and many more, called regularly to enquire after the ailing Una. Despite the loving care of her family, the visits of friends, and administration of quinine, she was slow to show any sign of improvement.

At the peak of the family's anxiety, Franklin Pierce arrived in Rome with Mrs. Pierce. The presence of this old friend was a great morale booster for Hawthorne and the entire

## REDCAR – "THE MOST SECLUDED SPOT I EVER MET WITH"
After the disastrous stay in Italy where Una almost died and Hawthorne's own health deteriorated, the family came back to England and took a modest house at Redcar. Here Hawthorne worked quietly and finished *The Marble Faun.*

family, although Pierce was now showing signs of advancing age. The two strolled about Rome, seeing St. Peter's and other sights, and talking over old times. The subject of American politics inevitably arose and Hawthorne suggested that Pierce run for president again; Pierce, however, was resolute in his determination not to allow his name to be put forward.

On the day of Pierce's departure from Rome, Hawthorne recorded what the visit had meant to him during the anxious period of Una's illness. "Never having had any trouble before that pierced into my very vitals," he said, "I did not know what comfort there might be in the manly sympathy of a friend, but Pierce has . . . so large and kindly a heart and is so tender and so strong that he really did me good, and I shall always love him the better for the recollection of his ministrations in these dark days. Thank God the thing we dreaded did not come to pass."[11]

Sophia, ever the perceptive wife, knew full well that Hawthorne's own health had been endangered, and that Frank Pierce's presence had been the right tonic. She gave the former president the lion's share of credit for enabling her husband to survive the ordeal of Una's almost fatal illness. Happily, Una's condition improved as quickly as she was stricken, and by the last week of May Hawthorne was able to make plans for the family's removal to England from which he hoped passage to the United States could be arranged in July.

Immediately upon arrival in England, Hawthorne set about preparing the manuscript of his Italian romance for the publishers. One week lapsed into the next and he was not long in realizing that the family would not be returning to the United States in 1859. ". . . for nearly three months," he wrote Ticknor in October, ". . . I have been constantly occupied with my book which required more work to be done upon it than I supposed. I am now, I think, within a fortnight of finishing it."[12]

Hawthorne had settled upon the tiny seaside resort of Redcar in Yorkshire as the place where he might find ideal conditions for completing his work. "It was," he said, "the most secluded spot I ever met with, and therefore very favorable to literary labor. We had not a single visitor or caller while we were there. This suited Mrs. Hawthorne as well as myself, for she was quite worn out with her anxiety and watching during Una's illness."[13]

While in Redcar Hawthorne was told by Henry Bright that their mutual friend, Richard Mockton Milnes, would be bringing before the House of Commons the matter of cruelty aboard British and American ships. In a letter to Milnes, Hawthorne said there was no more commendable discussion that could be undertaken by parliamentarians of the two countries.[14] Milnes kept his word, and in his speech cited the former consul by name and then went on to give the number of seamen confined in certain Liverpool hospitals.

Una prospered in the cooler climate and Hawthorne was able to report that she was "as plump and rosy as any English girl."[15] Sophia, meanwhile, busied herself by reading and re-reading the manuscript, all the time encouraging her husband in his effort to regain his old writing form. "Mrs. Hawthorne," said the novelist, ". . . speaks very much in its favor, but sometimes I suspect that she has a partiality for the author."[16] On November 8, 1859, Sophia recorded in her journal – pointedly in over-sized script – that her husband had completed the book.

By this time the family had quit Redcar for more familiar surroundings in Leamington, where they were to remain until just before sailing for the United States in the summer of the following year. The final winter in England was spent in negotiating with publishers and in trying to come up with titles which would attract readers both in Britain and America. Hawthorne suggested *The Romance of Monte Beni* to Smith and Elder in London, but told Ticknor that *St. Hilda's Shrine* might be more appropriate for the American edition. In the end neither title was acceptable; the British title became *Transformation* and the American one, *The Marble Faun*. Simultaneous publication on both sides of the Atlantic seemed appropriate, but this plan invited long delays because of the need to send proofs back and forth across the sea. By the time everyone was happy over the arrangements, Hawthorne was exhausted. "I shall really be glad to get home," he said, "although I do not doubt I shall be tortured with life-long wishes to cross the sea again. I fear I have lost the capacity of living contentedly in any one place."[17]

Early in 1860, with most problems pertaining to the book settled and his mind now firmly on departing for the United States, Hawthorne's thoughts turned once more to his financial condition. "I want to spend some money on books and other things before my return," he wrote Ticknor. "How much can I afford? Anything? Very little, I fear."[18]

With the coming of spring, Hawthorne's romance duly appeared in both countries and earned favourable reviews. "I have been much gratified by the kind feeling and generous praise contained in the notices you send me," he wrote Ticknor. "After so long absence and silence, I like to be praised too much. It sounds like a welcome back among my friends." Then his thoughts again drifted to the familiar home in New England. ". . . I already begin to count the days that intervene between now and our departure," he said, "and we are all restless and feverish with the thought of home. . . . If you happen to hear of a puppy-dog, of a large and good breed, I should like to get such a one."[19]

In April Hawthorne took the family to Bath for a few weeks in the hope of helping Sophia regain the vitality she had enjoyed in Rome. The stay proved to be restful, although the family's introduction to the town approached high comedy. On arrival at Bath station they asked a porter to recommend a good hotel. To their dismay he took them to the York House which, they quickly learned, was "not only the first hotel in Bath, but one famous

**BATH'S ROYAL YORK**
Before departing from Liverpool in 1860 the Hawthornes visited Bath. The station porter recommended the Royal Bath Hotel, but Sophia was terrified – when she saw its elegance – lest Hawthorne could not afford it.

throughout the land." There was little the family could do "but to take it grandly," remain only for twenty-four hours, and pray that the bill would not be too exorbitant.[20]

Then someone had a sudden notion: if, indeed, the family was stuck with grand surroundings for a full day, why not pretend to be grand persons – at least to themselves. After a hasty conference they decided that Hawthorne and Sophia would be the "Duke and Duchess of Maine," Una would be "Lady Raymond" (after their favourite haunt in Maine), Julian was to be "Lord Waldo" (for a county in Maine), while Rose was to be simply "Lady Rose." For the next twenty-four hours the family carried off their ducal pretenses as superbly as characters out of *Burke's Peerage*.

"I felt so grand," Sophia said, "that I was ready to shout with laughter – having gone full circle from the sublime to the ridiculous several times. I felt the ducal coronet on my brow, flashing fine flames from diamonds and emeralds. His Grace's diadems put my eyes out. . . ."[21] The staff of the York House may have been puzzled at the strange behaviour of their American guests, but if they were, the Hawthornes took no notice. When the day was over, they waited apprehensively for the account. When it was rendered a great sigh of relief went up, for the charges were more moderate than those of some much inferior accommodations.

While the family was still in Bath, John Motley wrote from London and invited Hawthorne to pass a few days in the capital before embarking for the United States. Hawthorne found it difficult to refuse this fellow New Englander who so recently had praised *The Marble Faun*. "I admire the book exceedingly," Motley had written. "I suppose that your ears are somewhat stunned with your praises, appearing as you do after so long an interval, but I hope that, amid the din, you will not disdain the whisper from such sincere admirers as I am myself, and my wife and daughter are."[22] Hawthorne was moved by Motley's sincerity and hastened to reply. "You are," he said, "certainly that Gentle Reader for whom all my books were exclusively written. Nobody else (my wife excepted, who speaks so near that I cannot tell her voice from my own) has ever said exactly what I loved to hear."[23]

While still consul, Hawthorne had seen the glories of Oxford in the company of Francis Bennoch. Now, with his time in England fast running out, he managed to see something of Cambridge with Henry Bright as companion. The occasion was the awarding of Bright's master's degree, and the arrangements could not have pleased Hawthorne more. "I am established here [Trinity College] in an ancient set of college rooms," he wrote Una in Bath, "which happen to be temporarily vacated by the rightful professor. I arrived yesterday evening and am pretty well wearied by a day of sight-seeing, – as you may suppose, Mr.

**TRINITY COLLEGE, CAMBRIDGE, WHERE HAWTHORNE STAYED**
Henry Bright, Hawthorne's Liverpool friend, returned to Cambridge in the spring of 1860 to receive his master's degree, and invited Hawthorne to accompany him.

Bright being the cicerone. I snatch just this moment to write before going to dine with one of the fellows of the college. . . . I heard a nightingale – two or three, indeed – last night!'"[24] Among the recorded sights Hawthorne saw in Cambridge were Byron's Pool, Cromwell's portrait in Sidney Sussex College, and the Cambridge Union.

With the family's passage booked for June 16 on the *Europa*, a sister ship of the *Niagara*, Hawthorne could not tarry long in London. The family wished to spend their last hours on British soil at Liverpool where many friends awaited them. Just how many merchants and civic officials Hawthorne saw is not known, but he did take the trouble to say farewell to two people he much admired. One was Henry Young, bookseller, whose shop in South Castle Street Hawthorne had frequented regularly while consul. "When the family left England," he said, "Mr. and Mrs. Hawthorne and, I think, Miss Una Hawthorne, called to shake hands and say good-bye."[25]

Although Hawthorne had been the guest of aristocratic families and civic officials of Liverpool during his time as consul, it was not to their elegant homes that he turned during the family's last days in the port, but the modest boarding house operated by Mary Blodget. There the family, for the last time, enjoyed the hospitality of the kindly lady who had so interwoven her own personality into the establishment on Duke Street as to give it a uniqueness in the world of commercial accommodation.

In mid-June the Hawthornes sailed from Liverpool aboard the *Europa*, as planned, and promptly met Captain John Leitch who had commanded the *Niagara* on the family's outward voyage in 1853. The genial captain, as dignified as ever, was basking in the praise gained from his extraordinary feats of navigational skill demonstrated while ferrying British troops to the Crimea. Other than the pleasant surprise of again being in the company of the ship's popular master, the family experienced no unusual adventures on the homeward voyage.

### "WE ARE ALL RESTLESS ... WITH THE THOUGHT OF HOME"

In June, 1860, the Hawthornes returned to The Wayside after a seven-year absence. A \$2,000 enlargement was not completed until the end of the year. A striking exterior feature was the tower room which Hawthorne hoped to use as a study. In the photograph above Sophia and Nathaniel are standing in front of the altered home.

Eventually the shores of New England and later, the docks of Boston, appeared and everyone waited apprehensively for the first look at the homeland in seven years. The parents had old memories to fall back upon, but to the children the New England countryside – even in summer – was a strange, new world. "When we drove from the station to The Wayside . . .," recalled Rose, "I distinctly remember the ugliness of the un-English landscape and the forlornness of the little cottage which was our home."[26]

While most New Englanders were preoccupied by the gathering clouds of conflict, Hawthorne had overriding domestic concerns. As in his pre-consular days, he found himself burdened with money problems. Thus, the cost of making the necessary enlargement and improvements to The Wayside came as a great shock. Week after week he was obliged to write Ticknor for advances. Before long the cost exceeded \$2,000, a sum several times more than he had originally estimated. "If I escape absolute beggary," he told Ticknor, "I shall thank Heaven and you." Then he added, ruefully: "What's the use of having a house if it costs me all my means of living in it?"[27]

Suddenly, while alterations were being made to the house, Una fell ill again. The new spell probably was a recurrence of the dreaded malaria with its accompanying fits of delirium. With her nervous system thus affected, Una presented a frightening aspect to her family. The sight of his first-born suffering, and perhaps afflicted thus for life, was almost more than Hawthorne could bear. Una's illness became his own. When her condition improved his own soared; when she became worse, he suffered as well. Eventually, after being subjected to electrical shock treatment, Una's condition improved. But the illness had severely ravaged her already frail constitution, and she was never to enjoy robust health again.

The strain of making ends meet and Una's weird illness had taken its toll. Hawthorne's energy now began to sag and though time and again he attempted to write, the old enthusiasm and will were missing. "I spend two or three hours a day in my sky-parlor and duly spread a quire of paper on my desk," he told Ticknor in February of 1861, "but no very important result has followed thus far."[28]

Abraham Lincoln was inaugurated as president on March 4, 1861 and a month later Fort Sumter fell to the Confederate forces. In both the North and South volunteers rushed to enlist, industry made hasty plans to expand, and agents were sent scurrying to foreign lands to obtain munitions. The first major battle, at Bull Run in July, was a victory for the newly formed Confederate States, but the many blunders on both sides foretold a long and bloody conflict.

When Hawthorne heard news of the South's victory at Bull Run, he communicated his morbid mood to James Russell Lowell. ". . . last evening's news will dull the edge of many a Northern appetite;" he said, "but if it puts all of us into the same grim and bloody humor that it does me, the South had better have suffered ten defeats than won this victory."[29] By October, when the magnitude of the fighting and the effect it might have on America's future were becoming apparent, Hawthorne evolved his own philosophy of the civil war — essentially a desire "to live and let live." To Horatio Bridge he wrote: "For my part, I don't hope (nor indeed wish) to see the Union restored as it was; amputation seems to me much the better plan. . . . I would fight to the death for the Northern slave states, and let the rest go."[30]

Extracts from Sophia's diary during this period reveal not only the major events in the family life, but a wife's growing concern for her husband's health:

> Letter and wine from General Pierce. . . . My husband made an anagram of the General's [Pierce's] name, 'Princelie Frank.' . . . My husband is not well. . . . I have been very anxious about him. . . . Mr. Thoreau died this morning. . . . Una's party took place tonight. . . . Papa illuminated it with his presence. . . . I went to the hilltop with my husband for a long time. Ineffable felicity. . . . Julian and I went to Boston. When I came home I found my husband looking very ill. . . . Everything seems sad when he is ill.[31]

The Civil War, indeed, cast a pall over both parents. News of the immense casualties was bound to depress Hawthorne, for few towns in New England were without some deaths. If Franklin Pierce's policies had not succeeded in averting the bloodshed which now engulfed the nation, Hawthorne never doubted his friend's intentions and patriotism. On one occasion the former president came to Concord to see his old friend. ". . . we mingled our tears and condolences for the state of the country," Hawthorne wrote Horatio Bridge; "Pierce is truly patriotic and thinks there is nothing left for us but to fight it out."[32]

Horatio Bridge had suggested that Hawthorne visit Washington early in 1862, but in February the former consul confessed to his friend that, although the invitation was tempting, he was "not very well, being mentally and physically languid . . ." He also offered another reason for not going to the capital: "I ought not to spend money needlessly in these hard times."[33] Nonetheless Hawthorne, accompanied by William Ticknor, set out in the first week of March for Washington via New York and Philadelphia.

The Washington stay, which lasted a month, was a great success. The capital was agog over the war and as Hawthorne and Ticknor neared the city they saw evidence of the conflict on every side – troops and tent cities, guards at stations, and weapons and supplies. A busy Abraham Lincoln took time out to meet Hawthorne. "On the whole," the author wrote afterwards, "I liked this sallow, queer, visage with the homely human sympathies that warmed it."[34] But he was disappointed not to see the President sit down and fold up his long legs, an act said to be an extraordinary spectacle in itself. Sophia was quick to hear of her husband's visit with the President. "Mary [Mann] has just sent me a note saying that there is a paragraph in the paper about your being at Washington," she wrote Hawthorne, "and that the President received you with especial graciousness. Stay as long as you can, and get great good."[35]

Although Hawthorne had now known or met the last three American Presidents, he was acquainted with very few military leaders on either side of the Civil War. There was, however, one general in the Confederate Army whose fortunes he may have followed with interest. He was Brigadier General Charles S. Winder who, as a young lieutenant in 1854, came ashore at Liverpool with survivors from the ill-fated troopship, the *San Francisco*. On that occasion Hawthorne had been much impressed with the officer's resourcefulness; if he had followed the course of the war, he would also have been impressed by Winder's record. He abandoned a promising career in the U.S. Army in April, 1861, to join the Confederate cause; he was promptly made a major of artillery. Afterwards he took part in the reduction of Fort Sumter and by July had become a colonel in the 6th South Carolina Infantry. Early in 1862 he was promoted to Brigadier General in the provisional army and assigned to General Thomas J. Jackson's "Stonewall Brigade." In the build-up to the Second Manassas campaign, Winder – while commanding Jackson's division – was hit by a shell at Cedar Mountain and died shortly afterwards. He was only 32 and, despite his youth, was regarded as one of the South's most able officers.[36]

One of the most remarkable letters ever written by Hawthorne was that sent to his friend Francis Bennoch on the subject of the American Civil War. A striking feature of the letter is Hawthorne's proposal that young men be excluded from fighting conflicts because their elders had allowed the wars to develop. Hawthorne began the letter to Bennoch by citing the precedent, during the French Revolution, of a people going to war "for an idea, – a very nice, if not an absolutely true idea." In the American Civil War, he told Bennoch, the same thing was happening.[37]

"We also have gone to war," he said, "and we seem to have little, or at least a very misty idea of what we are fighting for. It depends upon the speaker, and that again depends upon the section of the country in which his sympathies are enlisted. The Southern man will say: We fight for State rights, liberty, and independence. The Middle Western man will avow that he fights for the Union, whilst our Northern and Eastern man will swear that from the beginning his only idea was liberty to the Blacks and the annihilation of slavery. All are thoroughly in earnest, and all pray for the blessing of Heaven to rest upon the enterprise."[38]

Hawthorne admitted that the war had thoroughly aroused the spirit of young men and added, were it not for "certain silvery monitors hanging by my temples suggesting prudence," he would be inclined to join their ranks. Then he came to his novel notion of how armies should be raised. "Why draw from our young men in the bloom and heyday of their youth . . .?" he asked. "Had I my way, no man should go to war under fifty years of age, such men having already had their natural share of worldly pleasures and life's enjoy-

**A CHANGED MAN**
This portrait was executed in 1860 when Hawthorne returned to the United States. He was only 56, but anxiety over Una's serious illness and his family's security had made their mark.

ments. . . . Then I would add a premium in favor of recruits of three-score years and upwards as, virtually with one foot in the grave, they would not be likely to run away." He went on to ask Bennoch if, during the excitement which then reigned over the war, he could not pay the family a visit at The Wayside: "The room bearing your name is ready, the fire is laid, and here we are prepared to give you welcome. Come and occupy the apartment dedicated to you. Come and let us talk over the many pleasant evenings we spent together in dear Old England."[39]

Although many Americans still remembered Frank Pierce's lack-lustre administration and blamed the former president for his ineffectiveness in averting war, Hawthorne had no thought of abandoning his friend. Instead, loyalty to his Bowdoin classmate was soon to be put to an unexpected test. After Hawthorne's series of sketches about his consular experiences and life in England had appeared in *The Atlantic Monthly*, his co-publisher, James T. Fields, suggested adapting the articles so as to make a book of them. What the volume needed was a dedication to some well known personality. Fields no doubt hoped Hawthorne would turn to some prominent literary figure, but the author had a different notion. He proposed the man who had made his English sojourn possible – Frank Pierce. Fields was astounded, for he knew a dedication to such a controversial figure could not possibly help the book's sales.

Hawthorne refused to budge from his proposal. In a strongly worded reply to Field's objections, he left no doubt where he stood. ". . . it would be a piece of poltroonery in me to withdraw either the dedication or the dedicatory letter," he said. "My long and intimate personal relations with Pierce render the dedication altogether proper, especially as regards this book which would have had no existence without his kindness." Then he addressed himself to Field's concern about loss of profit on the book and, indeed, possible damage to Hawthorne's literary reputation. ". . . if he is so exceedingly unpopular that his name is enough to sink the volume," he said, "there is so much more need that an old friend should stand by him."[40]

The volume appeared under the title *Our Old Home* in both the United States and Britain. The dedication, untouched by Fields, read:

TO
FRANKLIN PIERCE
AS A SLIGHT MEMORIAL OF A COLLEGE FRIEND-
SHIP, PROLONGED THROUGH MANHOOD,
AND RETAINING ALL ITS VITALITY
IN OUR AUTUMNAL YEARS,
*This Volume*
IS INSCRIBED BY
NATHANIEL HAWTHORNE.

But it was the dedicatory letter itself, particularly the conclusion, which was to offend those who disagreed strongly with Pierce's political views. Hawthorne was careful to emphasize his relationship with Pierce as a *friend*. "And, now farewell, my dear friend," the last paragraph began, "excuse (if you think it needs any excuse) the freedom with which I thus publicly assert a personal friendship between a private individual and a statesman who has filled what was then the most august position in the world. But I dedicate my book to the Friend, and shall defer a colloquy with the Statesman till some calmer and sunnier hour."[41]

Apart from Hawthorne's insistence on retaining the laudatory references to Pierce, there was another aspect of the dedicatory letter which displeased the publishers. Among the sketches in the book were some that criticized physical aspects of the English people. Although his publishers may have wished these derogatory comments to be either toned down or omitted, Hawthorne refused. In the dedicatory letter he explained why. "I never stood in an English crowd without being conscious of hereditary sympathies," he said, "Nevertheless, it is undeniable that an American is continually thrown upon his national antagonism by some acrid quality in the moral atmosphere of England. . . . Jotting down the little acrimonies of the moment . . ., it is very possible that I may have said things which a profound observer of national character would hesitate to sanction, though never any, I verily believe, that had not more or less of truth. If they be true, there is no reason in the world why they should not be said."[42]

Hawthorne's novels had won him wide acclaim in the English-speaking world. This popularity was now at stake as Fields reluctantly proceeded to publish *Our Old Home* in the summer of 1863. Ostensibly, the work set out to narrate the adventures of the American Consul in Liverpool and to record his extensive travels in Britain. But was it – as Fields feared – a dangerous departure for an author whose works had charmed readers on both sides of the Atlantic for a decade past?

Hawthorne had not long to wait for the answer.

# XVII
## Condemnation and Death

Some biographers, Moncure Conway for one, have sought to excuse Hawthorne's *Our Old Home* on the grounds that it was written during a period of great anxiety and distraction for the author. Conway was a guest, along with Hawthorne, in the home of publisher James T. Fields some time after the former consul returned to the United States. On that occasion, during a memorable breakfast, Hawthorne captivated those present with "a charming flow of talk – most of it being about England." For Conway, there was no doubt how the author had allowed such a controversial volume to be published. "The sketches . . .," he said, "had unfortunately been hurried into a volume amid many worries, without such revision as we now got at the breakfast table where all his memories of England were happy."[1]

Whatever the reasons that allowed Hawthorne to leave the offending references intact, neither he nor Fields could have foreseen that the controversial passages would lead to greater sales than the pessimistic publisher imagined. Nonetheless, Hawthorne was stunned by the negative reception accorded the book in the United States. Some of the reviews were kind enough; The *North American Review*, for example, ignored the dedicatory references to Pierce and praised the work as "unequalled if not unsurpassed" as a narrative of experiences in foreign lands. The magazine, indeed, took note of the author's unsavoury observations, but saw them as an attractive aspect of Hawthorne's style of writing. "Things present themselves grotesquely to Mr. Hawthorne," the review said. "He takes hold of them by some other than the usual handle, and offers to our view just the parts and aspects of them which it is conventionally fit to keep out of sight."[2]

But it was private censure – especially in his native New England – that stung Hawthorne most. Though these piques did not always appear in print, they must have been a popular conversation piece in Boston's literary circle. Ralph Waldo Emerson, who told Conway that Hawthorne's chapter on Delia Bacon was the best thing he ever wrote, nonetheless cut out the references to Franklin Pierce from his copy of *Our Old Home*. Harriet Beecher Stowe criticized both Hawthorne, for his praise of Pierce, and Fields for publishing the book.

By the autumn of 1863 Hawthorne was a very sick man. In addition, everything in his life now seemed to go wrong. Una's illness, which he now realized could be chronic, was only one of several blows to his diminishing health. His lifelong dread of poverty in old age was now reality, and unless he could write again, his family seemed doomed to insecurity. He started one romance after the other, but was unable to bring any to satisfactory conclusion.

Then came an attack from an unexpected quarter, one which went far to quench any desire he still held to write. The reviews of the British edition of *Our Old Home* now arrived by steamer and they did not make pleasant reading. While a handful of publications praised Hawthorne's travel descriptions, most could not tolerate his criticism of English life and customs, and especially his portrayal of English women as solid, plump creatures.

"I have heard a good deal of the tenacity with which English ladies retain their personal beauty to a late period of life," wrote Hawthorne in *Our Old Home*, "but . . . it strikes me that an English lady of fifty is apt to become a creature less refined and delicate, so far as her physique goes, than anything that we Western people class under the name of woman."[3] Most national comparisons are odious; when the subject of comparison is women, the result in the offended nation can only be resentment. As a consul on active duty Hawthorne never once bared such thoughts, but now, in *Our Old Home*, he took the plunge. "... she [the English woman] has the effect of a seventy-four gun-ship in time of peace," he continued, "for, while you assure yourself that there is no real danger, you cannot help thinking how tremendous would be her onset if pugnaciously inclined, and how futile the effort to inflict any counter-injury. She certainly looks ten-fold – nay, a hundred-fold – better able to take care of herself than our slender-framed and haggard woman-kind."[4] By contrast, in the same chapter in which these offending passages were found Hawthorne had compliments about English girls. "... an English maiden in her teens," he said, "... possesses, to say the truth, a certain charm of half-blossom and delicately folded leaves, and tender womanhood shielded by maidenly reserves, with which, somehow or other, our American girls often fail to adorn themselves during an appreciable moment."[5]

Britain's literary world erupted in uproar when *Our Old Home* appeared. Few people took note of Hawthorne's praise of the nation's antiquity and her giants of literature, but most had a great deal to say about his references to English women. *Blackwood's* was kinder than most. "This [description of womanhood] ... is not exactly good-natured," it said. "We wish we could quote some pleasanter passages respecting our people, but there are really none ..."[6] The *Quarterly Review* was more to the point. "Mr. Hawthorne," it said, "in his ineffable coarseness, cannot even look on the budding beauty of English girlhood or the full flower of English womanhood without speculating upon the quantity of 'clay' that makes up the human form. ... A Yankee may think that his 'national paleness and lean habit of flesh' may give an advantage in an aesthetic point of view. We like to feel the radiating health and to hear the ring of it in the voice.'"[7]

It was left to *Punch*, the arch exponent of barbaric America, to strike the deadliest blow against Hawthorne. "We have often credited you with literary merit," it said, "and your style, dear boy, puts to shame a good many of our own writers who ought to write better than they do. ... You have written a book about England and into this book you have put all the caricatures and libels upon English folk which you collected while enjoying our hospitality. Your book is thoroughly saturated with what seems ill-nature and spite."[8]

With Hawthorne's reputation as a shy person in mind, *Punch* attacked the former consul for his remarks about English women. "... we ... give you credit ...," it said, "because you do not write of ladies whom you have seen at a distance, or in their carriages, or from the point of view of a shy and awkward man who skulks away at the rustle of a crinoline and hides himself among the ineligibles at the ball-room door. ... Everybody in the world knows that the gifted American Consul at Liverpool is an idoliser of the ladies and is one of the most ready, fluent, accomplished talkers of lady-talk that ever fascinated a sofa-full of smiling beauties. Consequently, his tribute has a value which would not appertain to the criticisms of a sheepish person ... No, no, this is the testimony of the lady-killer, the sparkling yet tender Liverpool Lovelace, NATHANIEL HAWTHORNE, to the merits of English women."[9]

Most of the unfavourable English criticism of *Our Old Home* had appeared by October of 1863. In the middle of the month, after having seen a fair sampling of what the critics on the other side of the Atlantic were saying about the book, Hawthorne was moved to write Fields. He told the publisher that he was not surprised that the English had taken him to task in such severe terms. "... it is perhaps natural that they should," he said, "because their self-conceit can accept nothing short of indiscriminate adulation." He went on to say that, in his view, Americans had more cause for complaint than the English. "Looking over the volume," he said, "I am rather surprised to find that whenever I draw a comparison between the two people I almost invariably cast the balance against ourselves. It is not a good nor a weighty book, nor does it deserve any great amount either of praise or censure. I don't care about seeing any more notices . . ."[10]

A few British publications, *The Times* among them, waited for the initial outrage over the book to pass before commenting. The respected London daily devoted almost three columns to *Our Old Home* and its tone was in marked contrast to that of *Punch*. "As we glide over these easy pages," the reviewer wrote, "we feel ourselves in the company of a gentle, kindly, pure-minded character who, however hard he may try to smite us, cannot hurt us much and might as well be pelting us with sugar plums and smothering us in roses. . . . Mr. Hawthorne's book is quite different from what – judging by the preface and some of the opinions that have been passed upon it, we were led to expect. . . . Mr. Hawthorne scarcely ever takes off his gloves; they are excellently well-padded and his blows fall on us like eider-down."[11]

Then *The Times* turned to Hawthorne's descriptions of English women. "The chief passages in which Mr. Hawthorne is supposed to have adopted an unduly deprecating tone are those in which he speaks of the personal appearance of English men and women," it said. "We hasten to re-assure this amiable Yankee. We can no more be offended with him because he says we are fat and rotund than we expect him to be offended with us because we think his countrymen lank and lean."[12]

The stir caused in English literary circles by *Our Old Home* led the novelist, Berkeley Aikin, to write to Hawthorne. After first complimenting the author on his previous works, she asked why – in his latest book – he dealt so harshly with members of her own sex. "Alas, my dear Sir," she said, "what have you been doing to the English ladies? . . . I have not seen your new book, but on every hand I hear, 'Mr. Hawthorne has written such a book! He says the English ladies are all like – like – beef!' I cannot make out even from literary folks that you have said anything else, but this bovine matter will not be forgiven to even so great a favorite as yourself. Oh, pray do write another romance to wipe out this *crime*!"[13]

If Hawthorne felt his two young friends in England would keep silent during the tempest over *Our Old Home*, he was to be mistaken. Henry Bright, in a review for the *Examiner*, must have been sorely distressed to write such harsh words about his friend's work. "Whatever Mr. Hawthorne may like in England," he said, "he certainly does not like us Englishmen." Then he came directly to the point. "With us," he continued, "he is neither struck nor pleased. Englishmen, and English women more especially, seem to be his positive aversion."[14]

Francis Bennoch did not have to await the publication of *Our Old Home* to vent his feelings, for he had read the sketches when they originally appeared in the *Atlantic Monthly*. ". . . you take the opportunity of having a fling at English beauty," he said, "contrasting it unfavourably with the fragile and most delicate fabric of American womanhood. This won't do! For either grace of loveliness, good bearing or refined gentleness, I'll back England's daughters against the world . . ."[15]

How is one to explain Hawthorne's criticisms when he knew so few English women? The inescapable conclusion is that his impressions came more from general observation than personal acquaintance.[16] No doubt many of the female passengers he saw aboard the ferry-boats, running every morning from Rock Ferry to Liverpool, were in domestic service in the homes of the city's wealthy families. Perhaps they, like the staff of Mrs. Blodget's boarding house, possessed the solid features that he chronicled. Likewise, he may have observed some women in Liverpool's poorer districts, which he often frequented, who cared more for their food and drink than in preserving their figures.

One happy event among so much disparagement was Julian's acceptance by Harvard

University. When his son was preparing to go to Cambridge to take the entrance examinations, Hawthorne said: "Mind you get in, but I don't expect you will!" Julian knew only too well that his father's words were meant to soften his humiliation in the event of failure. "Happily," said Julian, years later, "I succeeded after a fashion, but only afterwards learned that he would have been much cast down had my fate been different. I remember the happy expression with which he greeted the new-fledged collegian's return home."[17]

As December neared, the outcry attending the publication of *Our Old Home* was largely past. But there was to be one more ordeal for the ailing Hawthorne. Early in this month Mrs. Franklin Pierce died. For the former president, the loss of his wife was the crowning blow, for none of their three children had lived past the age of eleven. Hawthorne, although ill, could not abandon his old friend in his moment of loneliness and grief. On a bitterly cold day, he dragged himself to the funeral in New Hampshire. There the bereaved Pierce, burdened as he was with his wife's death, was seen to turn and pull up the collar of Hawthorne's coat to protect his friend against the chilling wind.

In the second half of December Una went away to spend the Christmas holidays, but Sophia – ever cognizant of the close bond between her husband and his first-born – kept her posted on Hawthorne's condition. On December 19 she told Una that her father felt well enough to read "in one of his huge books of the English State Trials," but shortly thereafter, looked very ill and obviously had been faint.[18] Two days later Sophia's letter sounded more like a hospital medical bulletin about someone who was critically ill. "Papa is comfortable today," she said, "but very thin and weak. . . . I am very impatient that he should see Dr. Vandersende, but he wants to go to see him himself, and he cannot go till it be good weather. How forever I shall bless the old German doctor if he can give papa again the zest of life he used to have!" Then she revealed that one of her husband's greatest delights, good food, no longer interested him. "I am amazed," she said, "that such a fortress as his digestion should give way."[19]

As the new year arrived, Hawthorne tried again and again to complete *The Dolliver Romance*, his tale about an old apothecary. In February he was obliged to tell Fields of his inability to continue. "I cannot finish it unless a great change comes over me," he said, "and if I make too great an effort to do so, it will be my death." Then, in an afterthought, his mind turned to the land on the other side of the Atlantic. "If I could but go to England now," he said, "I think that the sea-voyage and the 'old home' might set me all right."[20] Alas, it was far too late for an ocean voyage, and the only journeys Hawthorne would make were to be on the Atlantic seaboard, each in the company of a dear friend, and each of which would end in death for one of the partners. In both cases the trips were conceived as therapy for the ailing author.

William Ticknor, Hawthorne's faithful confidant over the years, felt a trip in the early spring, especially if pursued southwards through New York, might be just the tonic needed to restore his friend's health. On March 18 Hawthorne wrote he had "gained strength a little" and was fully resolved to start travelling. Frank Pierce originally hoped to accompany Ticknor and Hawthorne, but a note from him announced he was unable to get away just then. So the pair started out on their journey of hope, reaching New York without mishap. Then a violent storm broke, forcing them to remain indefinitely in the Astor Hotel. From this vantage point Ticknor sent Sophia an interim report on March 30, saying it was still too early to tell if the journey was having its desired effect – "but I can't but hope that it will prove the right medicine."[21]

The storm did not abate and the two friends were obliged to continue their enforced stay in the Astor. Four days later they were still in New York, and Ticknor sent Sophia another

## WILLIAM TICKNOR

When Hawthorne's health deteriorated rapidly in early 1864, Ticknor suggested that the former consul should join him in a trip to New York and Philadelphia. Bad weather led to Ticknor's own illness, from which he died while in Philadelphia. Hawthorne lived only two months more.

note. "I assure you," he said, "he is much improved, but he is yet very weak. The weather has been as bad as possible, and of course we have not been out much."[22]

Eventually the weather relented sufficiently to allow the two men to continue their journey southwards, and on April 7 Ticknor wrote Mrs. Ticknor that they had arrived safely in Philadelphia. The letter was brief, and must have left the recipient worried. "Excuse this short note," Ticknor said, "as I must look after my friend. I have a bad cold and feel disinclined to move at all."[23] Now Ticknor became the patient and Hawthorne the concerned friend. The following day Ticknor's condition worsened, and on April 10 he died. The crushed and ailing Hawthorne began his sad, lonely journey back to New England. He stopped briefly in Boston to give Fields a brief account of the tragic death, and then made his way wearily to Concord.

Sophia saw her husband as he reached the front porch, and his appearance sent terror into her heart. "He came back unlooked-for that day," she recalled, "and when I heard a step on the piazza, I was lying on a couch and feeling quite indisposed. But as soon as I saw him I was frightened out of all knowledge of myself, – so haggard, so white, so deeply scored with pain and fatigue was the face, so much more ill he looked than I ever saw him before. He had walked from the station because he saw no carriage there, and his brow was streaming with a perfect rain, so great had been the effort to walk so far. . . . He needed to get home to me where he could fling off all care of himself and give way to his feelings, pent up and kept back for so long, especially since his watch and ward of most excellent, kind Mr. Ticknor."[24]

As Hawthorne's condition deteriorated, Sophia's anxiety grew. In vain she begged him to see a doctor. Finally, she contrived a plan by which he, at least, would have a cursory examination. Writing to Fields, she asked if Dr. Oliver Wendell Holmes could be persuaded to see her husband "in some ingenious way on Wednesday as a friend."[25] Dr. Holmes readily agreed to the scheme and went to the Boston hotel where Hawthorne was staying before setting out the next day with Franklin Pierce on another therapeutic trip, this time to the mountains of Pierce's native New Hampshire.

Informed that Hawthorne had just left the hotel on foot, Holmes set out after him. Soon he saw the unmistakable figure of the author, except – Holmes noted – he now "seemed to

**PEMIGEWASSET HOUSE IN PLYMOUTH**
Here, in a connecting room shared with his old friend, Frank Pierce, Nathaniel Hawthorne
died on May 19, 1864.

have shrunken in all his dimensions and faltered with an uncertain, feeble step, as if every
movement was an effort." In the next half hour Holmes inquired into Hawthorne's condition as delicately as he could. "His aspect," he concluded, "was very unfavourable. There
were persistent local symptons, referred to especially to the stomach, – 'boring pain,'
distension, difficult digestion, with great wasting of flesh and strength. He was very gentle,
very willing to answer questions, very docile to such counsel as I offered him, but evidently
had no hope of recovering his health."[26]

The following day, according to plan, Hawthorne and Pierce left Boston on a journey
which the former president earnestly hoped would restore his old friend's vitality. The pace
was leisurely, first by train and then by Pierce's private carriage. On May 18 they reached
the town of Plymouth. Pierce's letter to Horatio Bridge relates what happened after they
had checked into the Pemigewasset House.

"After taking a little tea and toast in his room and sleeping for nearly an hour upon the
sofa," he said, ". . . [Hawthorne] retired. A door opened from my room to his and our beds
were not more than five or six feet apart. I remained up for an hour or two after he fell
asleep. He was apparently less restless than the night before. The light was left burning in

my room – the door open – and I could see him without moving from my bed. I went, however, between one and two o'clock to his bedside and supposed him to be in a profound slumber. His eyes were closed, his position and face perfectly natural. His face was turned towards my bed."

Pierce then retired himself, but sound sleep did not come. "I awoke again between three and four o'clock and was surprised – as he had generally been restless – to notice that his position was unchanged – exactly the same that it was two hours before," he said. "I went to his bedside, placed my hand upon his forehead and temple, and found that he was dead. He evidently had passed from natural to that sleep from which there is no awakening, without the slightest movement."[27] If Franklin Pierce needed some further manifestation of Hawthorne's respect for him, he now discovered it; while packing up his friend's belongings he came across an old pocket-book in the bottom of Hawthorne's valise. He picked it up, looked inside, and saw there his own picture which his friend obviously had taken with him wherever he had gone.

A hundred miles to the south, in The Wayside, an anxious family waited for news of Hawthorne – news which it dreaded to hear. Rose, writing later, remembered the impact of the event on her mother. She surmised, too, that on the day when her father left for the New Hampshire trip, both parents sensed the parting was to be forever. "I could hardly bear," she said, "to let my eyes rest upon [my mother's] shrunken, suffering form . . . [that] day of farewell. My father certainly knew, what she vaguely felt, that he would never return."[28]

Nor did Rose forget her own parting. "The last time I saw him," she said, "he was leaving the house to take the journey . . . Like a snow image of an unbending, but an old, old man, he stood for a moment gazing at me. My mother sobbed as she walked beside him to the carriage. We have missed him in the sunshine, in the storm, in the twilight, ever since."[29]

# XVIII
# Assessment of a Consul

It may be practicable in these days to assess the capacity of a diplomat through evaluation forms compiled by a reviewing officer or an inspector. For the work of a consul in the middle of the last century, however, there is insufficient evidence to contemplate such a judgment. Dispatches, correspondence and diaries provide merely the facade behind which hides the writer himself. Nor could such evidence as exists be given in a volume of this size.

Having been appointed to the Liverpool consulate through the patronage of President Pierce (his friend of college days), Nathaniel Hawthorne had achieved his immediate object – an assured position and income for the next four years. He could have sat back on the banks of the Mersey and drawn the fees from work done mainly by his English clerks. It says much for Hawthorne, however anxious he may have been about the amount and regularity of his remuneration, that he entered fully into activities incumbent on his appointment.

His dispatches, sometimes lengthy and emphatic, indicate his personal embroilment in problems which obtruded themselves on his attention. Notable was that of the condition of seamen on board American vessels calling at Liverpool. He returned to this matter many times, making personal appeals at the highest levels in Washington and elsewhere and continued to do so even after his retirement, not without success.

He was also prepared to bypass bureaucracy when there were strong arguments for so doing. For instance, he assisted in the relief and repatriation of soldiers stranded in Liverpool by the sinking of the *San Francisco*, although the regulations stipulated he could help only destitute sailors.

A consul is pre-eminently an administrative officer. He signs documents, he prepares dispatches, he succours his compatriots. But he should avoid becoming involved in politics. Such a deviation might affect the value of his official labours. Nevertheless Hawthorne on one notable occasion threw himself into an international turmoil and by certain speeches and private remarks was partially instrumental in easing the tension between Britain and America, over the Crampton imbroglio.

It must be remembered that Hawthorne came to England with an established reputation as an author. This, together with his position as consul, involved social obligations. He was not naturally a gregarious man. An affectionate husband and father, he preferred the pleasures of family life at Rock Ferry. But he was not unpopular with the business community of Liverpool. He was entertained by them and in his turn entertained, and appears to have enjoyed these junketings. There is little evidence to show what his acquaintances thought of him. Although he made many after-dinner speeches, mostly impromptu, it is doubtful whether he was invited for his humour and witty remarks.

By attending these functions which were mainly for men, Hawthorne kept in touch with public opinion. To this knowledge his travels around Britain contributed. The picture, in countless letters and dispatches of conditions in the towns and villages of England, conveyed to those in America information to counterbalance the prevailing acerbic press reports. There is no doubt but that Hawthorne liked England, what he saw of it.

By all these signs he may be judged to have been an assiduous consul carrying out his statutory duties but taking upon himself others that he considered required action. All in all he should be given considerable credit for his achievements.

All of which made, and still make, his outburst against English women so inexplicable. Notes in diaries may be accurate comments on the occasion described but need not appear in print. Hawthorne liked dining with males, but he did not mix with many of their women folk. He met very few during his official engagements and presumably only those acceptable to Sophia, his wife, would be welcome at his home.

Why, then, did he permit these criticisms to appear, criticisms which caused so much annoyance on both sides of the Atlantic? There was no need for it. Had his aversion towards English women been kept under cover during his stay in Britain by his natural courtesy, only to be vented on his return to his native land?

We do not know. We shall never know. He was an ageing man absorbed by consular worries and the seeds of his final illness may already have been sown, affecting his judgment and his mind. What is certain is that as a result of these ill considered remarks his reputation suffered notably at the time and in later years.

Although some critics berate Hawthorne for drastically changing his mode of life from literature to the consular service, what is certain is that his years at Liverpool were not wasted. His struggles for the seamen laid the foundations for future action, even if they did not bear immediate fruit.

What may be said in conclusion is that Nathaniel Hawthorne's last years were spent in the loving company of his wife and family and the congenial companionship of two of his oldest friends, William Ticknor and Franklin Pierce. These two stood by him to the end. A man who can lay his hand on his heart and say – "I have held two friends all my life" – is not without some claim to remembrance.

# Bibliography

Allison, W. A. G., Director, Glasgow District Libraries. Letters to the author, Sept. 13 and Aug. 25, 1975.

*The American Notebooks, The Centenary Edition of the Works of Nathaniel Hawthorne*, VIII.

*American Secretaries of State*. Ed., Samuel F. Bemis, 10 vols. New York: Alfred A. Knopp, 1927.

*The American Transcendental Quarterly*. II Quarter, no. 2, 1969.

Baines, Thomas, *History of the Commerce and Town of Liverpool*, Liverpool: published by the author; London: Longman, Brown, Green and Longman, 1852.

Baker, W. A., *From Paddle Steamer to Nuclear Ship*. London: Watts, 1965.

Barnes, Brian J., Birkenhead Central Library. Letters to the author, 1976–7.

Barnes, William, and Morgan, John Heath, *The Foreign Service of the United States*. Washington: Department of State, 1961.

Bede, Cuthbert (Edward Bradley), *The Adventures of Verdant Green*. London: James Blackwood & Co., 1853.

Bennoch, Francis, *A Few Lyrics*. London: published by the author, 1857.

———, *Poems, Lyrics, Songs, and Sonnets*. London: Hardwicke & Bogue, 1877.

Body, Geoffrey, *British Paddle Steamers*. Newton Abbot: David & Charles, 1971.

*Bowdoin College Matriculation Records, 1802–1866*. Brunswick: Bowdoin College Archives.

Bridge, Horatio, *Personal Recollections of Nathaniel Hawthorne*. New York: Harper & Brothers; London: James R. Osgood, McIlvaine & Co., 1893. Reprint, New York: Haskell House, 1968.

Buchanan, James, *The Works of James Buchanan*. Ed., John Bassett Moore. 12 vols. Philadelphia and London: J. P. Lippincott Co., 1908–11. Reprint, New York: The Antiquarian Press, 1960.

Churchill, R. C., *Shakespeare and His Betters*. London: Max Reinhardt, 1958.

*Circular to Consuls of the United States*. Washington: Department of State, June 1, 1853.

Clark, C. E. Frazer, Jr., Editor, *The Nathaniel Hawthorne Journal*. Letters to the author, 1972–83.

Cole, Lt. Col. Howard N., *The Origins of Military Aldershot*. Aldershot: Biddles, Ltd., 1972.

Coleman, Terry, *Passage to America*. London: Hutchinson, 1972.

Conn, Cary C., Military Archives Section, National Archives and Record Service, Washington, D.C. Letter to the author, Oct. 28, 1976.

Conway, Moncure D., *Emerson at Home and Abroad*. London: Trubner & Co., 1883.

———, *Life of Nathaniel Hawthorne*. London: Walter Scott, 1890.

*The Correspondence of J. L. Motley*. Ed., G. W. Curtis. New York: Harper & Brothers, 1889.

Cumming, J. W. V., Archivist, Government Secretariat, Gibraltar. Letter to the author, July 21, 1976.

"Cunard Steamers 100 Years Ago," (unsigned), *Sea Breezes*, III, Jan.–June, 1947.

Curtis, George Ticknor, *Life of James Buchanan*, 2 vols. New York: Harper & Brothers, 1883.

Dallas, George M., *Diary of George Mifflin Dallas While U.S. Minister to Russia*, 1837 to 1839, and to England, 1856–1861. Ed., Susan Dallas. Philadelphia: J. P. Lippincott, 1892.

———, *A Series of Letters from London*. Ed., Julia [Dallas]. 2 vols. Philadelphia: J. P. Lippincott, 1869.

*The Dictionary of English History*, Eds., Sidney J. Low and F. S. Pulling. London: Cassell & Co., 1884; revised 1897, 1928.

Dinan, T. M., Librarian, Lloyd's of London. Letter to the author, Apr. 24, 1975.

*Documents and Proceedings Connected with the Donation of A Free Public Library and Museum, by William Brown, Esq., to the Town of Liverpool*. Ed., A. Hume. Liverpool: T. Brakell, 1858.

Dodman, Frank, *Ships of the Cunard Line*. London: Harrap, 1955.

Duckworth, C. L. D., and Langmuir, G. E. *West Coast Steamers*. Prescot: T. Stephenson, 1956.

Dunn, Waldo H., *The Life of Donald G. Mitchell*. New York: Scribners, 1922.

Fields, James T., *Yesterdays with Authors*. Boston: Houghton, Mifflin, 1887, 1900.

Fraser, R. H., *Fraser's Guide to Liverpool and Birkenhead*. Liverpool: W. Kent & Co., 1855.
*The French and Italian Notebooks, The Centenary Edition of the Works of Nathaniel Hawthorne*, XIV. Eds., William Charvat, Roy Harvey Pearce, Claude M. Simpson, and Thomas Woodson. Columbus: Ohio State University Press, 1980.

*General Instructions to the Consul and Commercial Agents of the United States*. Washington: Department of State, 1855.
Gibbs, Commander C. R. Vernon, *British Passenger Liners of the Five Oceans*. London: Putnam, 1963.
*Gore's Directory of Liverpool and Its Environs*. Liverpool: J. Mawdsley, 1853.
Greenhill, Basil, Director, National Maritime Museum, London. Letter to the author, Apr. 2, 1975.

Hall, Lawrence S., *Hawthorne: Critic of Society*. New Haven: Yale University Press, 1944. Reprint, Gloucester, Mass.: Peter Smith, 1966.
Hall, S. C., *Retrospect of A Long Life*. 2 vols. London: Richard Bentley & Son, 1883.
*Hand Book to Liverpool*. Liverpool: Edward Howell, 1854.
Harwell, Richard, *Hawthorne and Longfellow: A Guide to An Exhibit*. Brunswick: Bowdoin College, 1966.
*Hawthorne: The Critical Heritage*. Ed., J. Donald Crowley. New York: Barnes & Noble; London: Routledge & Kegan Paul, 1970.
Hawthorne, Julian, *Hawthorne and His Circle*. New York and London: Harper & Brothers, 1903. Reprint, Hamden, Conn.: Archon Books, 1968.
———, *Hawthorne and His Wife*. 2 vols. Boston and New York: Houghton, Mifflin, 1884.
———, *Shapes That Pass*. Boston: Houghton, Mifflin; London: John Murray, 1928.
Hawthorne, Manning, "Nathaniel Hawthorne at Bowdoin," *New England Quarterly* XIII (June, 1940).
Hawthorne, Nathaniel, *The English Notebooks*. Ed., Randall Stewart. New York: Modern Languages Association, 1941; New York: Russell & Russell, 1962; Oxford: Oxford University Press, 1941.
———, *Passages from the American Notebooks*. London: Smith, Elder and Co., 1868 (2nd edn).
———, *Passages from the English Notebooks*. Boston: Houghton, Mifflin, 1883.
———, *Life of Franklin Pierce*. Boston: Ticknor, Reed, & Fields, 1852.
———, *Our Old Home*. Boston and New York: Houghton, Mifflin. 1907.
———, *Passages from the French and Italian Notebooks*. Boston: Houghton, Mifflin, 1883.
Hawthorne, Sophia, *English Account Book*. Unpublished record in the Essex Institute, Salem, Massachusetts.
Hull, Raymona E., *Nathaniel Hawthorne: The English Experience*. Pittsburgh: University of Pittsburgh Press, 1980.
Hume, Alexander, *Conditions of Liverpool, Religious and Social*. Liverpool: T. Brakell, 1858.

Lathrop, George Parsons, *A Study of Hawthorne*. Boston: James R. Osgood, 1876.
Lathrop, Rose Hawthorne, *Memories of Hawthorne*. Boston: Houghton, Mifflin; London: Kegan Paul, Trench, Trubner & Co., 1897.
Lester, Charles Edwards, "The Consular System of the United States," *Hunt's Magazine* (March, 1845).
*Letters of Hawthorne to William D. Ticknor*, 1851–1864. 2 vols. Newark: The Carteret Book Club, 1910. Reprint, Washington: NCR/Microcard Editions, 1972.
Ligoske, Christine F., U.S. Customs Service, Department of the Treasury. Letter to the author, Sept. 29, 1975.
Liverpool Record Office. Letters to the author, 1972–83.
*London at Dinner, or, Where to Dine*. London: Robert Hardwicke, 1858.
Love Letters of Nathaniel Hawthorne. 2 vols. Chicago: The Society of the DOFOBS, 1907. Reprint, Washington: NCR/Microcard Editions, 1972.

Manning, Elizabeth, "The Boyhood of Nathaniel Hawthorne," *Wide Awake* XXXIII (Nov., 1891).
Marx, Walter J., "The Consular Services of the United States," *Department of State Bulletin* XXXIII (Sept. 19, 1955).

Mellow, James R., *Nathaniel Hawthorne in His Times*. Boston: Houghton Mifflin, 1980.
*The Minute Book of the American Chamber of Commerce* [in Liverpool]. Unpublished record in the Liverpool Record Office.
Morley, Henry, *The Journal of A London Playgoer*. London: George Routledge and Sons, 1891.

*Nathaniel Hawthorne Journal.*
National Archives and Records Service. *Dispatches* by, and *Official Correspondence* relating to Nathaniel Hawthorne.
Nichols, Roy F., *Franklin Pierce: Young Hickory of the Granite Hills*. Philadelphia: University of Pennsylvania Press, 1958.
Nixson, A. P. M., Oxford City Secretary and Solicitor. Letter to the author, June 20, 1976.

Osborne, John Ball, "Nathaniel Hawthorne as American Consul," *American Review* XVI (Jan., 1903).


Parton, James, *Some Noted Princes, Authors, and Statesmen*. New York: Thomas Y. Crowell, 1885.
Pevsner, Nikolaus, and Hubbard, Edward, *Buildings of Cheshire*. London: Penguin Books, 1971.
Picton, J. A., *Memorials of Liverpool*. 2 vols. Liverpool: Gilbert G. Wamsley, 1903.
*The Profession of Authorship in America, 1800–1870: Papers of William Charvat*. Ed., Matthew J. Bruccoli. Columbus: Ohio State University Press, 1968.

Reed, Richard B. and O'Hern, John D., *Nathaniel Hawthorne at Bowdoin College*. Brunswick: Bowdoin College, n.d.
*Regulations Prescribed by the President for Consular Officers of the United States*. Washington: Department of State, 1856.
*The Royal Picturesque Hand-book of Liverpool*. Liverpool: Edward Howell, and London: Chapman & Hall, 1852.
Ryden, J. A., City Estates Surveyor, City of Liverpool. Letter to the author, July 14, 1975.

Schwass, Earl R., Director, U.S. Naval War College Library. Letter to the author, Aug. 4, 1976.
Smith, Henry Nash, *Democracy and the Novel*. New York: Oxford University Press, 1978.
Spratt, H. Philip, *Transatlantic Paddle Steamers*. Glasgow: Brown, Son & Ferguson, 1967.
Stewart, Randall, "Hawthorne's Speeches at Civic Banquets," *American Literature* VII (Jan., 1936).
———, *Nathaniel Hawthorne: A Biography*. New Haven: Yale University Press, 1948.
Stonefield, James, *The Streets of Liverpool*. Liverpool: William Lea, 1879.
Sweeney, Mark F., *An Annotated Edition of Nathaniel Hawthorne's Official Dispatches to the State Department*. Bowling Green: Bowling Green University, 1975.

Tarbuck, Miss J., Reference Librarian, Atkinson Library, Southport. Letters to the author, 1975–83.
Thompson, David P., *The Stranger's Vade Mecum or Liverpool Described*. Liverpool: H. Greenwood, 1854.
Ticknor, Caroline, *Hawthorne and His Publisher*. Boston and New York: Houghton, Miflin, 1913. Reprint, Port Washington, N.Y.: Kennikat Press, 1969.
Towson, J. T., "On the Deviation of the Compass and the Advantages to be Derived from Elevating the Compasses of Iron Ships," *Mercantile Marine Magazine* I (Dec., 1854).
Turner, Arlin, *Nathaniel Hawthorne: A Biography*. New York/Oxford: Oxford University Press, 1980.

*Vernon's*, house journal of W. Vernon & Sons, London and Liverpool. Christmas, 1905.

Warner, Ezra J., *Generals in Gray*. Baton Rouge: Louisiana State University Press, 1959.
Warner, Lee H., "With Pierce, and Hawthorne, in Mexico," *Essex Institute Historical Collections* III (July 1975).

Wood, John R., and Serres, Jean, *Diplomatic Ceremonial and Protocol.* New York: Columbia University Press, 1970.
*The Working Man's Friend and Family Instructor* V (Mar. 1, 1851).

Young, Harold E., *A Perambulation of the Hundred of Wirral in the County of Chester.* Liverpool: Henry Young & Sons, 1909.

# Abbreviations

The following abbreviations have been commonly used in the notes. For additional details about these works and others cited in the notes, see the bibliography.

*Account Book:* Hawthorne, Sophia, *English Account Book.*
Berg: Berg Collection, New York Public Library.
*Bowdoin Records: Bowdoin College Matriculation Records, 1802–1866.*
*Buchanan: The Works of James Buchanan*, edited by John Bassett Moore.
Caroline Ticknor: Ticknor, Caroline, *Hawthorne and His Publisher.*
*Circle:* Hawthorne, Julian, *Hawthorne and His Circle.*
Conway, *Emerson:* Conway, Moncure D., *Emerson at Home and Abroad.*
Conway, *Hawthorne:* Conway, Moncure D., *Life of Nathaniel Hawthorne.*
Dallas, *Letters: A Series of Letters from London.*
*DEH: The Dictionary of English History.*
*DNB: The Dictionary of National Biography.*
*EN:* Hawthorne, Nathaniel, *The English Notebooks*, edited by Randall Stewart.
*French and Italian: The French and Italian Notebooks* of Nathaniel Hawthorne.
Hall, *Critic:* Hall, Lawrence S., *Hawthorne: Critic of Society.*
Hall, *Retrospect:* Hall, S. C., *Retrospect of A Long Life.*
*Love Letters: Love Letters of Nathaniel Hawthorne.*
LRO: Liverpool Record Office.
*Memories:* Lathrop, Rose Hawthorne, *Memories of Hawthorne.*
*Minute Book: The Minute Book of the American Chamber of Commerce* [in Liverpool].
NARS: National Archives and Records Service.
*OOH:* Hawthorne, Nathaniel, *Our Old Home.*
*Royal Picturesque: The Royal Picturesque Hand-book of Liverpool.*
*Shapes:* Hawthorne, Julian, *Shapes That Pass.*
Stewart, *Hawthorne:* Stewart, Randall, *Nathaniel Hawthorne: A Biography.*
*Ticknor: Letters of Hawthorne to William D. Ticknor: 1851–1864.*
*Wife:* Hawthorne, Julian, *Nathaniel Hawthorne and His Wife.*

# Reference Notes

## Chapter I: The Future Consul at Bowdoin College

1  Bridge, 3–4.
2  Manning Hawthorne Collection, Essex Institute. This letter and others similarly cited in this chapter appeared in *The New England Quarterly*, June, 1940; they are now held by the Essex Institute.
3  *ibid.*
4  *ibid.*
5  Bridge, 38.
6  Harwell, 15.
7  Bridge, 37.
8  Manning Hawthorne Collection.
9  *ibid.*
10 Bridge, 184.
11 Hawthorne, *Pierce*, 17.
12 Bridge, 30.
13 Manning Hawthorne Collection.
14 Harwell, 10.
15 Manning Hawthorne, 261.
16 Manning Hawthorne Collection.
17 *Bowdoin Records*, May 17, 1824.
18 *Wife*, I, 116.
19 See dedication to *The Snow Image*.
20 Bridge, 16.
21 *ibid.*, 17.
22 Dedication to *The Snow Image*.
23 Manning Hawthorne Collection.
24 *ibid.*
25 Bridge, 46–7.

## Chapter II: Of Love and the Custom House

1  Hawthorne to Pierce (Boston Public Library), June 28, 1832.
2  *Wife*, I, 135.
3  Harwell, 61–2.
4  Bridge, 7.
5  *Wife*, I, 148.
6  Harwell, 62
7  *Wife*, I, 148.
8  *ibid.*, 147.
9  Bridge, 82–3.
10 Conway, *Hawthorne*, 78.
11 *Love Letters*, I, 31.
12 Conway, *Hawthorne*, 79.
13 *The American Notebooks*, May 30, 1839.
14 *ibid.*, 194.
15 *ibid.*, 193.
16 *Wife*, I, 202.
17 *Love Letters*, I, 14.
18 *ibid.*, I, 46.
19 *ibid.*, 122–3.
20 *ibid.*, 209.
21 *Love Letters*, II, 3–4.
22 *Love Letters*, I, 201.
23 *Love Letters*, II, 91.
24 *ibid.*, 94.
25 *Memories*, 50–51.
26 *ibid.*, 52–4.
27 *ibid.*, 56.
28 *ibid.*, 59–60.
29 *ibid.*, 67–8.
30 Hawthorne to Hillard (Maine Hist. Soc.), Mar. 24, 1844.
31 *Memories*, 73.
32 *ibid.*, 74.
33 *ibid.*, 74–5.
34 *ibid.*, 76.
35 *ibid.*, 80.
36 Conway, *Hawthorne*, 102.
37 Bridge, 95.
38 *Wife*, I, 281.
39 *ibid.*
40 Sophia to her mother (Berg), Sept. 7, 1845.
41 Conway, *Hawthorne*, 109–10.
42 *ibid.*
43 *ibid.*, 106.
44 Hawthorne to Hillard (Maine Hist. Soc.), Mar. 5, 1849.
45 Hawthorne to Hillard (Maine Hist. Soc.), June 8, 1849.

## Chapter III: A Pen Helps a Friend

1  Sophia to her father (Berg), June 8, 1849.
2  Sophia to her mother (Berg), June 8, 1849.
3  Sophia to her father (Berg), June 10, 1849.
4  *ibid.*
5  *Wife*, I, 354–5.
6  Conway, *Hawthorne*, 118–19.
7  *ibid.*, 125.
8  Hawthorne to Hillard (Berg), Mar. 28, 1850.
9  See introduction to *The Scarlet Letter*.
10 *Ticknor* (foreword to 1972 reprint).
11 *Wife*, I, 394.
12 Hawthorne to his sister Louisa (Maine Hist. Soc.), May 25, 1851.
13 *ibid.*
14 Sophia to her mother (Berg), June 6, 1852.
15 Conway, *Hawthorne*, 141.
16 *Ticknor*, I, 2.
17 *ibid*, 4.
18 Conway, *Hawthorne*, 146.
19 Hawthorne to Pierce (Boston Public Library), June 28, 1852.
20 Hawthorne to Bridge (Bowdoin College Library), Oct. 18, 1852.
21 *Wife*, I, 484.
22 Conway, *Hawthorne*, 144.
23 Hawthorne to Bridge (Bowdoin College Library), Oct. 18, 1852.
24 *Ticknor*, I, 4.
25 *ibid.*, 5.
26 Hawthorne to Pierce (New Hampshire Hist. Soc.), July 27, 1852.
27 *Memories*, 199–201.
28 See preface to *Life of Pierce*.
29 Bridge, 63–4.
30 *Love Letters*, II, 219.
31 *Memories*, 204–5.
32 Stewart, *Hawthorne*, 132–3.
33 Conway, *Hawthorne*, 144.
34 *ibid.*, 144.

35  *Democratic Review*, Sept., 1852.
36  *Literary World*, Sept. 25, 1852.
37  *Manchester Review*, Jan. 1, 1853.
38  Hawthorne to Bridge (Bowdoin College Library), Oct. 18, 1852.
39  Warner, Lee H., 220.
40  Hawthorne to Bridge (Bowdoin College Library), Oct. 18, 1852.
41  Fields, 72.
42  Marx, 450.
43  Charvat, 294.
44  *Ticknor*, I, 8.
45  *ibid.*, 8–9.
46  *Home Journal*, Mar. 26, 1853.
47  Sumner to Hawthorne (Yale University Library), Mar. 26, 1853.
48  Stewart, *Hawthorne*, 142.
49  Sophia to her father (Berg), Apr. 3, 1853.
50  *Ticknor*, I, 9.

## Chapter IV: Mr. Hawthorne Sails for England

1   Conway, 148–9.
2   *Memories*, 208.
3   *ibid.*, 211.
4   *Love Letters*, II, 221–2.
5   Caroline Ticknor, 43.
6   *ibid.*
7   *ibid.*, 44.
8   *ibid.*, 46.
9   *Love Letters*, II, 225.
10  *Wife*, II, 13.
11  Hawthorne to Hackley (University of Virginia Library), June 22, 1853.
12  Sophia to her father (Berg), May 8, 1853.
13  NARS.
14  Bennoch, *Poems*, 87 (note).
15  Bennoch, *Lyrics*, 6–7.
16  Samuel Longfellow, *Life of Henry Wadsworth Longfellow with Extracts from His Journals and Correspondence*, 2 vols. (Boston, 1886), II, 234.
17  Hawthorne to William Manning (Essex Institute), July 2, 1853.
18  Boston *Daily Courier*, July 7, 1853.
19  *Memories*, 220.
20  Lloyd's of London and The Mitchell Library, Glasgow.
21  Towson, 450.
22  *Memories*, 221.
23  *ibid.*, 219.
24  Caroline Ticknor, 50.
25  *Memories*, 219.
26  *ibid.*, 219.
27  Sophia to her father (Berg), July 7, 1853.
28  *ibid.*
28  *ibid.*
30  *Shapes*, 7–8.
31  *Wife*, II, 17.
32  Body, 202.
33  Sophia to her father (Berg), [July, 1853].
34  *ibid.*
35  *Circle*, 79.
36  *Shapes*, 6.
37  *Memories*, 218.
38  Body, 70.
39  *ibid.*
40  Sophia to her father (Berg), [July, 1853].
41  *Circle*, 83–4.
42  *ibid.*, 80.
43  Caroline Ticknor, 51–2.
44  Sophia to her father (Berg), [July, 1853].
45  *Shapes*, 9–10.
46  *ibid.*
47  *ibid.*, 11.

## Chapter V: The Consul's "Parish"

1   Thompson, 180–1.
2   *London at Dinner*, 26–7.
3   *Shapes*, 11–12.
4   *Memories*, 224.
5   Liverpool *Mercury*, Aug. 5, 1853.
6   *Memories*, 223.
7   Sophia to her father (Berg), Aug. 5, 1853.
8   *Shapes*, 12.
9   Caroline Ticknor, 51–2.
10  *EN*, 17.
11  Conway, *Hawthorne*, 151–2.
12  *EN*, 17.
13  *OOH*, 473–4.
14  *ibid.*, 474–5.
15  *Friend and Instructor*, 232–3.
16  *ibid.*
17  *Royal Picturesque*, 28.
18  *ibid.*, 53.
19  Thompson, 132.
20  *ibid.*, 19.
21  *ibid.*, 179–80.
22  See Dickens, *American Notes*, Ch. 1.
23  Picton, II, 270.
24  *EN*, 26.
25  John Lewis Griffiths, *The Greater Patriotism* (London, 1918), 57–8.
26  *EN*, 13.
27  *ibid.*, 17.
28  *ibid.*, 43.
29  *ibid.*, 9.
30  *ibid.*
31  Picton, II, 100.
32  Thompson, 168.
33  *ibid.*, 167.
34  Hume, 26–7.
35  *OOH*, 472–3.
36  Baines, 772–3.
37  *Memories*, 234.

## Chapter VI: The Consul's Open Door

1   *OOH*, 6.
2   *ibid.*, 2.
3   *ibid.*, 4–5.
4   *ibid.*, 5.
5   *Shapes*, 15.
6   *Memories*, 283.
7   *EN*, 3.
8   Conway, *Hawthorne*, 119–20.
9   *ibid.*, 150.
10  Lester, 211–24.
11  *EN*, 11.
12  Liverpool *Mercury*, Oct. 14, 1853.
13  Sweeney, 21.
14  *EN*, 11.

15  *ibid.*, 442.
16  *ibid.*, 349
17  *ibid.*, 35
18  *ibid.*, 98.
19  *OOH*, 9–10.
20  *ibid.*, 13–17.
21  *ibid.*, 17–22.

22  *EN*, 113.
23  *Ticknor*, II, 52.
24  *EN*, 35–6.
25  *ibid.*, 14.
26  *ibid.*, 49
27  *Minute Book*, Aug. 5, 1853.

28  *ibid.*, Aug. 30, 1853.
29  *ibid.*, Jan. 11, Sept. 1, 1854; May 7, 1856.
30  *ibid.*, Mar. 12, 1857.
31  *EN*, 190.
32  *OOH*, 51–2.

## Chapter VII: Of Shipwrecks and Bureaucracy

1  *Memories*, 282.
2  *Ticknor*, I, 101.
3  NARS, Haw. *Disp. No. 2.*
4  *ibid.*, *Off. Cor.*, State Dept. to Hawthorne, June 26, 1856.
5  State Dept. *Cir. No. 9*, Nove. 20, 1854.
6  NARS, Haw. *Disp. No. 32.*
7  *ibid.*, *Off. Cor.*, State Dept. to Hawthorne, May 29, 1855.
8  *ibid.*, Haw. *Disp. No. 60.*
9  *ibid.*, *Off. Cor.*, State Dept. to Hawthorne, June 24, 1856.
10  *ibid.*, Haw. *Disp. No. 79.*

11  *ibid.*, No. 81.
12  *ibid.*, No. 34.
13  *ibid.*, No. 38.
14  *ibid.*, No. 41.
15  *ibid.*, No. 68.
16  *ibid.*, No. 51.
17  *ibid.*, No. 75.
18  *ibid.*, No. 78.
19  *ibid.*, No. 22.
20  *ibid.*
21  *ibid.*
22  *ibid.*
23  *ibid.*
24  *ibid.*

25  Sweeney, 21.
26  NARS, *Off. Cor.*, Treasury to Hawthorne, Sept. 18, 1855.
27  *ibid.*, Marcy to Hawthorne, Nov. 23, 1855.
28  *ibid.*, Thomas to Hawthorne, Jan. 18, 1856.
29  *ibid.*, Haw. *Disp. No. 62.*
30  *ibid.*
31  *ibid.*
32  *ibid.*, *Off. Cor.*, Thomas to Hawthorne, Dec. 24, 1855.
33  *Ticknor*, I, 121.
34  NARS, Haw. *Disp. No. 76.*

## Chapter VIII: The Hawthornes at Home

1  Sophia to her father (Berg), Aug. 26, 1853.
2  Pevsner and Hubbard, 103.
3  Curtis, II, 102.
4  Sophia to her father (Berg), Aug. 17, 1853.
5  *EN*, 22.
6  *Shapes*, 21.
7  *Ticknor*, I, 17.
8  *Memories*, 242.
9  *Shapes*, 20.
10  *EN*, 22.
11  *ibid.*, 23.
12  *ibid.*, 28.
13  *ibid.*, 31.
14  *Wife*, II, 30–1.
15  *ibid.*, 27.
16  *ibid.*, 31.
17  *Shapes*, 51–2.
18  *Memories*, 262.
19  *ibid.*

20  *ibid.*, 263–4.
21  *Account Book.*
22  *Memories*, 287.
23  *Circle*, 130.
24  Sophia to her father (Berg), Aug. 26, 1853.
25  *Memories*, 305–6.
26  *ibid.*, 250.
27  Sophia to her father (Berg), Dec., 1854.
28  *Memories*, 299–300.
29  *Wife*, II, 79.
30  LRO, Channing to Jevons, Sept. 18, 1854.
31  *Memories*, 284.
32  LRO.
33  *Memories*, 255–6.
34  *Ticknor*, I, 71.
35  *Memories*, 260–1.
36  *EN*, 98.
37  *ibid.*, 35.

38  *ibid.*, 98.
39  Duckworth and Langmuir, 35.
40  *EN*, 48.
41  *ibid.*, 119.
42  *ibid.*, 30.
43  *Memories*, 284–5.
44  *EN*, 397–8.
45  *ibid.*, 425.
46  *Ticknor*, II, 28.
47  *ibid.*, 37.
48  *Memories*, 324.
49  *ibid.*, 324–5.
50  *EN*, 432.
51  *Circle*, 225–6.
52  *ibid.*, 227–8.
53  *EN*, 443.
54  *ibid.*, 444.
55  *ibid.*
56  *ibid.*, 495.
57  *ibid.*, 461.

## Chapter IX: The Consul and the Future President

1  *The Times*, Jan. 24, 1854.
2  *Memories*, 281–2.
3  Liverpool *Chronicle*, Jan. 30, 1854.

4  *Ticknor*, I, 28.
5  *The Times*, Feb. 7, 1854.
6  Portsmouth (N, H.) *Journal*, Mar. 4, 1854.

7  NARS, Haw. *Disp. No. 10.*
8  *Ticknor*, I, 32–5.
9  *Buchanan*, IX, 36.
10  *ibid.*, 42.

11 *ibid.*
12 NARS, Hawthorne to Buchanan, Sept. 8, 1853.
13 *Buchanan*, IX, 79.
14 *ibid.*, 98.
15 NARS, Hawthorne to Buchanan, Mar. 6, 1854.
16 *Buchanan*, IX, 158–9.

17 *Ticknor*, I, 39.
18 *EN*, 99.
19 *The Times*, Jan. 5, 1855.
20 *Memories*, 290.
21 *EN*, 100.
22 *ibid.*
23 *ibid.*, 221.

24 *ibid.*, 234.
25 *ibid.*
26 *ibid.*, 237.
27 *ibid.*, 253.
28 Buchanan to Hawthorne (University of Iowa Libraries), Dec. 3, 1855.

## Chapter X: Mischief at Sea

1 *OOH*, 44.
2 *ibid.*, 45.
3 NARS, Haw. *Disp. No. 11.*
4 *ibid.*, *No. 22.*
5 *Ticknor*, I, 60.
6 NARS, Haw. *Disp. No. 35.*
7 *EN*, 109–112.
8 NARS, Haw. *Disp. No. 37.*
9 Hawthorne to Sumner (Houghton Library, Harvard), May 23, 1855.
10 NARS, Haw. *Disp. No. 54.*

11 *EN*, 267.
12 *ibid.*
13 NARS, Haw. *Disp. No. 55.*
14 *Ticknor*, II, 38.
15 *ibid.*, II, 41.
16 NARS, Haw. *Disp. No. 83.*
17 *ibid.*, *Off. Cor.*, Hawthorne to Messrs. Rathbone Bros. & Co., Feb. 13, 1857.
18 NARS, Haw. *Disp. No. 86.*
19 *ibid.*

20 *ibid.*
21 NARS, Haw. *Disps. No. 82 & 89.*
22 *The Times*, July 13, 1857.
23 NARS, Haw. *Disp. No. 90.*
24 *ibid.*
25 *ibid.*
26 *Harper's*, CVIII (Mar., 1904), 602–7.
27 *Wife*, II, 161–2.
28 *OOH*, 45.

## Chapter XI: The Peregrinations of a Consul

1 The *Examiner*, Oct. 17, 1863, 662–3.
2 *Ticknor*, I, 22.
3 *EN*, 64–5.
4 *ibid.*, 66.
5 *ibid.*, 70.
6 *Memories*, 273–4.
7 *Ticknor*, I, 56.
8 *EN*, 77–9.
9 *ibid.*, 80.
10 *Memories*, 288–9.
11 *ibid.*, 337.
12 *EN*, 121.
13 *Ticknor*, I, 97.
14 *EN*, 131–2.
15 *ibid.*, 147–9.
16 *ibid.*, 152.
17 *ibid.*, 155–6.
18 *Ticknor*, I, 99.
19 *EN*, 163.
20 *Memories*, 318–322.
21 *EN*, 168.
22 *ibid.*, 165.
23 *ibid.*, 184.

24 *ibid.*, 185.
25 *ibid.*, 172.
26 *ibid.*, 199.
27 *ibid.*, 203.
28 *OOH*, 362.
29 *EN*, 203–5.
30 *ibid.*, 252–3.
31 *ibid.*, 213.
32 *ibid.*, 264–5.
33 *Love Letters*, II, 251.
34 *EN*, 286.
35 *ibid.*, 293–4.
36 *ibid.*, 342.
37 *ibid.*, 355.
38 *ibid.*, 359.
39 *ibid.*, 360.
40 *ibid.*, 398–9.
41 *Alden's Guide*, 1874.
42 Bede, 89–90.
43 *EN*, 399.
44 *ibid.*, 402.
45 *OOH*, 281–299.
46 *ibid.*, 305–12.

47 *EN*, 419–21.
48 *OOH*, 322–4.
49 *Ticknor*, II, 22–4.
50 *OOH*, 324.
51 *EN*, 451.
52 *ibid.*, 467.
53 *OOH*, 240–1.
54 *EN*, 474.
55 *OOH*, 269.
56 *Ticknor*, II, 55.
57 *EN*, 481–3.
58 *ibid.*, 498–9.
59 *OOH*, 327.
60 *EN*, 502.
61 *OOH*, 349.
62 *ibid.*, 357.
63 *EN*, 544.
64 *OOH*, 358.
65 *Wife*, II, 54–5.
66 *ibid.*, 374.
67 *OOH*, 374.
68 *EN*, 554.
69 *ibid.*, 182.

## Chapter XII: Mrs. Blodget and the Lonely Consul

1 *Shapes*, 33.
2 *Circle*, 173.
3 Cummings, letter to author.

4 *EN*, 496.
5 *Circle*, 176.
6 *Shapes*, 31.

7 *ibid.*, 33.
8 *EN*, 258.
9 *Shapes*, 37.

10  *ibid.*, 34–5.
11  *Wife*, II, 80–1.
12  *Ticknor*, I, 113.
13  Hawthorne to Longfellow (Houghton Library, Harvard), Nov. 22, 1855.
14  *EN*, 270.
15  *Ticknor*, II, 3.
16  *Shapes*, 37.
17  *Circle*, 175.

18  *ibid.*, 184.
19  *EN*, 227.
20  *ibid.*, 353–4.
21  *Circle*, 179.
22  *ibid.*, 38–9.
23  *Love Letters*, II, 245–6.
24  *ibid.*, 249–251.
25  *Memories*, 294.
26  *ibid.*, 323–4.

27  *Love Letters*, II, 259.
28  *ibid.*
29  *ibid.*, 265–70.
30  *ibid.*, 256–7.
31  *EN*, 363.
32  *ibid.*, 496.
33  *ibid.*
34  *ibid.*
35  *ibid.*, 573.

## Chapter XIII: War Fears and Calming Words

1  Van Alstyne, 494–5.
2  *Ticknor*, I, 79–80.
3  Van Alstyne, 498.
4  *Punch*, XXX, June 14, 1856, 239.
5  *Buchanan*, IX, 425.
6  *Love Letters*, II, 233–5.
7  *Wife*, II, 83.
8  *Ticknor*, I, 112–13.
9  *Love Letters*, II, 237.
10  *Ticknor*, I, 116.
11  Bemis, VI, 257.
12  Curtis, II, 116–7.
13  *ibid.*, 167.
14  *Ticknor*, II, 4.
15  *Love Letters*, II, 249.
16  *EN*, 295.
17  *ibid.*
18  *ibid.*, 298.
19  *ibid.*, 296.

20  *ibid.*, 298.
21  *ibid.*, 311–2.
22  *Illustrated London News*, XXVIII, Apr. 5, 1856, 342.
23  *EN*, 313.
24  *ibid.*, 325.
25  *DNB*, L, 211.
26  *Love Letters*, II, 254.
27  *EN*, 319–20.
28  *ibid.*, 320.
29  *ibid.*, 320–21.
30  *ibid.*, 322.
31  Hall, *Retrospect*, II, 202.
32  *EN*, 323.
33  Stewart, "Speeches," 417–9.
34  *EN*, 323.
35  *The Times*, June 6, 1856.
36  Dallas, *Letters*, I, 61.
37  *ibid.*, 58.
38  *The Times*, June 6, 1856.

39  *ibid.*, June 11, 1856.
40  *ibid.*, June 12, 1856.
41  *Dallas*, Letters, I, 77–8.
42  *Ticknor*, II, 17.
43  *Punch*, XXX, June 14, 1856, 238.
44  *ibid.*
45  *Quarterly Review*, XCIX, No. CXCVII, 282.
46  *Blackwood's*, LXXX, June 1856, 126.
47  *Hansard*, CXLII, June 16, 1856, 1511.
48  Dallas, *Letters*, I, 48.
49  *Ticknor*, II, 19–20.
50  Hawthorne to Bridge (Bowdoin College Library), June 20, 1856.
51  Dallas, *Letters*, II, 51.
52  *DEH*, 332.

## Chapter XIV: The Lion of Liverpool

1  *EN*, 4.
2  *ibid.*, 12.
3  *Memories*, 237.
4  *EN*, 8.
5  *ibid.*, 31.
6  *Memories*, 246–7.
7  *EN*, 49.
8  *ibid.*, 56.
9  *Ticknor*, I, 43.
10  NARS, *Haw. Disps. 14, 15 and 18.*

11  *EN*, 89–90.
12  Liverpool *Mercury*, Oct. 6, 1854.
13  *EN*, 102.
14  *ibid.*, 103.
15  *ibid.*, 108.
16  *ibid.*, 198.
17  *ibid.*, 278.
18  *ibid.*, 429.
19  *Ticknor*, II, 30–1.

20  *OOH*, 539–40.
21  *EN*, 440.
22  *ibid.*, 441.
23  *ibid.*, 458.
24  *ibid.*, 458–9.
25  *ibid.*, 460.
26  *ibid.*
27  *Ticknor*, II, 64.
28  Conway, *Hawthorne*, 155–6.

## Chapter XV: Provide, Provide, Provide

1  Churchill: see Chapter 2.
2  *Ticknor*, II, 48.
3  *ibid.*, 53–4.
4  Caroline Ticknor, 141.
5  *Buchanan*, IX, 87.
6  *Ticknor*, I, 14.

7  *ibid.*, 16.
8  *ibid.*, 22.
9  *ibid.*, 23–4.
10  *ibid.*, 24.
11  *ibid.*, 25.
12  *ibid.*, 29.

13  *ibid.*, 30.
14  *ibid.*, 31–2.
15  *ibid.*, 37.
16  *ibid.*, 39–40.
17  *ibid.*, 46.
18  *ibid.*

19  *ibid.*, 49.
20  *ibid.*, 56.
21  *ibid.*, 60.
22  *ibid.*, 62.
23  *ibid.*, 63.
24  *ibid.*, 65.
25  *ibid.*, 66.
26  *ibid.*, 73–5.

27  *ibid.*, 81.
28  *ibid.*, 83.
29  *ibid.*, 85.
30  *ibid.*, 95.
31  NARS, *Off. Cor.*, Hawthorne to Pierce, June 7, 1855.
32  *ibid.*
33  *ibid.*

34  *ibid.*
35  *Ticknor*, I, 104.
36  *ibid.*, 111.
37  *ibid.*, 123.
38  *Ticknor*, II, 45.
39  *ibid.*, 61.
40  *ibid.*, 66.

## Chapter XVI: Near Tragedy and Tribulation

1   *Ticknor*, II, 69.
2   Conway, *Hawthorne*, 158–9.
3   *Ticknor*, II, 71–2.
4   *ibid.*, 75.
5   *Memories*, 353–4.
6   *New York Times*, Apr. 4, 1859.
7   *Ticknor*, II, 75.
8   *ibid.*, 76.
9   *ibid.*, 78.
10  *Memories*, 370.
11  *French and Italian*, 518.
12  *Ticknor*, II, 81.
13  *ibid.*, 82–3.
14  Hall, *Critic*, 24.
15  *Ticknor*, II, 83.
16  *ibid.*, 81.

17  *ibid.*, 90.
18  *ibid.*
19  *ibid.*, 99–101.
20  *Memories*, 343.
21  *ibid.*, 345.
22  *ibid.*, 407.
23  Motley, 339.
24  *Wife*, II, 259–60.
25  Young, 22.
26  *Memories*, 421.
27  *Ticknor*, II, 112.
28  *ibid.*, 113.
29  Lathrop, 270.
30  Hawthorne to Bridge (Bowdoin College Library), Oct. 12, 1861.

31  *Memories*, 429–30.
32  Hawthorne to Bridge (Bowdoin College Library), Feb. 14, 1862.
33  *ibid*
34  Caroline Ticknor, 272.
35  *Memories*, 437–8.
36  Warner, Ezra, J., 340.
37  Conway, *Emerson*, 221–3.
38  *ibid.*
39  *ibid.*
40  Fields, 107–8.
41  See dedication to *Our Old Home.*
42  *ibid*

## Chapter XVII: Condemnation and Death

1   Conway, *Hawthorne*, 205.
2   *North American Review*, XCVIII, Oct., 1863, 588–9.
3   *OOH*, 73.
4   *ibid.*, 73–4.
5   *ibid.*, 75.
6   *Blackwood's*, XCIV, Nov., 1863, 610–23.
7   *Quarterly Review*, CXV, Jan., 1864, 42–68.
8   *Punch*, XLV, Oct. 17, 1863, 161.

9   *ibid.*
10  Fields, 109.
11  *The Times*, Nov. 9, 1863.
12  *ibid.*
13  *Wife*, II, 306.
14  The *Examiner*, Oct. 17, 1863, 662–3.
15  *Wife*, II, 308.
16  *EN* (introduction: xxvii–xviii).
17  *Wife*, II, 330–1.
18  *ibid.*, 332.

19  *ibid.*, 333.
20  Conway, *Hawthorne*, 211.
21  *Wife*, II, 340.
22  *ibid.*, 341.
23  Caroline Ticknor, 320.
24  Fields, 118–9.
25  *ibid.*, 121.
26  *ibid.*, 121–2.
27  Bridge, 179.
28  *Memories*, 480.
29  *ibid.*

# Index

[The abbreviation NH has been used in the Index to denote Nathaniel Hawthorne.]